Finally, a leadership book that speaks to CFOs. It's smart, grounded, and gets to the heart of what it really takes to lead people – not just manage results.

Andrew Bonfield, *CFO, Caterpillar Inc.*

Leadership varies according to context. So how do things look for CFOs who wish to lead? Blending experience, expertise and research this book provides thoughtful insight and pragmatic advice for CFOs – and all those who aspire to the role.

Rob Goffee, *Emeritus Professor of Organizational Behavior, London Business School and co-author of* Why Should Anyone Be Led by You?

This book perfectly illustrates how strategic finance teams aren't just scorekeepers, they proactively engage to put points on the board. Dr. Bunea delivers an insightful reflection on how the next generation of CFOs can lead by driving growth, preserving value, and empowering talent to truly unlock an organization's full potential.

Sandeep Aujla, *CFO, Intuit*

A must-read for modern CFOs, this book offers a sharp and timely rethinking of leadership in the financial sector.

Arun Sivaramakrishnan, *CFO, NN Leven*

Most finance leadership books focus on numbers; this one focuses on people. It offers finance leaders an unflinching look at the psychological and political dynamics they must master to truly lead.

Andrea Burlacu, *Vice President – Global Finance Operations, The Coca-Cola Company*

LEADERSHIP FOR THE CFO

Most leadership books are not written with finance in mind. This one is. Written by a seasoned CFO with deep research expertise, *Leadership for the CFO* speaks directly to the realities of leading from the top finance seat.

The CFO role is changing, requiring new levels of influence across the C-suite and in organizations. More than ever, CFOs need to raise their leadership game. What motivates finance teams? What tools can a CFO use to influence non-finance stakeholders? How can finance leaders communicate with impact? What are some blind spots CFOs have when developing talent? How can finance leaders avoid being pigeonholed in their roles? How do CFOs best prepare for a CEO role? Grounded in cutting-edge leadership research, the book answers these and many other questions. It combines clear frameworks with practical tools tailored to finance leaders. These ideas are brought to life through real-world cases of finance leaders. The book includes exclusive access to selected scenes from *Crossroads Life* – an award-winning film, not available outside executive education, that portrays a CFO's real-world leadership journey.

Essential reading for CFOs, aspiring finance executives, and anyone aiming to lead in finance.

Emilia Bunea, Ph.D., CFA, is a leadership scholar, board member, and entrepreneur whose nearly two-decade-long corporate career as CFO and CEO included overseeing a €20 billion balance sheet and leading an organization serving two million customers. Dr. Bunea's research has been published in prominent academic and practitioner outlets. She lectures on leadership at business schools, corporations, and events around the world and has written and produced the first-ever cinematic case study on leadership. Her TED Talk at London Business School on how top CEOs fuel their leadership has drawn wide attention. She holds an MBA from the University of Washington and a doctorate from VU University Amsterdam.

LEADERSHIP FOR THE CFO

Influence. Motivate. Inspire.

Emilia Bunea, Ph.D.

Routledge
Taylor & Francis Group
LONDON AND NEW YORK

Designed cover image: Cover design by Luana Iosif and Freepik

First published 2026
by Routledge
4 Park Square, Milton Park, Abingdon, Oxon OX14 4RN

and by Routledge
605 Third Avenue, New York, NY 10158

Routledge is an imprint of the Taylor & Francis Group, an informa business

British Library Cataloguing-in-Publication Data
A catalogue record for this book is available from the British Library

ISBN: 978-1-032-94778-5 (hbk)
ISBN: 978-1-032-90309-5 (pbk)
ISBN: 978-1-003-58173-4 (ebk)

DOI: 10.4324/9781003581734

Typeset in Joanna
by SPi Technologies India Pvt Ltd (Straive)

CONTENTS

INTRODUCTION

Some years ago, while serving as CFO at a financial services corporation, I enrolled in a senior executive development program at a renowned business school. The experience was enlightening. I absorbed frameworks on change management and strategy formation, and soon after, I applied them with some success. Yet there was one subject that felt oddly remote, like studying the rituals of an Amazonian tribe: leadership. The concepts were fascinating, rooted in universal values and profound reflections on human nature. But they felt distant from my day-to-day world. The stories of transformative leadership seemed to feature leaders cut from a different cloth, guiding employees who behaved in ways I could not imagine my finance teams ever behave.

For a while, I assumed the fault was mine. Perhaps, I reasoned, a more inspiring leader could transcend these differences – ignoring the specifics of finance with grand, universal recipes. Perhaps leadership was just about whether or not you had that *je ne sais quoi* that made anyone – finance or not finance – enthusiastically follow you.

DOI: 10.4324/9781003581734-1

Fast forward ten years. By then, I had moved into leadership academia and had even produced a film about the trials and tribulations of a newly promoted CFO. I used this film as part of a leadership course for managers. The course wasn't designed specifically for finance leaders, but a pattern emerged: whenever a CFO was in the room, they'd approach me afterward and say, "This is so me" or "Why didn't I know about these things five years ago?"

It became clear to me that, just as "women are not small men," finance leaders are not merely leaders with a pocket protector. Their challenges, contexts, and opportunities are distinct. This book is my attempt to distill from the vast body of leadership knowledge the insights most relevant to (aspiring) CFOs and to explore how leadership truly plays out in the nuanced world of finance.

Why leadership?

1. **Because leadership pays off**
   Leadership is not just a pleasant ideal; it has measurable impacts:
   - Leaders who motivate and inspire foster **knowledge-sharing** (1), strengthen **resilience** (2), encourage **openness to change** (3), enhance success in **international projects** (4), and **reduce turnover** (5).
   - Firms named among the "100 Best Companies to Work For" tend to see **higher future abnormal stock returns**. And intriguingly, the market **undervalues** this intangible (6).
   - Consider Jamie Dimon, CEO of JPMorgan Chase, who has decided to hire "professional managers" because those super-smart financial wizards cannot do it properly (7). Or Ben Horowitz, co-founder of venture capital firm Andreessen Horowitz, who emphasizes the importance of soft skills for emerging leaders (8). These are **no-nonsense, show-me-the-money** leaders, unlikely to indulge in lofty slogans about "becoming the best version of yourself," yet they speak emphatically about **the centrality of people skills**.
2. **Because leadership is increasingly essential for CFOs**
   Over half of today's CFOs in Fortune 500 and S&P 500 companies hold an MBA, up from 40% a decade ago. Yet the proportion with a CPA has remained steady at around 35% (9). This shift reflects the

evolving demands on finance leaders: technical excellence is still necessary, but it is no longer sufficient. Leadership capability is becoming a key differentiator.

Who is this for?

This book is for **finance leaders at any stage of their journey**. If you're experienced, it offers an opportunity to map your practical insights against research-based frameworks, identifying potential blind spots. If you're earlier in your career, it offers stories and guidance to help you navigate the path ahead.

All through what follows, I write as though you are already a CFO or on the path to becoming one. However, much of this book will also resonate with those aspiring to **broader leadership roles**. Perhaps you aim to transition from leading FP&A to heading operations or from overseeing finance to managing a business unit. The insights here will still be relevant to your leadership.

This book is also for **young finance professionals** wondering if the CFO path is for them. It certainly doesn't gloss over the difficulties and setbacks waiting for them on this path, but I am confident that this will not discourage them and that they might even be emboldened by the challenge.

What's inside?

Part 1 introduces the LIFE model of leadership: Leader, Interaction, Followers, and Environment. Each section is tailored to the finance context, with topics such as

- Personal characteristics essential for finance leaders.
- Leadership styles that shape leader–follower dynamics, with a focus on transformational leadership.
- The traits and mindsets of finance professionals and how they influence your leadership.
- The environmental forces – culture, power, politics, and business context – that shape leadership outcomes in finance.

Part 2 provides tools for CFOs to apply while engaged in the LIFE mechanism of leadership, including

- Communication skills
- Charismatic leadership tactics
- Techniques for understanding and motivating individuals
- Networking, influencing, and political skills
- Talent selection and development
- Relationship with the CEO and the board
- Self-leadership

Each chapter includes practical advice, finance-specific insights, and real-life leadership stories from CFOs (including the numerous finance leaders I interviewed for this book).

Throughout the book, I've woven in scenes from **Crossroads Life** https://www.ed.movie/cine-cases, an award-winning cinematic case study that follows the real-life leadership journey of a CFO. These moments invite you to engage with the emotions, dilemmas, and decisions faced on screen, offering an immediate way to test the book's ideas against the messy, high-stakes reality of life in the CFO seat.

Why me?

My biography appears separately, but the simplest explanation can be visualized in Figure 0.1.

Books about leadership are often written by authors who fall into just one of these categories (and occasionally by those who fit none). I occupy the intersection of all four, combining real-world CFO, general management, and board experience with leadership research, academic rigor, and practical teaching.

Why does this matter? Because

- Leadership academics often lack management experience and struggle to make research relatable and actionable.
- Practicing leaders and board members share war stories but have a hard time abstracting to a level beyond their own experience as well as connecting their anecdotes to the vast body of leadership research.
- CFOs rarely write about leadership, and when they do, they face the same challenges as generalist leaders.

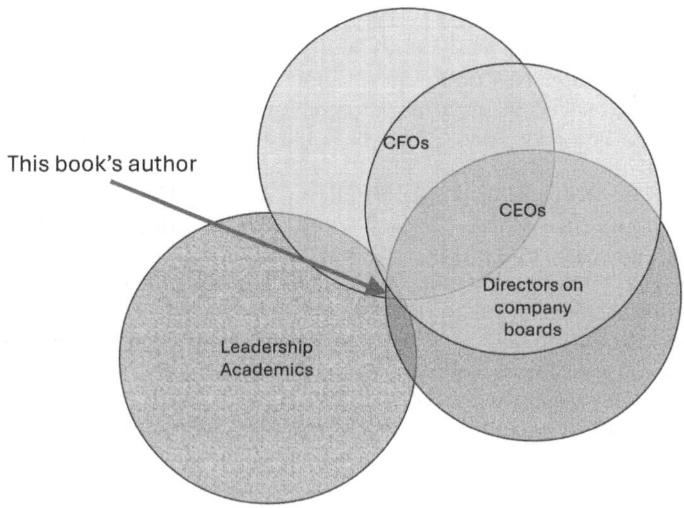

Figure 0.1 Why me.

Here, you will find a perspective that is both grounded and informed, combining the best of theory and practice.

One topic is absent from these pages: AI. This is intended. Writing about AI in a book nowadays would be like getting a tattoo of a joke you've just heard: it makes you look cool for 5 minutes and silly forever after.

Instead, I will post updates on the latest leadership+finance research (including research on AI and its impact) at www.emiliabunea.com. Find me there to continue the conversation.

References

(1) Jiang, Y., & Chen, C. Integrating knowledge activities for team innovation: Effects of transformational leadership. *Journal of Management* 2018, 44 (5), 1819–1847. DOI: 10.1177/0149206316628641

(2) McCombs, K., & Williams, E. The resilient effects of transformational leadership on well-being: Examining the moderating effects of anxiety during the COVID-19 crisis. *Leadership & Organization Development Journal* 2021, 42 (8), 1254–1266. DOI: 10.1108/LODJ-02-2021-0092

(3) Zainab, B., Akbar, W., & Siddiqui, F. Impact of transformational leadership and transparent communication on employee openness to change: Mediating role of employee organization trust and moderated role of change-related self-efficacy. *Leadership & Organization Development Journal* 2022, 43 (1), 1–13. DOI: 10.1108/LODJ-08-2020-0355

(4) Kabore, S., Sane, S., & Abo, P. Transformational leadership and success of international development projects (ID projects): Moderating role of the project team

size. *Leadership & Organization Development Journal* 2021, 42 (4), 517–530. DOI: 10.1108/LODJ-06-2020-0236
(5) Oh, J., & Chhinzer, N. Is turnover contagious? The impact of transformational leadership and collective turnover on employee turnover decisions. *Leadership & Organization Development Journal* 2021, 42 (7), 1089–1103. DOI: 10.1108/LODJ-12-2020-0548
(6) Edmans, A. Does the stock market fully value intangibles? Employee satisfaction and equity prices. *Journal of Financial Economics* 2011, *101* (3), 621–640. DOI: 10.1016/j.jfineco.2011.03.021
(7) Dimon, J. Jamie Dimon, Chairman, President, and CEO of JPMorgan Chase: Stanford Graduate School of Business. https://www.youtube.com/watch?v=IyEadGANbgM, 2017.
(8) Horowitz, B. *Nailing the hard things*. Stanford e-corner: https://www.youtube.com/watch?v=F2e3RqL4VWs. 2014.
(9) *Cristkolder Volatility Report*; https://www.cristkolder.com/volatility-report, 2024.

PART 1

A FULL LEADERSHIP FRAMEWORK

"But what exactly do you mean by 'leadership'?"

I once put this very question to my LinkedIn community, inviting them to suggest a film they instinctively associated with leadership. Their answers, mostly coming from experienced managers, were intriguingly varied: some evoked scenes of heroic behavior amid crisis, while others conjured images of imposing displays of power. Such diverse associations make perfect sense; they certainly evoke notions connected to leadership. Yet, crucially, they are not leadership itself.

The term "leadership" frequently appears in business book titles, often chosen perhaps because it carries greater prestige than the humbler "management". Books pairing "leadership" with "CFO" commonly delve into such management topics as audit processes, cash management, mergers and acquisitions, or strategic planning. Undoubtedly, strategic management is essential for senior leaders, and I have yet to meet a truly effective leader who was not also an adept manager. Also, I am fiercely against the

DOI: 10.4324/9781003581734-2

simplistic mantra that commands us to "be leaders, not mere managers," as if managers were a lower species that occasionally, under rare and mysterious circumstances, evolves into the nobler *Leader sapiens*. Yet management, though vital, is not leadership.

What, then, is leadership?

> Leadership refers to a **social influence** process in which leaders attempt to motivate and enable followers toward achieving collective goals[1].

This definition is hardly contentious. Indeed, most leadership scholars seem to converge on it these days – and leadership scholars hardly ever converge on anything. Yet, despite this clarity, we often revert to viewing leadership as a trait buried deep within an individual, something inherent and permanent. Popular books detailing the lives of "great leaders" imply that these individuals would invariably succeed regardless of context. This myth is sometimes embarrassingly disproven when the same revered figures stumble dramatically after publication, but this seems not to trouble anyone much.

My intention here is not to dismiss the value of experience or proven leadership skills. Rather, when we say, "Joe is a great leader," we should approach this statement with the same caution we might reserve for declaring, "General Joe is a winner". We understand intuitively that General Joe's past victories do not guarantee future success, irrespective of context or opponent. Instead, we mean simply that Joe has an impressive history of triumphs, rendering him suitably equipped for battles yet unknown.

This book is your "prepared for combat" checklist. It cannot promise victory in every battle you may face, but it ensures that no critical preparatory step is overlooked. It also provides tools for navigating setbacks – or, perhaps even more dangerously, spectacular successes – with composure and insight. And importantly, it does so through the unique lens of financial leadership, because CFOs have their own, specific battles to win.

The LIFE model of leadership

To bring clarity to your leadership journey, I have distilled the key determinants of leadership effectiveness into one framework: the LIFE model. Its ambition is nothing less than to capture all the moving parts of the leadership mechanism, a more comprehensive approach than commonly found in popular leadership texts. Many such books tend to offer oversimplified lists – seven habits, five golden rules – focused almost exclusively on leader behaviors or on inner characteristics like values or confidence. Such perspectives inevitably remain partial, leaving gaps between the promise and the lived experience of leadership.

The LIFE model synthesizes **the current state of the research** on leadership effectiveness. Rest assured, this will not be a tedious theoretical lecture; we will have **three ingredients** to spice it up:

1. Every concept presented is explicitly **tailored** to the context of financial leadership. For instance, when discussing the impact of followers' personality, we will look at what research says about the personalities of finance employees, and we will interpret what this may mean for your leadership. Every theoretical idea included in this text has been carefully selected for its **practical** application and is accompanied by tangible, actionable insights. For example, we will not spend any time on academic issues such as the impossibility of a "true self" or the complex interaction between leader development and identity development – although they are far from trivial in leadership research – because they help little in your daily professional life.
2. There will be **real-world illustrations**, gathered from my interviews with CFOs, from public cases of finance leaders, and occasionally from my personal experiences as a CFO. These stories, including my own – which are often about missteps rather than triumphs – should not be mistaken for blueprints of perfect leadership. Even renowned figures such as Luca Maestri at Apple or Ruth Porat at Alphabet remain enigmatic in their day-to-day people leadership despite media acclaim. We lack sufficient insight to confidently label them exemplary leaders. Therefore, take their words and stories only as additions to the rich trove of leadership cases that you will have accumulated by the end of this book, that *together* can help shape your leadership choices.
3. You will have scenes from **Crossroads Life** (https://www.imdb.com/title/tt15548102/), an award-winning film based on the real-life leadership journey of a finance executive, to accompany your learning and to test how the research applies to the messy reality of a CFO's experience.

Ready, then, for the LIFE "lecture"? Here we go.

Reference

(1) Liden, R.; Wang, X.; Wang, Y. The evolution of leadership: Past insights, present trends, and future directions. *Journal of Business Research* 2025, 186. DOI: 10.1016/j.jbusres.2024.115036

1

LEADERSHIP IS ABOUT LIFE

In 2014, the Denver Broncos walked onto the field of the Super Bowl, favored to win. They had the best offense in the league. Their quarterback, Peyton Manning, had just finished a record-breaking season. It should have been a coronation. Instead, they lost. Badly.

The Seattle Seahawks – a younger, scrappier, less flashy team – stunned everyone with a 43–8 victory. Why? Because while the Broncos brought an extraordinary offense, the Seahawks brought something else: an acute understanding of their own abilities, of their opponent, and of the environment they were stepping into. They studied the field. They adapted.

Leadership is like that. It's not just about you or about those you are trying to lead. It's also about the interaction you have with them – and the context in which you operate. That context can lift your leadership to new heights or grind it to a halt.

LIFE stands for **Leader, Interaction, Followers**, and **Environment**. Think of it not as a list of ingredients but as a living ecosystem. Every part influences every other part. Leadership is an evolving interaction between leader and followers, shaped by who they are and the world they move through.

DOI: 10.4324/9781003581734-3

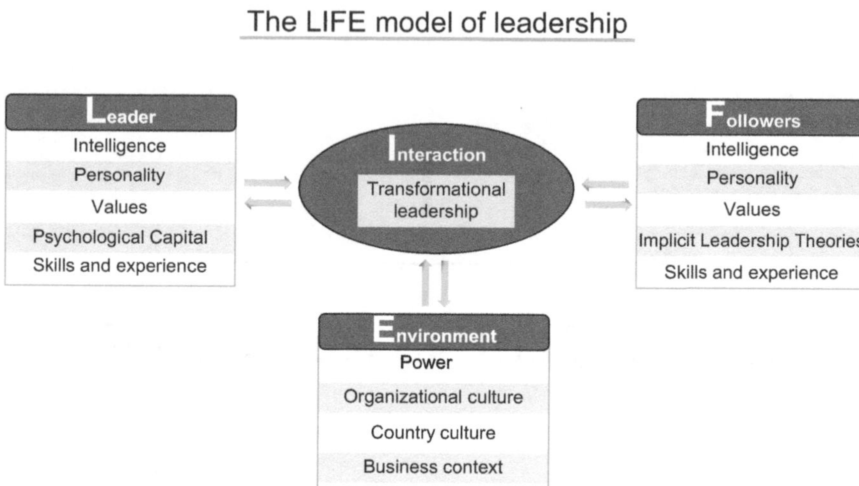

Figure 1.1 The LIFE model of leadership.

Figure 1.1 illustrates the four components of LIFE. Let's briefly unbox each of them here; they will later each have their own dedicated chapter.

The Leader

The first part of LIFE is everything *inside* the leader: personality traits, values, psychological capital, knowledge, skills. For decades, leadership was believed to reside here – and only here. Leadership was all about some mystical, innate power bestowed upon a select few – cue the early 20th-century "**Great Man**" theories (1). In those days, people assumed that either you won the genetic lottery and popped out as a dazzling leader or you did not. Even the legendary management thinker Peter Drucker once proclaimed: "Leadership cannot be created or promoted. It cannot be taught or learned" (2). Such a perspective can be a bit discouraging for anyone not born with the letter L on their foreheads.

In all fairness, they are not entirely wrong. As with athletic prowess, some leaders do come equipped with innate advantages. For example, extraversion consistently shows up as being helpful for leadership. Watch, for example, an interview (3) with Steve Presley (CEO of Nestlé North America, former CFO for Nestlé), and you will quickly sense his extraversion shining through. Clearly, that didn't hurt his climb from auditor to executive suite.

However, as every athlete knows, natural gifts get you only so far. Just as future Olympic swimmers have to train in the pool until their fingers resemble raisins, so too must leaders develop their craft. Furthermore, in leadership, putting in the hard work can get you far even if you're not great at those natural abilities. Dr. Lisa Su, CEO of AMD, is a self-proclaimed introvert. Yet she commands admiration as an inspirational leader, showing that introversion can cohabit with formidable leadership. There are other personality traits, such as neuroticism (how sensitive you are to every challenge the world hurls at you), that do not make leadership easier. Ultimately, self-awareness is key: know which personality cards you hold, so you can skillfully play the best possible hand in the leadership game.

By the mid-1900s, researchers began dismantling the myth of the "born leader." They argued that leadership could be learned. The prevailing view of leadership shifted to a set of **skills** that can be learned and honed. The focus was still very much on the leaders, specifically on their knowledge and skills, only now they could work on developing these skills.

Today leadership research, when it focuses on the leader's characteristics, covers a wide array of topics, from individual traits that are practically fixed, such as personality, to characteristics that can change, but only slowly (such as values), to those that can be managed and optimized (such as energy, self-confidence, resilience, and optimism) to those that can be intentionally accumulated and developed (such as knowledge, skills, and abilities). All of them matter in leadership success and will be the topic of Chapter 2, including what might set finance leaders apart in these respects.

The Interaction

Imagine a manager unveiling her new vision to her team. The leadership interaction begins with her behavior – depicting the vision – and then hinges on how the team responds. Will they nod enthusiastically and happily hop aboard? In doing so, they would *accept* their respective roles as leader and followers in this interaction. Or will they implicitly (or even explicitly) *decline* this assigned role as followers and go back to playing Candy Crush at their desks?

Many well-intentioned leadership books skip over the accept/decline role of followers, focusing solely on the heroic manager's actions. In doing so, they ignore an axiom that I will keep pestering you with throughout this book: leadership is in the eye of the beholder. A manager can brandish her vision passionately, but if her employees collectively shrug and mutter, "meh," that behavior is not experienced as leadership by them.

As research on leadership marched on, it shifted from studying *who effective leaders are* to looking at *what effective leaders do*. This is called the **behavioral** approach to leadership research. Academics examined the sets of behaviors that effective leaders tend to consistently enact and distilled these behaviors into "leadership styles". We will cover the heavyweights of these styles – particularly the champion, transformational leadership – in Chapter 3, along with what the data says about how they work in finance teams. Throughout, keep in mind that how followers *respond* to your behavior is what decides whether it represents effective leadership.

But even this is only part of the picture. *Who* your followers are plays an equally important role in your leadership.

The Followers

Professor Boas Shamir was a respected scholar of leadership. He would give lectures on charisma, and he noticed something odd. At the beginning of his talk, listeners' eyes were bright with anticipation. They were preparing to learn how leaders use their charisma to lead, how they influence their followers, and how this influence develops. But then, as Boas started to talk about followers and their motivation, one by one the lights in those eyes dimmed (4).

Why "followers," a word that may suggest advice about social media rather than about leadership? This is the best term we researchers have to include not only your direct or indirect reports but also any peers or other stakeholders whom you may attempt to lead (or, more humbly, to influence in the direction of a common goal) at various points in your career journey.

This part of the LIFE framework is about followers' individual characteristics, motives, and preferences as well as about characteristics of the team. Is Jim in FP&A driven by insatiable intellectual curiosity or by a desire to climb the corporate ladder? Does your accounting team think the ideal leader is essentially invisible – someone who steps aside and trusts them to do their work unmolested – or do they prefer a visionary presence who routinely pushes them to aim higher? These aren't side questions – they are the terrain you're leading across.

I hope your eyes will stay alert and bright as you go through Chapter 4, in which we dive into followers' characteristics. Surely you want to know, for example, what research tells us about what makes finance professionals tick?

The Environment

Finally, we arrive at the fourth component of the LIFE model: the environment, the context that can either blow a friendly wind in your sails or tie those same sails into a hopeless knot. What is the *culture* of your company? How does *country culture* interact with your *company's culture?* If you hold a management role, how much *position power* do you actually have? For example, are you in a matrix organization where the people you manage also report to two other people named Bob? Is your company in a *growth* phase that encourages all sorts of glorious risk-taking or in a *cost-cutting* one where each dollar is spent with a sigh? There are many ways in which the environment plays a role in the success of your leadership.

For example, David Gibbs, when starting in finance at Yum! Brands, realized early on that the company had a culture that valued sales and marketing talent at a premium, so that top leadership positions tended to be less accessible to, for instance, someone coming from finance. David navigated these environmental straits with great skill all the way to becoming CFO and ultimately CEO of the company, by building a personal brand as "the growth finance guy", pushing against the stereotype of finance as a "sales prevention" function (5). But would David have equally succeeded if, say, the business environment had required drastic cost cuts, and how would he have adapted his personal brand strategy? We will cover the environment and its many challenges in Chapter 5.

The environment shapes what kind of leadership is possible – and what kind is needed.

Where do we place LIFE in research?

Let's summarize how the LIFE model brings together the evolution of thought in leadership research, as the focus moved from traits to skills, then to behavior, to followers and finally to the environment:

- The **trait-focused** view, the oldest conceptualization of what makes effective leaders, gradually declined in importance in leadership research but is currently experiencing a revival. It focuses primarily on the "**L**" in LIFE.
- The **skills-focused** view was introduced when the idea that leaders might be made, not just born, started to get traction, and has been consistently accounted for, in scientific studies. Like the trait-based view, it's about the leader, therefore the "**L**" in LIFE.
- The **behavior-focused** view followed, leading to the proliferation of leadership styles, and is still going strong today. It moves the focus to the "**I**" in LIFE.
- The **follower-focused** view is a more recent addition, recognizing the active and sometimes decisive role of followers in leadership effectiveness. It deals with the "**F**" in LIFE.
- The **environment-focused** view, the newest kid on the block, aims to draw attention to the make-or-break role that the environment can play in leadership. It considers the "**E**" in LIFE.

Figure 1.2 illustrates this historical evolution of leadership researchers' focus.[1]

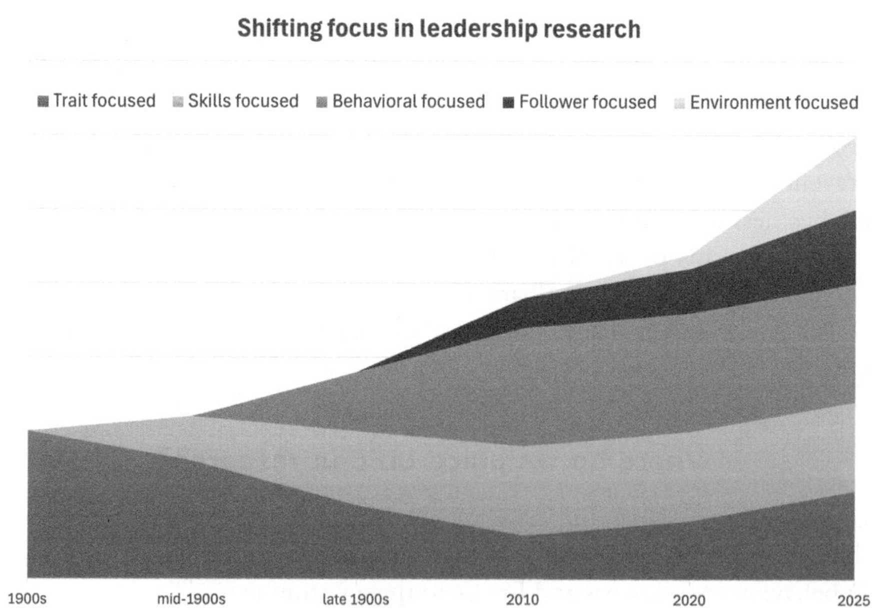

Figure 1.2 Shifting focus in leadership research.

So far, in presenting the LIFE model, I only spoke about a one-way influence, whereby the leadership interaction is impacted by leader, follower, and environmental characteristics. However, there is also **a feedback loop**, whereby the leadership interaction impacts the characteristics of the leader, the followers, and the environment. Your leadership experiences will alter your knowledge and skills, impact your energy and motivation, and color your mindsets and values. Followers' ideas of what makes a good leader are shaped by their own interactions with leaders in the past. And you, as a leader, might try to mold the environment by, for example, shifting the company culture or inspiring the team to achieve more favorable business conditions.

Many popular books about leadership propose some structure, a set of, say, seven rules or ten principles, guaranteed to solve every leadership conundrum you might ever face. These prescriptions tend to revolve around leadership behaviors and the related skills. Now, that isn't entirely misguided – after all, your own behavior is the most direct lever you can pull. But, without considering your traits, your followers' characteristics, and the environment, it's incomplete.

This holistic perspective is especially relevant given the mission of this book: unpacking what leadership means in finance. As we will see in the following chapters, there are specifics in finance leaders' and finance followers' characteristics, as well as in the environment surrounding the CFO role, that are important to leadership success.

Note

1 The figure is not at scale but is only meant to give a broad idea of the relative importance accorded to each of the five views on leadership during a particular period.

References

(1) Carlyle, T. *On heroes, hero-worship, and the heroic in history*. Boston, MA: Houghton Mifflin: 1907.
(2) Drucker, P. T. *The practice of management*. New York: Harper & Brothers: 1954.
(3) Presley, S. *2023 USF alumni awards: Steve Presley '90 - Distinguished alumni award*. USF Alumni Association: 2023.
(4) Eilam-Shamir, G., Kark, R., & Popper, M. Boas Shamir: The person, his impact and legacy. *Leadership Quarterly* 2017, 28 (4), 563–577. DOI: 10.1016/j.leaqua.2016.03.004
(5) Novak, D. David Gibbs, Yum! Brands CEO - Flip the script in tough situations. https://youtu.be/1bgneW-d_F4?t=183: 2024.

2

THE LEADER

We begin our examination of the LIFE model by magnifying the L in LIFE: what does a leader have that helps or hinders their leadership? From immutable characteristics such as intelligence to evolving ones such as values, to those actively developed such as knowledge and skills, each leader brings a complex and unique configuration to the table. Throughout, we ask: *Are finance leaders different?*

Leaders' traits: Are finance leaders different?

We used to believe that most of a leader's secret power came from their individual traits, such as intelligence and personality. As explained in Chapter 1, these days we know better. Still, leaders' unique characteristics can make an important difference in the LIFE equation. Some of these, we can do little about but should still be aware of: for example, *better looking CFOs receive more favorable loan contracts from their banks!* (1). Of these fixed traits, intelligence plays the biggest role in leaders' success, although not always in the direction you would expect.

DOI: 10.4324/9781003581734-4

Intelligence: A leadership asset – unless you're too smart

It will surprise no one that intelligence is correlated with successful leadership (2). However, when it comes to leadership, there is such a thing as being *too* intelligent. Research suggests that while intelligence enhances leadership perceptions, this advantage hits a ceiling at 12 IQ points above a team's average—beyond which, a leader may seem brilliant but perplexingly out of touch (3). The study examined people leadership, rather than strategic brilliance or visionary thinking, which can still benefit from sky-high IQs.

What does this mean for CFOs? Well, the average IQ of accounting professionals is 115 (4), meaning that your ideal leadership IQ hovers around 127. But let's be honest: if you're reading this, your problem is unlikely to be *insufficient* intelligence. If anything, you might be too smart for your own good – at least when it comes to leading people. The broader and more diverse your area of responsibility, the more you must remind yourself that your audience is not made up exclusively of front-row A-students.

Clarity is your ally. Use simple language. Explain things that seem self-evident. No one, in the history of finance, has ever complained about "that CFO who over-explains". More importantly, communicate with both the heart and the head. Numbers rarely inspire; stories do (more on this in Chapter 6 on communication).

Otherwise, since there isn't much we can do about our own IQ level,[1] we move on to other traits of leaders.

Personality: The leadership cocktail

Personality traits are often summarized by the Big Five model: extraversion, conscientiousness, emotional stability, openness to experience, and agreeableness. A newer model, HEXACO, adds a sixth trait: honesty-humility. Here's what they mean for leadership:

1. **Honesty-Humility (H)** – Sincerity, fairness, greed avoidance, modesty. High scorers are honest and modest; low scorers, manipulative and self-serving. As you would expect, individuals high in honesty-humility make better leaders. What may be surprising is the strength of this relationship, with honesty-humility being one of the strongest predictors of leader effectiveness (6).

However, as with all of the HEXACO traits, the "too much of a good thing" rule applies. For example, even in the most egalitarian and least political of cultures, good leaders have trust in their abilities and know when honesty may not be the best policy.

2. **Emotionality (E)** – Fearfulness, anxiety, dependence, sentimentality. High scorers are sensitive and anxious; low scorers are emotionally stable and independent. While lower emotionality makes you a better leader, this relationship also takes an inverse U shape, with extreme emotional stability not serving your leadership because it tends to make you less empathetic and less likely to adapt to your environment. Leaders must strike a balance: enough composure to steer the ship but enough sensitivity to stay connected with the crew.
3. **eXtraversion (X)** – Consists of two subdimensions: sociability (being talkative, needing and thriving in the presence of others) and agency (being assertive, energetic, bold). High scorers are outgoing and energetic; low scorers are reserved and quiet.

   Extraversion shows the highest correlation with leadership, most consistently across studies (6–9). While there is such a thing as too much extraversion when it comes to leadership, this applies mostly to individuals who score extremely high on the sociability (not the agency) subdimension of extraversion.

   Although we habitually divide the world around us into extraverts and introverts, there are many individuals who fall somewhere in the middle, sometimes called "ambiverts".[2]
4. **Agreeableness (A)** – Forgiveness, patience, tolerance. High scorers are cooperative and lenient; low scorers are critical and unconcerned with others' feelings. Agreeableness is the least correlated with leadership, although this varies depending on culture, and some countries such as China or Central American countries assign more value to leaders higher in agreeableness (6).
5. **Conscientiousness (C)** – Organization, diligence, responsibility. High scorers are disciplined and goal-oriented; low scorers are impulsive and careless. Conscientiousness is one of the strongest predictors of leadership, alongside extraversion and honesty-humility (6). Again, the hump curve pattern applies: too much conscientiousness could hamper your leadership (e.g., by cutting off your appetite for risk).

6. **Openness to experience (O)** – Creativity, curiosity, unconventionality. High scorers are imaginative and open-minded; low scorers prefer routine and tradition. Leaders higher in openness are more likely to inspire others, but there is variation across studies as to the strength of this relationship.

Statistically, finance professionals tend to be more emotionally stable, more conscientious, and less extraverted than other professionals (11). Given the importance of extraversion in leadership, let's examine it and what you can do if you are an introvert.

Extraversion: The currency of leadership?

Extraversion is leadership's equivalent of tallness in basketball: a definite advantage though not strictly mandatory. Extraverts are more likely to be promoted to leadership roles (12) as well as to emerge as leaders in a peer group (13).

Although much has been made in the popular literature of an "introvert advantage", there is little evidence that introverted leaders are more successful or effective. The most widely cited research study in support of the introvert superiority theory (14) found indeed that leaders lower in extraversion tended to foster higher team performance, but only when their teams were highly proactive (i.e., the team spoke up or took action to improve results without waiting to be prompted by the leader). More importantly, a closer look at the study's real-life sample, comprising managers of pizza stores and their teams, shows that 84% of them were extraverted and the remaining 16% were only slightly introverted. In other words, the study found at most a "mild introvert" advantage, and, even then, only when the team does not need much leading to begin with.

The importance of extraversion in leadership seems to be confirmed by the sparse research on personality of finance people. Finance professionals, and accountants in particular, score lower than the general population on extraversion (11, 15). Yet most S&P 500 CFOs appear to be extraverted, almost as much as CEOs (16). This suggests that extraverted finance professionals are more likely to reach the CFO role. But could it also mean that some CFOs learned to *act* extraverted?

Personality is practically unchangeable[3]; therefore, introverted finance professionals are unlikely to morph into extraverts on their way to the CFO seat. However, while each of us has a given level of long-term ("trait") extraversion, there is high variability in our momentary ("state") levels of extraversion. Even trait introverts have numerous moments of state extraversion as they go about their day (18).

A closer look at those studies that assess CFO personalities shows that they all rely on indirect methods, based on videos or transcripts of earnings calls (usually the Q&A section). This raises the question: are most CFOs really extraverted, or do some of them only act extraverted during the earnings calls? Introverted CFOs would likely want to act extraverted (which, as we have seen, means not only sociable but also energetic, bold, and assertive) in front of investors. They could probably sustain high levels of extraversion for the short duration of earnings calls. They could succeed in being perceived as extraverts by an audience that rarely sees them outside of these predetermined interactions.

Should introverted leaders act extraverted?

If you are an introverted leader, should you act extraverted? At first sight, research seems to suggest that you should. Acting extraverted when you are an introvert is apparently good not only for your interaction with others but also for your own happiness (18). An experiment in which introverts were instructed to act extraverted showed that they were more likely to be perceived as leaders by the team (19).

However, the experiment consisted of a one-off, 20-minute interaction within groups whose members did not know each other. Again, as in the CFO personality study above, it should be possible for all but the most introverted of individuals to act extraverted for a short time, in front of an audience that has never seen them outside of this controlled interaction. This is a very different context from how leaders interact with their teams at work.

Moreover, the "act extraverted to be happy" study by Fleeson and colleagues (2002) explored *naturally occurring* moments of extraversion in the subjects' lives over the previous day/week (i.e., when the subjects acted extraverted without being asked to by the researcher). This may mean, as the authors admit, that causality could go the other way: we tend to act more extraverted in those moments when we are happier. Another study found that introverts reported being more tired, less happy, and feeling less authentic when having to act extraverted (20).

In short, acting extraverted when you are not may exact a toll.

Nevertheless, as CFO, you will be well served by strategic bursts of extraversion. For example, Monish Patolawala, CFO of ADM, passionately advocates proactive engagement: "Go out and meet your people listen to pain points. [...] Go out, reach out, reach out to people. It's amazing what you'll hear" (21).

Monish's advice works only if you engage in the kind of extraverted interaction that invites people to open up. Many of us were subjected to the odd ritual of sitting through an "informal chat" with an introverted top boss whose relief, when it was over, was even greater than ours. Acting extraverted on such occasions (and feeling it!) is a must.

British thinkers Rob Goffee and Gareth Jones posed a disarmingly simple question: Why should anyone be led by you? (22). It is a question that should haunt all leaders more than their unread Slack messages. Their answer – equally elegant – was that great leaders must "be themselves, more, with skill". This is not an invitation to overshare your fondness for spreadsheets. It's a call to *know yourself so well* that you can amplify the right parts of your personality at the right time – without feeling like a fraud. And this brings us back to extraversion. You may be a self-identified introvert. But, as we saw, research (and lived experience) shows that introverts do, in fact, have bursts of extraversion – moments of energy, boldness, and assertion. Goffee and Jones help us see that using those moments deliberately is not acting out a role. You're not becoming someone else – only spotlighting the traits the moment calls for.

Here are several practical tips for introverted leaders:

- **Know your baseline**. If you are unsure, take a personality test. You can find a list of research-based personality tests at https://ipip.ori.org/ (23),[4]
- **Draw on agency rather than sociability**. Remember that "extravert" means not only sociable but also energetic, enthusiastic, bold, active, and assertive (traits that psychologists group together under "agentic"). It may come more naturally to you to be agentic than to be sociable. Most studies agree that the agentic subdimension of extraversion is correlated with leadership, while there is less research agreement about what being sociable means for leadership (8, 25).

- **Strategically "turn it on"**. Be confident that, unless you are an extreme introvert, you are perfectly capable of behaving extraverted over short periods of time. But choose when to act extraverted wisely. The ideal audiences for your extraverted persona are stakeholders who are important to you but with whom you interact infrequently enough to be able to consistently maintain an extraverted behavior.
- **Stay authentic with direct reports**. When interacting with those you lead directly on a day-to-day basis, it is best not to act extraverted unless it comes naturally, as they would likely soon sniff you out as inauthentic.
- **Finance allows some leeway**. You might be less penalized for introversion as a leader in finance, since introverts (more often found among finance employees) are readier to accept and follow introverted leaders. However, as your area of responsibility grows, diversity of distribution on the introversion–extraversion continuum also increases, and while introverts are OK, albeit not ecstatic, about having an extraverted leader, extraverts are not happy with being led by an introvert.

We delve further into how followers' personality influences their response to the leader's personality, and the specifics of finance employees in this respect, in Chapter 4.

Personal values: A rocky topic

Your values are your rock. "Anchor your leadership in your values", enjoin leadership gurus, coffee mugs, and every other source of unsolicited wisdom. But what if your top values fall squarely in the "self-enhancement" category – prioritizing personal success and happiness over noble altruism? Are some values inherently better than others? And if so, shouldn't you try to lead by those superior values instead?

This is rocky terrain to explore, and doing so comprehensively would take its own book (there's a reason why ethics is a branch of philosophy). For our practical purposes, we will first define your personal values and ways to determine them, then we will separate moral absolutes from personal values, and finally, we will discuss how your values are your "rock" and the pitfalls of (in)authenticity.

Your personal values

They are "desirable, trans-situational goals, varying in importance, that serve as guiding principles in people's lives" (26). Whether or not you are fully aware what yours are, they inform your behavior and aspirations. Schwartz's model of Basic Human Values (Figure 2.1) organizes values along two principal dimensions:

1. **Self-enhancement versus self-transcendence**. This dimension concerns whether values serve individual or collective interests. When values center on the individual, they highlight power, achievement, and

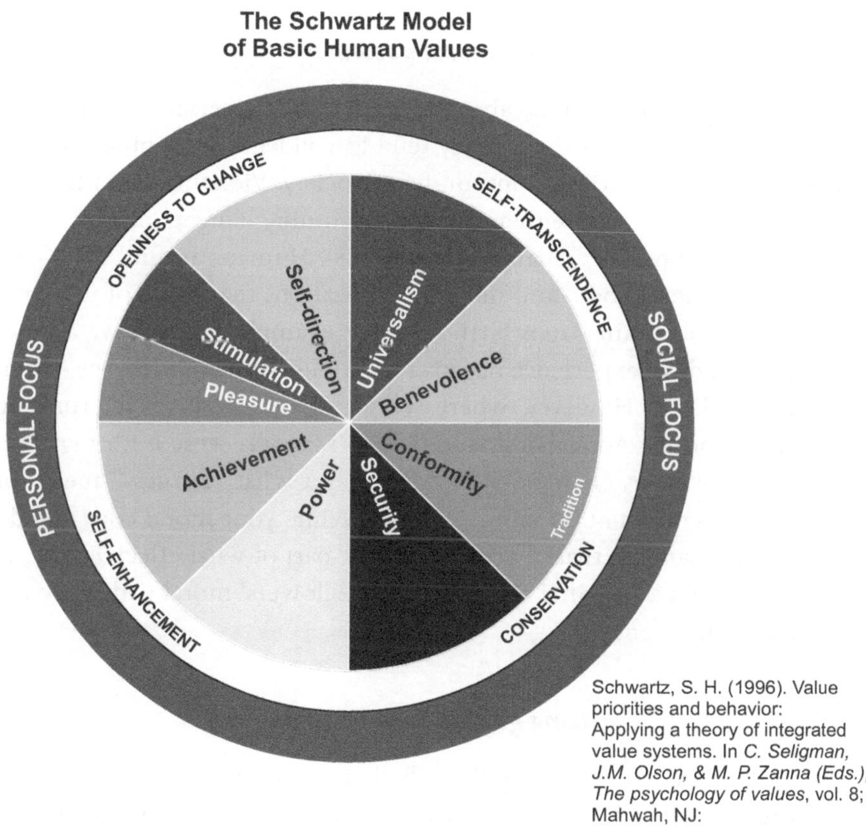

Figure 2.1 The Schwartz model of basic human values.

success; when they emphasize the collective, they stress altruism, care, and universalism.

2. **Openness to change versus conservation**. This dimension contrasts values oriented toward novelty, experimentation, and flexibility with those that uphold tradition, fulfill social obligations, and favor conformity.

You can find out more about Schwartz's values and take the corresponding test for free (27). Alternatively, you may have taken Hogan's MVPI (Motives, Values, Preferences Inventory) test, which yields a more detailed assessment of your motives, expressed similarly (though not identically) with Schwartz's values.

Your moral absolutes

Unlike personal values, moral absolutes tend to be universal and often take the form of "Thou shalt nots". They tend to condemn wronging others – individually or as a group, community, or society. Violating them triggers strong moral emotions, either other-condemning (anger, disgust, contempt) or self-conscious (shame or guilt) (28). Humans around the world share a basic moral code, and there are indications that some of it is programmed in our brains from birth (29). For example, we all have a sense of fairness, and we experience negative emotions, from an early age, when we see it violated. However, where we get in trouble is in interpreting what "fair" means. Adolf Hitler and Nelson Mandela were both regarded by their followers as champions of fairness, yet what "fairness" meant in the two cases could not be more different. While your moral code should be largely the same as that of your followers, part of what effective leaders do is to interpret and frame their and their followers' moral codes so as to emphasize alignment.

Being guided by your values

If your values inform your behavior whether you want it or not, don't you, by definition, always lead in accordance with your values without having to go into deep soul-searching when faced, for example, with difficult choices? Not if your context pushes in a different direction. If, for example, your top values are benevolence (caring for and about others around you) and conformity (respecting rules and not ruffling feathers) but you are leading in a context that requires a strong hand, you might attempt to behave or make difficult choices more in accordance with power- and change-oriented values. Inevitably, this will result in feelings of inauthenticity. Consider François's case and the taste of compromise.

CASE: FRANÇOIS PAVIOT AT AURORA FIRST TRUST[5]

François joined Aurora First Trust, an insurance company, as CFO after several senior investment banking roles. He soon realized the strategic importance of shorter pricing cycles for Aurora and saw that this required more detailed and more frequent information on the company's main revenue drivers than the accounting systems were able to provide.

Peter, the Chief Accounting Officer, did not agree with François's assessment. Peter saw the younger François as an ambitious man who had little experience or knowledge of the day-to-day workings of an insurance company and who was eager to make his mark by fixing something that wasn't broken. Peter's behavior, though polite, left no doubt as to how unimpressed he was with the new CFO.

François would have fired Peter but, with no accounting experience and a sprawling mess of the company's various accounting systems that only Peter seemed to understand, was forced to take the long roundabout route. And so François had to compromise ("swallow his pride" as he put it) and endure 18 months of strategic patience, navigating an awkward alliance while the accounting change was being implemented.

Did François stay true to his values? Not exactly. His top values were achievement (being successful, aiming for excellence) and transparency (part of "security" in Schwartz's circle), and he felt he was badly trampling over them during that one-and-a-half-year period. But leadership may sometimes require that you hold your values more loosely, to adapt to reality.

Values are not habits

If you feel inauthentic at work, it might be a sign that you are straying too far from your values, and this cannot be sustained for long. However, be aware that sometimes discomfort arises not because you're betraying your values but because you're **shedding old habits** that masqueraded as values.

CROSSROADS LIFE: CLARA'S WORK ETHIC

Clara is the CFO of the Romanian subsidiary of Crossroads Life, a major insurance corporation. The film opens with her recalling a saying from her mother – an echo of the values we often inherit without realizing it. "My mother always said: What's the point of doing anything, unless you give it your best?" becomes Clara's unconscious mantra, shaping her beliefs about what real work looks like.

For Clara, "real work" excludes idle chatter. She disdains gossip – broadly defined as any conversation about others, even if well meaning – and steers clear of the watercooler crowd. This principle sets her apart when she's promoted to regional CFO for Crossroads Life in Europe. In this new role, she's surrounded by colleagues who linger in corridors, chatting freely. Clara holds fast to her code but in doing so misses out on vital relationship-building and informal intelligence-gathering.

It takes a major turning point – a so-called *crucible of leadership*, a transformative trial that can either break or remake a leader – for Clara to confront a hard truth: informal conversation, when not malicious, can be a crucial part of leadership. In high-level roles, political acumen often begins with small talk.

Ultimately, Clara learns that what she thought was a core value – avoiding gossip and casual conversation – was just a habit. Her true value is rigorous, high-quality work. And she can uphold it while embracing a broader definition of what "work" looks like at the top.

Watch the scene selection at: https://www.ed.movie/clara-values (or scan the QR code).

Leadership demands continuous adaptation, and that includes shedding those comfortable old habits.

The leader's psychological capital

You are likely familiar with **financial capital** (money), **human capital** (skills and experience), and **social capital** (connections). But how much thought have you given to **psychological capital** (**PsyCap** to its friends)?

In the early 2000s, psychologists observed that some people seemed not only better equipped to deal with whatever life threw at them but also eager to throw something back with equal enthusiasm. These individuals exhibited high levels of **optimism, self-confidence, resourcefulness**, and **resilience** – a combination now known as PsyCap.

Among your colleagues, you will easily recognize the lucky winners of the PsyCap lottery. When a deal collapses, they see it as a temporary setback. When faced with uncertainty, they assume things will work out. If life drops a big boulder in their pathway to a goal, they take it as a great opportunity to find another, even better path. They are self-assured without arrogance, certain that they have what it takes or at least can get what it takes. And when they fail at something and fall flat on their faces, they cheerfully spring back up, grateful for the opportunity to have practiced doing a burpee.

Leadership thrives on PsyCap

Getting people enthusiastic about a goal starts with being twice as enthusiastic about it yourself. Helping teams build resilience in the face of adversity starts with your own resilience. Think about a leader who inspired you, and you will likely recall that they were unwaveringly optimistic.

Is PsyCap an unfair genetic advantage, or can it be cultivated? The answer is both. While genes and childhood experiences play a role, PsyCap can be protected and grown intentionally.

If you are curious about your levels of PsyCap, MindGarden offers the scientifically validated self-test.[6] However, you do not have to scientifically assess your current levels of PsyCap in order to learn how to manage it. We discuss ways to protect and increase your PsyCap in Chapter 11, "Leading yourself".

But… should CFOs be unwaveringly optimistic?

The CFO personality paradox

We've shown that leadership success is associated with optimistic, risk-taking personalities and that, to some extent, you can intentionally grow your optimism and enthusiasm. Yet the CFO role seems to require a very different profile: a cool-headed, prudent gatekeeper, a solid counterbalance to the passionate, visionary CEO.

This is how real-life examples of successful CEO–CFO duos are always portrayed. For example, here is Alfred Lumsdaine, CFO of Ardent Health, describing how he complements Marty Bonick, the CEO:

> Marty is strategic and focused on the long-term, but we must continually focus on the now. [...] Marty continually pushes the organization long-term, while I push based on the next 30 days. This complimentary relationship helps us hit our major milestones.

Marty, for his part, sees Alfred as the adult in the room:

> I look to Alfred to be our critical-eye and litmus test to make sure we are making good business decisions. He is the conscience that sits on my shoulder, and we must have that tug-of-war to be successful (30).

Research supports the advantages of nose-to-the-ground, killjoy CFOs. For example, creditors are not amused when the CFO signals an optimistic, forward-looking personality (31). Moreover, companies seem to perform better when their risk-taking, visionary CEOs are grounded by risk-averse, facts-only CFOs (32) Ominously, CFOs are more likely to show optimism in an earnings call when they sell their stock holdings shortly after (33).

In short, the personality required from a CFO seems to be the exact opposite of the personality of an inspiring leader. Yet today's CFOs need to lead and inspire more than ever.

Furthermore, if you plan to transition to a CEO role someday, that same dig-your-heels-in personality that made you an ideal CFO would make you a far-from-ideal CEO. David Gibbs was CFO of Yum! Brands before becoming its CEO. He mentions his reluctance in taking the CFO role, afraid that the stereotypes associated with it would rub onto perceptions about his own potential:

> I had ambitions to be a big general manager, and there's always a little bit of fear about becoming pigeonholed in a functional role, particularly when you take the top role in that function, you sort of limit your options (34).

Here are three tips for dealing with the CFO personality paradox:

- **Separate role from self.** This is not unfamiliar to you. We play multiple roles in our lives, and we often display different "personalities" in each, without feeling less authentic. You might play a stern, rules-based parent role with your rebel teenage son yet be a goofy, adventurous companion to your friend since high school.

  Similarly, when you crash-land, with financial arguments, the CEO's high-flying dream of a new investment, you should be aware that you are doing it because being the pessimist in the room is a vital role to play at that moment, for the good of the organization, rather than because you are inherently a pessimist. If that distinction is clear to you, it will also be seen by others. Adding a bit of humor to your analysis (while staying away from sarcasm, the most corrosive form of humor for leaders!), or simply showing an upbeat disposition even while your message is sobering, can help make the distinction between role and self even clearer.

  Sandeep Aujla, CFO of Intuit, makes a mantra out of separating role from self:

  > Take your responsibility seriously but don't take yourself too seriously. I take my role and responsibilities – professional and personal – very seriously and aim to perform them exceptionally well. Yet, I also believe in being easy-going, appreciating humor and not overly worrying about things that I cannot control.[7]

- **Segment your audiences.** A quarterly investor call will always benefit from an optimistic CEO–realistic CFO dynamic. On the other hand, when talking to your team about launching a big change program in finance, you want to be the optimistic, visionary leader they need, and for that you will need to mobilize and grow your PsyCap.

- **Fight the stereotype**. Even your best-intended colleagues, after having seen you say "no" several times, may fall back on the stereotype of CFOs as pessimistic, lacking long-term strategic thinking, or even worse, lacking imagination. Purposefully hunt for those opportunities (however small) to say "yes" and ensure that they are noted by your teammates. When bringing a "no" message, take some time to show why it might actually support the company's strategic direction. Use storytelling to make others see things your way and to break the "numbers only" CFO stereotype (more on this in Chapter 7 on inspiring and motivating tools for the CFO).

David Gibbs puts it as consciously working on your personal brand:

> I decided early on that I would make my brand, the David Gibbs brand, all about driving growth. I was going to be the CFO that figured out how to invest money to make even more money. I think a lot of people don't think about their own brand within the company, but everybody has one. [...] And then, when I got into a position where I could influence others, I would come up with some pithy ways to describe what we wanted to be, like "find a way to say 'yes'". You know, the Finance department, as some people I've heard call it, can often be the "sales prevention department". We don't want to be the Sales Prevention Department; we want to be the Find-a-Way-to-Say-Yes department" (34).

Leaders' skills, knowledge, and experience

Hard skills: still essential (despite the Ted Lasso effect)

A lot has been said about the importance of soft skills in leadership, to the point where hard skills are sometimes portrayed as optional for great leaders. The popular TV character Ted Lasso, an American football coach who somehow ends up leading a British soccer team (despite knowing *nothing* about soccer), was hailed as an exemplar of leadership even by the business press, including the *Financial Times* (35). He somehow conveys the notion that good people management is so important that leaders should focus on honing those skills and none other, leaving the technical wizardry to their employees.

Granted, the readers of the *Financial Times*, many of them experts in the finance field, hardly need reminding about sharpening their cashflow projection knowledge but often do need prodding to develop their soft skills. Nevertheless, technical expertise *is* important in leadership. Employees are more satisfied when their boss is technically competent, especially entry-level employees, who prefer leaders who can answer their *actual* work-related questions (36).

Among senior executives, the CFO is especially expected to draw on strong technical knowledge. But does that mean a CFO must be a master of all financial domains? Not necessarily. The "halo effect" suggests that strong expertise in one area creates the perception of competence in others (37). Moreover, you might benefit from an "accelerating expertise" effect, as described by Joseph Nelson, CFO of Delta Corp Holdings:

> What I've found is that, once you've grabbed an area of expertise in one place, whether it's accounting or corporate finance or whatever, after you really went deep into that one, those skills allow you to ramp up to the next functional area faster. You won't maybe have the same level of depth, but you'll get up the learning curve a lot faster.[8]

So CFOs don't need to be omniscient – but they *do* need one or two deep areas of expertise to establish credibility. Of course, some basic understanding of all finance areas is required. Accounting employees do not take kindly to CFOs completely ignorant of their trade: advice to an employee complaining about a new CFO not knowing "basic accounting" includes such gems as "recognize him as a liability" or, more worryingly, "switch to cash basis" (38).

The credits and debits of accounting expertise

CFOs with accounting backgrounds, such as CPAs and former Chief Accounting Officers, bring clear benefits: their companies tend to be more compliant and handle regulatory matters more efficiently (39). However, the proportion of CPAs among the CFOs of large US public companies has been declining, from 46% in 2014 to 38% in 2024 (40, 41).

Studies indicate that "accounting expert CFOs" are less likely to succeed in the top finance role and even less likely to be promoted to CEO (42).

Why? Because while they are brilliant at ensuring financial compliance, they tend to have less exposure to areas such as strategy, business development, global operations, and technology, compared with nonaccounting expert CFOs. They are also less likely to sit on the board of a public company and less likely to have an MBA degree, which is increasingly valued in CFOs (as of 2024, 52% of CFOs of large US public companies had an MBA (41)). In short, it appears that mastering accounting can be so time-consuming that it prevents CFOs from developing the other skills needed to move beyond the finance function (42).

Similarly, a study by Datta & Iskandar-Datta (43) finds that CFOs with "generalist", "strategic" profiles (such as having an MBA from an elite school) command a compensation premium compared with CFOs with "specialist" profiles (such as having an accounting degree or a non-MBA master's degree, even when the latter is from an elite school). Large companies are almost three times more likely to promote a nonaccounting finance executive (e.g., Financial Planning and Analysis, VP of Finance) to CFO than to elevate a Corporate Controller or Chief Accounting Officer (41).

The key takeaway? Accounting is a fantastic foundation, but it must be complemented with broader business acumen to avoid career stagnation.

From expert to leader: Stepping "into the wild"

As managers grow in seniority, they start drawing less on their "hard" subject matter expertise and more on generalist, "soft" skills such as social effectiveness, influencing and networking, and ability to get followership (44). As a CFO put it, "Congratulations! You've stepped into a senior managerial role. You are a relationship manager now".

Often, this transition is not gradual but rather brutal, like being hurled into a managerial wilderness with little more than a compass and some PowerPoint slides. Many of the CFOs I interviewed did not have much use for "soft" skills before they stepped into the C-suite. They were typically recruited externally, often from the investments or consulting industries, after having led smaller, high-performing teams filled with people much like themselves: smart, ambitious, self-motivated. Suddenly, as CFOs, they found themselves managing massive teams with widely varying levels of skill, motivation, and engagement, embedded in complicated organizational structures and practices. They needed to navigate corporate politics, influence colleagues over whom they had no formal authority, and – most distressingly – motivate employees who seemed more excited about getting home for dinner than achieving peak financial efficiency.

Nevertheless, while taking this "crash course" in soft skills, many CFOs found that their expertise provided a comforting anchor. As Mark Hawkins, former CFO of Salesforce, sees it:

> For a first-time CFO, intimate knowledge of how your business makes money – and what it spends money on – is what you fall back on when you don't yet have all the requisite soft skills (45).

We will open the CFO's leadership toolbox and bring to light and examine soft skills, such as communication, charismatic tactics, understanding individual motivation, influencing, networking, and political skill, in Part 2 of this book.

What this means for you

As a CFO, your technical expertise builds your credibility, but your leadership abilities determine your success. In short:

- **Be excellent at one thing**. Develop deep expertise in at least one financial domain – it will create a halo effect for everything else.
- **Don't let accounting define you**. If you're an outstanding accounting expert, make sure you actively seek broader business experience and avoid getting pigeonholed in your role.
- **You do not need to let go of expertise, but make it one of your many leadership tools**. Expertise is important for leaders' credibility, and especially important for CFOs, but at some point it will become insufficient.
- **Develop your soft skills**. Communication, influencing and inspiring others, motivation, political skill, and networking may be "soft", but lacking them makes for a hard landing. Learn more about each of these in Part 2 of this book.

In short: you need to be good at finance to become a CFO, but you need to be great at leadership to stay there.

Emotional intelligence: Trait or skill?

Picture this: you are having a meeting with Martin, one of your most brilliant and dedicated team members. Martin admires you immensely – he sees you as a paragon of principle, an unwavering champion of what is right. Today you inform him about your decision to delay implementing an important but unpopular measure that Martin had worked on fleshing out. You expect a few questions, maybe a sigh, but instead you get a short nod and a clipped "Got it". Meeting over. You return to your inbox, pleased at how smoothly that went.

Two months later, Martin resigns.

You're baffled. Where did this come from? You retrace your steps, going over that meeting again in your head. To you, the decision was strategic – delaying implementation was a politically astute move that would prevent unnecessary fallout. But to Martin, it was something far more damning: a violation of the principles he thought you embodied. Your ability to pragmatically navigate corporate landscapes was, to him, not wisdom but betrayal. And unfortunately, disillusioned protégés – especially when they are young and have a fierce, no-compromise life philosophy – do not tend to send follow-up emails outlining their grievances. They simply vanish.

To prevent this debacle, you would have ideally reflected on all of these considerations before your meeting with Martin. But if you had not – maybe because several strategic priorities were competing for your attention – you could have at least picked up on his emotional cues – the subtle stiffening of his shoulders, the slight hesitation before his curt response – and you might have sensed the brewing storm. Had you connected the dots between his deep sense of integrity and his reaction, you might have found a way to reassure him, to explain your reasoning in a way that acknowledged his perspective. Emotional intelligence (EI) could have saved the day.

In recent years, EI has been hailed as the magic ingredient of leadership. Books have been written. Seminars have been sold out. If leadership were a superhero franchise, EI would be the secret serum that turns the ordinary manager into an extraordinary one. Yet not everyone is convinced. Some academic purists remain skeptical – not about the importance of managing emotions but about how we define and measure this elusive skill (46).

However, if, as practitioners, we squint a little when looking at all the academic wrangling, we can tease out some consensus that EI is made of four distinct abilities (46, 47):

1. **Emotion recognition**: The ability to read the silent language of facial expressions, body language, and tone – decoding emotions as swiftly as a poker player reads a bluff.
2. **Understanding of emotions**: Recognizing not just *what* someone is feeling but *why*. This is the difference between thinking "Martin is irritated" and realizing "Martin is irritated because he feels I've betrayed my core values".
3. **Emotion regulation**: The inner art of keeping one's cool. Not letting irritation bubble into an email typed too hastily.
4. **Emotion management**: Navigating emotionally charged situations with finesse, defusing tensions, and fostering constructive outcomes.

But is EI an innate gift, bestowed upon the lucky few like good hair? Or is it a skill that can be nurtured? The answer, unsurprisingly, is both. While genetics and early upbringing lay the groundwork, EI is not a fixed trait. Research shows it can be cultivated through deliberate effort, from bite-sized online interventions to immersive leadership development programs (48).

Yet there's a paradox. Those who most need to improve their EI are often the least inclined to do so. Individuals scoring low on EI tests often dismiss the tests as pseudo-science, brush off feedback, and show little interest in increasing their EI. Meanwhile, those already high in EI eagerly sign up for workshops, keen to sharpen an already strong skill (49). The result? The emotionally aware become even more so, while the oblivious continue their blissfully unaware (and often destructive) journey through leadership.

So, where does that leave us?

- **Consider taking an EI test**. The Geneva Emotional Competence Test (47) is currently favored by researchers (46). Alternatively, the MSCEIT (Mayer-Salovey-Caruso Emotional Intelligence Test) remains widely used despite occasional criticism.
- **Practice mindful awareness**. Simply being conscious of EI's importance can subtly elevate your leadership.

- **Choose the right program**. If you are serious about developing your EI, seek programs that measure your EI before and after the intervention and that do so using ability-based questionnaires and not ones based on your perceptions or those of others. Ability-based EI assessments have right and wrong answers, akin to IQ tests. Perception-based tests could be summarized in one question, "Do you believe you are emotionally intelligent?"

In the end, whether you were born with the EI of a sage or of a bulldozer, there is always room to grow. In leadership, the ability to navigate emotions – your own and those of others – is often what separates those who inspire from those who bewilder their teams into quitting.

In closing

As we have seen, leadership involves a constant calibration of personal strengths and weaknesses, of natural tendencies and deliberate effort.

The best CFOs are a walking paradox: numbers-driven realists yet also enthusiastic motivators. Acting extraverted in certain situations but not in others. Emotionally intelligent but also coldly rational.

So what separates those who thrive from those who stall? Adaptability. Knowing when to lean into your strengths, when to stretch beyond them, and – perhaps most importantly – when to rewrite the rules altogether.

Notes

1 Unless it is about contending with cognitive decline as we grow older (for which the most effective intervention appears to be aerobic exercise) (5).
2 The "ambivert" term is "personality non grata" with most psychologists, as it seems to imply distinct behaviors from what one would expect from a normal person between the introvert/extravert extremes (10).
3 This long-standing paradigm may crumble in the future, as there are exciting new developments in research on volitional personality shifts (17). The research is still young, and it is too early to talk about practical applications, but if you are interested in changing some of your personality, you may want to watch this space.
4 Note that the MBTI (Myers–Briggs Type Indicator), a personality assessment tool that is still popular among employers, especially in North America, has been disproven by research (24).
5 Interviewed CFO, anonymized.
6 https://www.mindgarden.com/136-psychological-capital-questionnaire.

7 https://www.cfo.com/news/the-6-am-cfo-how-intuit-sandeep-aujla-starts-his-day-turbo-tax-quickbooks-software/734490/.
8 Interview with the author.

References

(1) Hrazdil, K., Li, J., Lobo, G., & Zhang, R. CFO facial beauty and bank loan contracting. *Accounting and Finance* 2024, 64, 975–1009. DOI: 10.1111/acfi.13168

(2) Cavazotte, F., Moreno, V., & Hickmann, M. Effects of leader intelligence, personality and emotional intelligence on transformational leadership and managerial performance. *Leadership Quarterly* 2012, 23 (3), 443–455. DOI: 10.1016/j.leaqua.2011.10.003

(3) Antonakis, J., House, R. J., & Simonton, D. K. Can super smart leaders suffer from too much of a good thing? The curvilinear effect of intelligence on perceived leadership behavior. *Journal of Applied Psychology* 2017, 102 (7), 1003–1021. DOI: 10.1037/apl0000221

(4) Gottfredson, L. S. Implications of cognitive differences for schooling within diverse societies. In C. L. Frisby & C. R. Reynolds (Eds.) *Comprehensive handbook of multicultural school psychology*, New York: Wiley, 2005, pp 517–554.

(5) Nisbett, R. E., Aronson, J., Blair, C., Dickens, W., Flynn, J., Halpern, D. F., & Turkheimer, E. Intelligence: New findings and theoretical developments. *American Psychologist* 2012, 67 (2), 130–159. DOI: 10.1037/a0026699

(6) Javalagi, A., Newman, D., & Li, M. Personality and leadership: Meta-analytic review of cross-cultural moderation, behavioral mediation, and honesty-humility. *Journal of Applied Psychology* 2024, 109 (9), 1489–1511. DOI: 10.1037/apl0001182

(7) Judge, T. A., Bono, J. E., Ilies, R., & Gerhardt, M. W. Personality and leadership: A qualitative and quantitative review. *Journal of Applied Psychology* 2002, 87 (4), 765–780. DOI: 10.1037/0021-9010.87.4.765

(8) Do, M., & Minbashian, A. A meta-analytic examination of the effects of the agentic and affiliative aspects of extraversion on leadership outcomes. *Leadership Quarterly* 2014, 25 (5), 1040–1053. DOI: 10.1016/j.leaqua.2014.04.004

(9) Bono, J., & Judge, T. Personality and transformational and transactional leadership: A meta-analysis. *Journal of Applied Psychology* 2004, 89 (5), 901–910.

(10) Davidson, I. The ambivert: A failed attempt at a normal personality. *Journal of the History of the Behavioral Sciences* 2017, 53 (4), 313–331. DOI: 10.1002/jhbs.21868

(11) Anni, K., Vainik, U., & Mottus, R. Personality Profiles of 263 Occupations. *Journal of Applied Psychology* 2024. DOI: 10.1037/apl0001249

(12) Spark, A., O'Connor, P., Jimmieson, N., & Niessen, C. Is the transition to formal leadership caused by trait extraversion? A counterfactual hazard analysis using two large panel datasets. *Leadership Quarterly* 2022, 33 (2). DOI: 10.1016/j.leaqua.2021.101565

(13) Härtel, T., Hoch, F., & Back, M. Differential behavioral pathways linking personality to leadership emergence and effectiveness in groups. *Personality and Social Psychology Bulletin* 2024. DOI: 10.1177/01461672241246388

(14) Grant, A., Gino, F., & Hofmann, D. Reversing the extraverted leadership advantage: The role of employee proactivity. *Academy of Management Journal* 2011, 54 (3), 528–550.

(15) Burton, H., Daugherty, B., Dickins, D., & Schisler, D. Dominant personality types in public accounting: selection bias or indoctrinated? *Accounting Education* 2016, 25 (2), 167–184. DOI: 10.1080/09639284.2015.1127768
(16) Harrison, J., & Malhotra, S. Complementarity in the CEO-CFO interface: The joint influence of CEO and CFO personality and structural power on firm financial leverage. *Leadership Quarterly* 2024, 35. DOI: 10.1016/j.leaqua.2023.101711
(17) Perossa, A., & Connelly, B. Volitional trait change in selection: It's about time, but also degree and perspective. *International Journal of Selection and Assessment* 2025, 33 (1). DOI: 10.1111/ijsa.12509
(18) Fleeson, W., Malanos, A., & Achille, N. An intraindividual process approach to the relationship between extraversion and positive affect: Is acting extraverted as "good" as being extraverted? *Journal of Personality and Social Psychology* 2002, 83 (6), 1409–1422. DOI: 10.1037//0022-3514.83.6.1409
(19) Spark, A., & O'Connor, P. State extraversion and emergent leadership: Do introverts emerge as leaders when they act like extraverts? *Leadership Quarterly* 2021, 32 (3). DOI: 10.1016/j.leaqua.2020.101474
(20) Jacques-Hamilton, R., Sun, J., & Smillie, L. Costs and benefits of acting extraverted: A randomized controlled trial. *Journal of Experimental Psychology-General* 2019, 148 (9), 1538–1556. DOI: 10.1037/xge0000516
(21) Patolawala, M. Manage the X to get the Y. https://epthoughtleaders.com/manage-the-x-to-get-the-y/, 2022.
(22) Goffee, R., & Jones, G. *Why should anyone be led by you?*, Harvard Business Review Press, 2015.
(23) IPIP. IPIP Implementations Around the Web. https://ipip.ori.org/
(24) Stein, R., & Swan, A. Evaluating the validity of Myers-Briggs Type Indicator theory: A teaching tool and window into intuitive psychology. *Social and Personality Psychology Compass* 2019, 13 (2). DOI: 10.1111/spc3.12434
(25) Karlsen, H., & Langvik, E. Facet level effects of extraversion on leadership behaviours rated by subordinates. *Cogent Psychology* 2021, 8 (1). DOI: 10.1080/23311908.2021.1930712
(26) Schwartz, S. H. Value priorities and behavior: Applying a theory of integrated value systems. In C. Seligman, J. M. Olson, & M. P. Zanna (Eds.), *The psychology of values*, Vol. 8, Mahwah, NJ: Erlbaum, 1996, pp 1–24.
(27) PVQ_Test. Portrait Values Questionnaire. n.d. https://aidaform.com/templates/pvq-test.html
(28) Greenbaum, R., Bonner, J., Gray, T., & Mawritz, M. Moral emotions: A review and research agenda for management scholarship. *Journal of Organizational Behavior* 2020, 41 (2), 95–114. DOI: 10.1002/job.2367
(29) de Waal, F. *Primates and philosophers: How morality evolved*. Princeton, NJ: University Press., 2006.
(30) Unknown. *The Powerful CEO/CFO Relationship*. CFO Forum, 2023. (accessed).
(31) Um, C. T., Guo, S. L., Lumineau, F., Shi, W., & Song, R. X. The downside of CFO function-based language incongruity. *Academy of Management Journal* 2022, 65 (6), 1984–2013. DOI: 10.5465/amj.2019.0943
(32) Firk, S., Detzen, N., Hennig, J., & Wolff, M. Strengthening the CEO-CFO interplay: The role of regulatory focus and similar compensation plans. *Accounting Organizations and Society* 2024, 113. DOI: 10.1016/j.aos.2024.101563

(33) Sextroh, C., & Wutzler, J. Speaking with one voice? Individual preferences and managers' personal communication style. *Journal of Business Finance & Accounting* 2025, 52 (1), 5–47. DOI: 10.1111/jbfa.12792
(34) Novak, D. David Gibbs, Yum! Brands CEO - Flip the script in tough situations. https://youtu.be/1bgneW-d_F4?t=183, 2024.
(35) Clark, P. Ted Lasso's leadership lessons. In *The Financial Times*, https://www.ft.com/content/238bca26-c48e-4d36-b00a-6e30eee28250, 2021.
(36) Artz, B., Goodall, A., & Oswald, A. Boss competence and worker well-being. *ILR Review* 2017, 70 (2), 419–450. DOI: 10.1177/0019793916650451
(37) Köhler, D., Rausch, A., Biemann, T., & Büchsenschuss, R. Expertise and specialization in organizations: A social network analysis. *European Journal of Work and Organizational Psychology* 2024. DOI: 10.1080/1359432X.2024.2387874
(38) Reddit. My new accounting boss does not know accounting. https://www.reddit.com/r/Accounting/comments/1e3ji40/my_new_accounting_the_cfo_boss_doesnt_know/, 2024.
(39) Kwon, S., Lim, J., & Park, J. CFO accounting expertise and SEC comment letter process. *Journal of Accounting Auditing and Finance* 2024. DOI: 10.1177/0148558X231215912
(40) Derrick, L. The CPA population stalls. In *Insight*, https://www.icpas.org/information/copy-desk/insight/article/digital-exclusive---2021/cpa-2027-the-cpa-population-stalls, 2021.
(41) Cristkolder Volatility Report. Associates, C., Ed., https://www.cristkolder.com/volatility-report, 2024.
(42) Bernard, D., Ge, W., Matsumoto, D., & Toynbee, S. Implied tradeoffs of chief financial officer accounting expertise: Evidence from firm-manager matching. *Management Science* 2021, 67, 5776–5799. DOI: 10.1287/mnsc.2020.3738
(43) Datta, S., & Iskandar-Datta, M. Upper-echelon executive human capital and compensation: Generalist vs. specialist skills. *Strategic Management Journal* 2014, 35 (12), 1853–1866. DOI: 10.1002/smj.2267
(44) Sadun, R., Fuller, J., Hansen, S., & Neal, P. J. The C-Suite skills that matter most more than ever, companies need leaders who are good with people. *Harvard Business Review* 2022, 100 (7–8), 42–50.
(45) Gustafson, C. J. What I wish I knew as a first year CFO. https://www.mostlymetrics.com/p/what-i-wish-i-knew-as-a-first-year, 2023.
(46) Dasborough, M. T., Ashkanasy, N. M., Humphrey, R. H., Harms, P. D., Credc, M., & Wood, D. Does leadership still not need emotional intelligence? Continuing The Great EI Debate. *Leadership Quarterly* 2022, 33 (6). DOI: 10.1016/j.leaqua.2021.101539
(47) Schlegel, K., & Mortillaro, M. The Geneva Emotional Competence Test (GECo): An ability measure of workplace emotional intelligence. *Journal of Applied Psychology* 2019, 104 (4), 559–580. DOI: 10.1037/apl0000365
(48) Mattingly, V., & Kraiger, K. Can emotional intelligence be trained? A meta-analytical investigation. *Human Resource Management Review* 2019, 29 (2), 140–155. DOI: 10.1016/j.hrmr.2018.03.002
(49) Sheldon, O. J., Dunning, D., & Ames, D. R. Emotionally unskilled, unaware, and uninterested in learning more: Reactions to feedback about deficits in emotional intelligence. *Journal of Applied Psychology* 2014, 99 (1), 125–137. DOI: 10.1037/a0034138

3

THE LEADER–FOLLOWER INTERACTION

In our journey through the LIFE model, we now enter the realm of the I in LIFE: the interaction between leaders and followers. While we focus on leaders' behaviors, especially on those comprising transformational leadership, it is important to not lose sight of how followers fundamentally impact the behavior of the leader and ultimately decide who is, and who is not, a leader.

It's a two-way street

We (researchers and practitioners alike) often think of leadership as an action–reaction dynamic: the leader acts, and followers react. Certainly, we acknowledge that effective leaders adapt their leadership based on their followers' characteristics; we even accept that the leader may refocus their approach depending on followers' response. The image that comes to mind is that of a soccer forward preparing to shoot at goal: the player's strategy

DOI: 10.4324/9781003581734-5

will depend on the goalkeeper's position and knowledge of the goalkeeper's habits and tendencies. Still, it is clear who acts and who reacts in the ensuing interaction.

In reality, however, followers frequently play an active role in shaping the leadership relationship. Their behaviors significantly impact your leadership, sometimes even without your being aware of it.

A common example is the *ingratiation-favoritism* dynamic. Of course, you are immune to flattery. I wasn't. During my time as an executive, I thought myself completely impartial, treating employees equally regardless of how much they seemed to appreciate or admire me. Reflecting now from an academic perspective and with some distance, I'm no longer so confident of that impartiality.

There are many other ways in which followers influence the leader's behaviors. Consider the newly appointed leader who begins their tenure with a warm-hearted, empowering leadership style but gradually becomes distant and authoritarian as employees grow dissatisfied with necessary yet unpopular decisions. (Marissa Mayer's tenure as CEO of Yahoo! provides an example, among many others.) Of course, followers can also influence leaders positively, such as when proactive teams encourage traditional command-and-control leaders to adopt more collaborative leadership styles.

In this chapter, we will briefly talk about patterns of leader behaviors ("leadership styles"), and we will then focus on the most extensively studied and – in most circumstances – consistently effective combination of leader behaviors known as "transformational leadership". As we explore this topic, remember that it is ultimately followers who decide whether you embody transformational leadership and that they contribute to shaping your leadership behaviors.

Leadership styles

Researchers have long been looking for that elusive Holy Grail, a combination of leadership behaviors, or "leadership style", that would consistently ensure leader success.

This led to a bewildering multiplication of leadership styles. You may have heard about **charismatic, authentic, humble, ethical, change-oriented, empowering, participative, servant**, or **paradoxical** leadership – and the list goes on. Each of these styles was particularly fashionable in research and the media at one point in time. Ethical leadership, for example, was a favorite in the wake of corporate scandals such as Enron and WorldCom.

More recently, **servant** leadership has been all the rage, so much so that researchers each wanted to coin their own measure of it, which led to "at least 16 different measures, based on diverse models that contain at least 44 dimensions" (1). More troublingly, once cause and effect are properly separated, servant leadership simply does not seem to affect follower performance (2). Understandably, managers are also confused about what "servant leadership" really means. For example, Carol Tomé, Home Depot CFO for 18 years and then CEO of UPS, swears by servant leadership but describes it as "you, the leader, take responsibility for the decisions that they [employees] make and the actions that they take." (3) This seems to be not so much about servant leadership as about that time-honored law articulated in Pixar's *A Bug's Life*: "First rule of leadership: everything is your fault".

The lifecycle of most leadership styles in academic research typically follows this pattern: (1) "we've finally found *the* leadership style that's always effective", (2) "OK, there are some situations in which it might not work", and finally (3) "actually, this new style does not add much to the classics".

Which brings us to **the classics**: **Task-oriented vs. people-oriented** leadership[1] and **the full-range leadership model** (transactional + transformational leadership). They seem to be at the root of many other leadership styles proposed over the years (4). I will also cover **charismatic leadership** as a component of transformational leadership.

I believe that, after completing this chapter, you will be sufficiently equipped in terms of practical understanding of leadership styles. However, if you want to dig deeper into styles, such as authentic, ethical, or servant leadership, here are a few reading suggestions:

- *Authentic Leadership* (2017) by Bill George, Herminia Ibarra, Rob Goffee, and Gareth Jones. Harvard Business Review Press.
- *Advances in Authentic and Ethical Leadership* (2014), Linda L. Neider and Chester A. Schriesheim (editors). Information Age Publishing.
- *Handbook of Servant Leadership: Developments in Theory and Research* (2019). Dirk van Dierendonck and Kathleen Patterson (editors). Palgrave McMillan.

Task-oriented vs. people-oriented leadership: The Blake Mouton grid

In the 1960s, two researchers – Robert Blake and Jane Mouton – sat down to chart a map of leadership. What they came up with was "the managerial grid", a deceptively simple two-axis model that divided leadership into two essential types of behaviors: one axis for **task**, the other for **people**.

Task-oriented behaviors are about organizing, structuring, monitoring performance, and more generally problem-solving. People-oriented behaviors are about offering encouragement, showing concern, and empowering.

The good news is that the two types of behavior are not in conflict, as it might look at first glance. You can score high on both task and people orientation, and that is what according to research (and common sense) makes for the most effective leadership. Too little task orientation and lots of people focus will turn you and the team into a "country club". Too little people orientation and only focusing on task will make you a dictator. Too little of both behaviors probably means you have given up on this leadership business altogether.

Now, if you're like most finance leaders, you're probably already nodding. Of course – tasks and people. Spreadsheets and soft skills. Deliverables and development.

In practice, most finance leaders I interviewed admit to spending too little time on the people side. I recently spoke to Hong Wha, a CFO at a mid-sized manufacturing company. I asked him how much time he spends on the people side of leadership.

"Honestly? Not as much as I'd like," he admitted. "There's just so much work to do every day."

Classic response. But then he paused.

> Although... I guess sometimes it's both, isn't it? Like when I give someone extra responsibility, I always try to praise them. Or when we're pushing toward a deadline, I make sure to show appreciation.

There it was. Without realizing it, Hong Wha was weaving people into the fabric of the task. Not in separate blocks but simultaneously. And then he told me something that stuck.

> One time, a team member came to me upset. Said he wasn't being taken seriously by sales. I had a lot on my plate, but I listened. Later, he took the initiative to meet with sales. Said it was because I'd made time for him.

One conversation, one decision to listen, and it changed the dynamic in his team. So why don't leaders do more of this?

The answer isn't a lack of knowledge. It's tunnel vision (overestimating the importance and urgency of the task at hand) and often also the irresistible pull of being uber busy. They push for the task-oriented side of leadership and sabotage the people side.

Tunnel vision and busyness: Enemies of the people

It is a truth universally acknowledged that, at any point in time, you will have more on your desk than you can solve on any given day. Finance leaders tend to dislike loose ends and unfinished work. So it's easy to become stressed and task-obsessed and neglect your people-oriented duties.

Karen Lynch, until recently CEO of CVS Health, started out as an accountant in an insurance company. She told me that, early on, she received the best leadership advice from a senior finance manager:

> If you are working a lot of hours and you look harried, people aren't going to follow you.[2]

Over time, she distilled this and similar experiences into a personal mantra: maintain "grace under pressure". This calm attitude allowed her to dedicate time to important but not urgent things, such as investing in building trust and openness with her teams.

If you are in a junior or mid-management finance role, there may be another reason why you often look harried, other than having too much on your plate. Could you sometimes *enjoy* having more to do than you can handle, so that you feel important and in demand? I definitely did, in my first management roles. And, since I did not have a wise mentor like Karen's to tell me any different, I thought that it was good to show others how busy and stressed out I was, that it would make me more of a leader in their eyes. It took me years to realize that the opposite was true.

My example may not be the norm, but the phenomenon of people actually *wanting* to have their plate always overflow with work, and to always be seen as very busy, is prevalent enough to deserve a research term, "**busyness**". Worse, research shows that busyness might also be encouraged by your organization, as many companies still reward activity/input over achievement/output (5). Finance managers often come from those industries that turn busyness into a competitive sport: audit, consulting, investments, and banking. As a partner at a leading global auditing firm puts it:

> I've nearly always got things that are urgent because I've slipped them time and time again because other urgent things, important things have come in that are urgent and so there is always this nagging thing that says, well, actually, I could sit down now and I could work solidly for 48 hours with nothing new coming in and still I wouldn't actually clear the backlog (6).

But once leadership becomes your most important responsibility, busyness can harm it a great deal. Your people need to know that they are important to you, that they take space in your mind, instead of being crowded out by all those to-do's. The more senior you become, the more you'll need to perfect the art of walking around looking like you have all the time in the world for your team while moving mountains of work.

Experience makes a big difference: both overall experience in leadership roles and how long you've been in your current job. Most managers I interviewed (including Fortune 500 CEOs and CFOs) talked about how, in the beginning of their career but also every time they changed jobs, **everything seemed equally urgent** to them. It took them some time to be able to separate the wheat from the chaff. The good news is that, as you accumulate senior experience, the "calibration" periods you need after taking a new position become shorter and shorter.

The full-range leadership model

The full-range leadership model refers to combining two leadership styles: transactional and transformational leadership (7).[3] Leaders are most effective when they use a combination of the two styles, varying the emphasis on one or the other depending on – you've guessed it – followers and the environment.

We quickly overview transactional leadership before focusing on the most important set of leadership behaviors, transformational leadership.

Transactional leadership

Transactional leadership means setting up and honoring an (often implicit) **contract** between the leader and the followers. It entails behaviors such as clarifying expectations, rewarding performance, enforcing rules, and correcting underperformance.

Transactional leadership gets a bad rap in the popular literature. Indeed, if a leader relies only on transactional behaviors, they will not get very far in terms of followers' engagement and performance.

However, it is essential to keep in mind, as we move on to discussing transformational leadership, that a fully effective leader needs to practice *both* transactional and transformational leadership. It is of little use, for example, to communicate a great vision, to show that you care about the individuals in your team, or to challenge them to think outside the box (all of these being transformational leadership behaviors) if you haven't first sorted out things such as a good performance appraisal system. Transactional leadership is a necessary (though not sufficient) basis for establishing trust in the leader.

Good transactional leadership requires an organized and methodical mind, consistency in behavior, and making good on one's promises. As an (aspiring) CFO, you probably already do well on these, if only because you likely score high on the "conscientiousness" personality trait. A 2024 study that inventoried personality profiles by occupation found that **finance managers have the highest median conscientiousness of all managers** (intriguingly, on par with construction managers) (8). Therefore, since I trust you've already "got" transactional leadership, we move on to the focus of this chapter: transformational leadership.

Transformational leadership

Transformational leadership is about leading humans toward achieving more than their job description requires. Of course, "more" does not have to be about working harder. It can be about your direct reports taking initiative, finding creative solutions, and thriving on a new challenge. It can be about the team working so well together that it becomes the envy of other teams, inside and outside your company, allowing you to attract top talent.

Why transformational leadership?

Transformational leadership (9) is probably **the most influential leadership theory in management studies**. Only in the past decade, over **two thousand academic research studies** focused on it. They show an impressive range of benefits, from inspiring and engaging employees (10) to encouraging employees' innovative behavior as well as selfless behavior for the benefit of the organization (11). Transformational leadership has also been shown to promote knowledge-sharing in the team (12), strengthen employee resilience (13), facilitate openness to change (14), ensure the success of international projects (15), and lower employee turnover (16).

Under attack?

Given the central role I assign to transformational leadership in this book, we first need to address recent challenges thrown at it in the research community. An emerging school of thought (I will call it "the signaling school" as it draws on signaling theory) has been pointing to methodological weaknesses in transformational leadership research and is urging the academic community to go back to the drawing board and re-examine what transformational leadership is made of, how it is measured, and how its outcomes are determined (17, 18).

One key issue they identify is the over-reliance on questionnaires: employees are asked to what extent their leader displays a list of behaviors, such as "expresses confidence that goals can be achieved". The problem is that employees may be swayed, in their answers, by how happy they are with their leader overall. At the end of the day, the signaling school says, the entire 45-item transformational leadership questionnaire might amount to one single question: "How much do you like your leader?"

The solution of the signaling school is to **replace questionnaires with experiments**. Experiments are a superior method because they allow one to control the behaviors displayed by the leader and to tease out causality instead of just correlation. However, they necessarily have to isolate only those behaviors that could be enacted in an experimental context: short and easily measurable tasks assigned to teams that meet each other and their leader for the first time. Moreover, since the leader's behaviors need to be standardized across all teams in the experiment, the experiments always end up having the leader "do" leadership by delivering a speech. As you well know, most real-life leadership is not delivered through speeches.

In short, the new signaling school can only research the leader's speeches and only in an artificial setting.

Reconciled

The good news is that the new signaling school also finds that transformational leadership (as they redefine it) brings team and performance benefits (17, 18).[4] Moreover, for our practical purposes, we can map most of the traditional transformational leadership model onto what the signaling school calls transformational and charismatic leadership, with minimal changes compared with the original framework. For the organizational psychology geek in you, Appendix 1 describes the mapping between the traditional and the signaling approach.

The four I's of transformational leadership

There are 16 behaviors composing transformational leadership, grouped in four buckets, that the fathers of transformational leadership theory, Bernard Bass and Bruce Avolio, worked hard to name alliteratively: Idealized Influence (who the leader is), Inspirational Motivation (what the leader wants to achieve), Individual Consideration (how the leader supports their people), and Intellectual Stimulation (how the leader encourages innovative thinking) (19). Each of them is powerful in itself, but together, like the Planeteers, they are so much stronger.

Figure 3.1 presents the four I's and the behaviors that compose them.

Idealized Influence: Being the leader they quote

If you find yourself quoting from a leader who inspired you, they probably signaled the following qualities:

1. Demonstrates strong values
2. Puts the team before self interest
3. Represents the team
4. Displays a sense of power and confidence

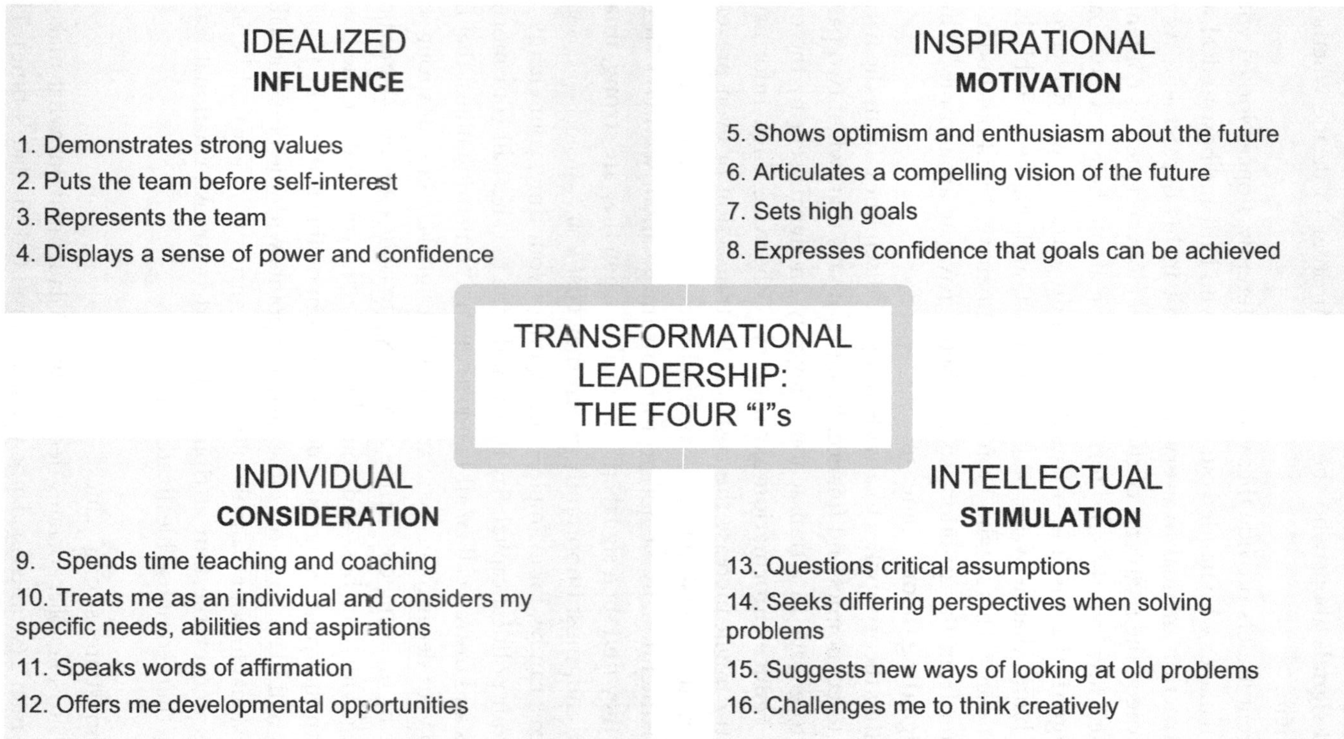

Figure 3.1 The Four "I"s of Transformational Leadership (20).

Why "signaled"? Since leadership is a process of social interaction, **followers need signals** about who the leader is, in order to decide whether to follow them.

Different leaders provide these signals differently. I once worked with a finance manager who handed out a "This is who I am and how to deal with me" instruction manual to every new recruit in his department. As you would expect, the recipients of that booklet seldom accepted its contents at face value. However, they did form an opinion about their new boss based on the **signals** that his "me" manual was sending: that he was direct to the point of blunt, that he was a bit of a narcissist, and that he probably had a fixed mindset: "This is who I am and how I behave, I will not budge one millimeter from this position, so you better navigate around me". This is where **signaling theory** comes in.

Signaling theory applies to a wide range of disciplines, from the natural sciences to economics and finance. In short, it says that, when two parties prepare to engage in a transaction, they rely on signals sent by the other party to **reduce information asymmetry**. Otherwise, high information asymmetry might increase the costs of the transaction or even prevent it altogether.[5] In leadership terms, your followers rely on signals sent by you (whether intentionally or not) to form an image about who you "really" are, and they find such signals most valuable when they are **strong**, **unambiguous**, and, most importantly, when they **cost** you.[6]

This cost can be, for example, coming out of your time, your energy, and maybe your political capital. Say that you decide to cancel all your morning meetings and instead call an all-hands to discuss something unjust that happened in your department – you are sending a signal about your strong sense of justice by investing costly time and energy to right a wrong. Or maybe, in a meeting with your boss and your direct reports, you disabuse the boss of the notion that your team could deliver the impossible feat that he is asking for. This will likely cost you some brownie points with the boss but will be a strong signal to your team about your commitment to their well-being.

Let us unpack the four attributes signaled by transformational leaders that, together, compose Idealized Influence.

1. Demonstrates strong values
   In Plato's *Republic*, Socrates debates with Glaucon about what makes "a just man" (women had not yet been invented in Plato's time). Their

conclusion is that a man is most truly just when, while genuinely virtuous, he is stripped of his reputation for justice. Instead, everyone believes he is profoundly unjust. He is scorned and punished and faces suffering, despite his actual moral integrity (21). I don't mean to pick a fight with Plato, but for you to be an effective leader, your followers need to *notice* your strong values. Leadership is a process of social influence in which, as the adage says, **perception is reality**. Therefore, you need to be aware of, and actively initiate and manage, signaling your values to your followers.

Actions speak louder than words, but they could still be misheard

You might be tempted to say, "I'll let my actions speak for my strong value system". Indeed, demonstrating your values through your behavior is a stronger signal than just talking about them. However, you may simply not have enough early opportunities to act in ways that signal your values to your followers. Moreover, when you let actions speak for you, they might come across very differently from what you had in mind. Take Joost's case.

CASE: JOOST BAKKER AT TRANSVELO[7]

Joost, the newly appointed CFO of Transvelo, a transportation company, soon got a sense that the amount of work put in by the various sub-teams and members of the finance team (spread out around the globe) varied wildly. This was also a source of frustration to the harder-working members of the team (or at least those who thought of themselves that way).

To address the issue, Joost decided to introduce FloQast, a monthly closing software, to streamline and monitor the closing process. He thought this would give a strong signal to the team about his sense of fairness.

The team, however, saw the introduction of FloQast as signaling Joost's desire to ingratiate himself with the board by showing decisive action toward "change for the sake of change". They resisted the implementation, making it twice as lengthy and costly as it had been initially estimated.

In retrospect, Joost realizes that he should have invested more time in communicating his belief in fairness, the fact that he was responding to fairness concerns from the team, and the benefits of the new software in ensuring fairness.

In short, you need to be aware of, and actively manage, how your value system is perceived by followers. Do not be afraid to **state your values** out loud. Your employees might joke about it ("of course John reminded us how his grandfather instilled in him a passion for excellence"). Nevertheless, if you are consistent in communicating your values and, more importantly, if your actions are perceived as consistent with those values, your team will appreciate your spelling them out.

Which values?

Having strong values seems to be more important than what those values are. In a study of corporate managers, whether their top values were tradition and conformity, or they primarily valued achievement and power, or they put care for others first, mattered little for their leadership. What really mattered was how **intensely** they felt about those values: the stronger their values, the more their followers saw them as charismatic leaders (22).

However, there are two conditions:

a. Your moral absolutes should be the same as those of your followers. (We discussed the difference between your personal values and your moral absolutes in Chapter 2.)
b. You have to have at least some self-transcendence (meaning, as you recall from Chapter 2, showing some concern for people other than yourself) in your value system, even if it does not take first place (23).

This is confirmed by another study (see Figure 3.2): when CEOs were low in self-transcendent values, their attempts to secure the commitment of middle management by engaging in transformational leadership behaviors fell flat (or at best got modest results). Having high self-enhancement values such as ambition and desire for power was not a deal-breaker for effective leadership as long as they were accompanied by high self-transcendent values.

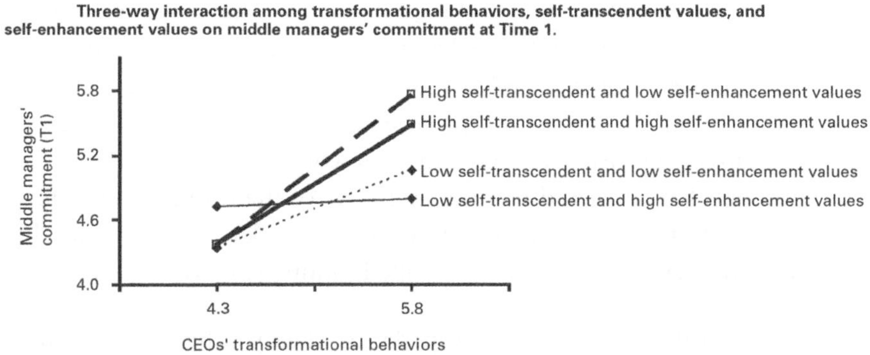

Figure 3.2 Transformational leadership and leader values.
Reproduced with permission from Fu et al., 2021 (24)

Simply put, if you are an egomaniac, no amount of intensity in your value system can get your employees to follow you.

2. Puts the team before self

   Self-sacrifice has distinguished great leaders since time immemorial. At work, leader self-sacrifice does not need to reach Joan of Arc or Leonidas of Sparta proportions. For many finance leaders, it takes the more mundane form of working later and harder than anyone else on the team. Or maybe protecting your team from emotional exhaustion by absorbing the pressure coming from the higher ranks of your organization.

   This latter example is trickier than it appears because, as you well know by now, what is not seen does not exist – at least from an Idealized Influence perspective. Here as before, you have to be aware of, and manage, the signals that your team receives about you and how they are interpreted. You don't want to toot your own horn, but you don't want to be the Unknown Hero either.

3. Represents the team

   You know it: once you have taken the helm, your pronouns change to we/us/our. Transformational leaders embody who the team is and what it is about. They convey what researchers call "the sentiment of the collective": shaping, sharing, and communicating the emotions, values, and beliefs of the group.

When asked about you at the cafeteria, your team members should be able to say things like "she has a lot in common with people in my team" or "she represents what is characteristic about us as a team" (just not in academese but in workplace speak – "she's one of us"). This will not happen by itself. Chances are that you and your team are more different than alike and that the members of the team, as your area of responsibility increases, may be quite dissimilar among themselves. Richard Galanti, Costco's CFO, recalled joining Costco:

> One of the things that you experience when you have worked in banking or consulting is that you are around a fairly homogeneous group of people who all have the same levels of motivation to work hard to get ahead. In most businesses, not everybody has the same level of skill or the same level of motivation, they all bring their own issues to work, both personal and business, and boy, have I learned how inadequate I am as a manager (25).

Your Idealized Influence mission is to find, communicate, and, to some extent, co-create the characteristics, emotions, experiences, and implicit rules of behavior that the team – including you – have in common. Note that this is not yet about emphasizing the team's work goals and your vision for what it can achieve (which goes under "Inspirational Motivation") but about identity, who they are as a team.

4. Displays a sense of power and confidence
Power, often maligned as a corrupting force, is in truth the quiet architect of leadership, shaping the conditions under which vision can be translated into action. You would not want to wield power for its own sake, but without it, ambition never rises above the realm of private dreams.

Even much-praised behaviors such as servant or humble leadership, that are seemingly about de-emphasizing power, work only when followers perceive the leader as having considerable sway in the organization (26, 27).

In Chapter 5, we unpack power and where it comes from when you are a finance leader.

Inspirational Motivation. turning goals into goosebumps

Inspirational motivation is about energizing others to achieve a common goal. It relies on four key behaviors:

5. Shows optimism and enthusiasm about the future
6. Articulates a compelling vision of the future
7. Sets high goals
8. Expresses confidence that goals can be achieved

Let's see how each of these works.

5. Shows optimism and enthusiasm about the future

CASE: GABOR BALASZ AT ELLINGFORD[8]

Gabor was a young manager I coached, who worked for a British medical device organization and had recently moved to the UK with his family to manage an important project for his company.

The project progressed at a good pace, and Gabor was hopeful that senior management would appreciate his performance and consider him for a permanent position at headquarters. Yet the informal feedback he received from "upstairs" was that, while he was appreciated as a hard worker, there were some hesitations because "he didn't seem very enthusiastic".

He was confused about this, and so was I. He seemed a sprightly, optimistic young man to me. It took a while to realize what the problem was: while he spoke perfect English, his every sentence had a downwards intonation, characteristic of Hungarian speakers. In his interactions with senior management, he had mostly been delivering presentations, which made his falling tone stand out. A few voice lessons and, presto! his enthusiasm ratings shot up.

Gabor's story speaks to an important issue: optimism needs to be not just felt but shown. As a leader, you will need to consistently show what Warren Bennis called "unwarranted amounts of optimism", and even a small slippage such as downwards voice intonation can cost you.

But what if you don't really feel that optimistic? I put this question to Matt, a CEO I had previously worked with.

CASE: MATT'S ADVICE[9]

Matt was my CEO when I was a quite young CFO. He was a true inspiration: an unwavering optimist, even as we waddled through a thickening marsh of difficult business conditions.

Interestingly, at the time, I took his enthusiasm as a given: he was the leader; of course, he would see every setback as an opportunity.

It was only later that I reconsidered Matt's perpetual optimism, when, as CFO in a significantly more complex, and more political, environment, I launched a massive change program. I soon realized that, to get others to embrace it, I had to keep feeding it massive amounts of enthusiasm and energy, like the stoker on a steam locomotive. I asked Matt: what if you really don't feel that optimistic about the future?

Matt answered my question without missing a beat: "Fake it". Then he elaborated,

> It's a virtuous circle. You show optimism, you will feel more optimistic, which will open you up to new ideas for reaching your goal. But, of course, don't lie. If the writing is on the wall, it's on the wall no matter how many smileys you slap on it.

Matt's approach may not work for everyone, so take it as an illustration rather than as a prescription; for some, it could have adverse effects, such as stabbing pangs of inauthenticity.

Nevertheless, the fact remains that inspiring leaders need to have optimism on tap. As we saw in Chapter 2, optimism and enthusiasm are part of your psychological capital (PsyCap) which, while partly a given, can partly also be managed and increased. In Chapter 11 ("Leading yourself"), we discuss how to protect and grow your PsyCap.

6. Articulates a compelling vision of the future

In most organizations, "the Vision" with capital V is the remit of the CEO. Granted, the best CEOs do not just dream up a vision but involve their organization in creating it, through a combination of top-down and bottom-up iterations. But it is nevertheless the CEO who is, if not the author, at least a guardian of the Vision. Your job, as a finance leader, is to articulate for your team how their work and goals contribute to achieving the Vision. Sometimes – and especially for support functions such as finance – spelling out a convincing and consequential connection to the Vision is not easy. In the famous story of the NASA janitor who described his work as "helping put a man on the moon", the unsung hero may be that janitor's boss.

However, if you are to inspire your team to greatness, connecting their work to the Vision is only half of the job. You still need to formulate a vision specifically for your team, their own ideal state to reach. This team vision should support the Vision but also have standalone meaning, be specific and consequential, to give the team a sense of what they, together, are striving for. For example, for many CFOs, their vision for their teams is about making finance a strategic business partner. However, to make this vision compelling to your teams, you need to paint a more specific picture. For example, Monish Patolawala, ADM's CFO, says:

> I want my finance team to have a seat at the table. They should be sought out for having an active voice. I want the operating team to be calling our finance folks and say: 'What do you think? Do you think we can do this or not?' (28)

This is a scene that we can picture in our heads. Granted, with some difficulty. (Do those operations people currently even know the finance folks' names, let alone what they do?) But after all, a vision should have an element of reaching beyond the possible. It can spark the team's commitment to draw up and follow a roadmap for getting there.

7. Sets high goals
   Picture Nadine, a department leader who ticks off all the other boxes of transformational leadership behaviors except for this one: setting high goals. Her approach is rather "just do your best, and results will follow". Nadine's team might describe her as people-oriented, principled, enthusiastic, knowing how to create a tight-knit team. However, they would probably not use words such as "transformational" or "inspiring". High goals are a required part of transformational leadership.

When Jack Welch, the legendary CEO of General Electric, introduced the concept of "**stretch**", he described it as "using dreams to set business targets, with no real idea how to get there". Stretch targets did not replace traditional budget objectives. The point was that, while people would not be punished if they didn't reach the dream, they would be rewarded if they did. The sheer ambition of the stretch goal made it clear that just working a bit harder, pushing people to search for innovative approaches, would not cut it. The audacity of "aiming for the stars" added to Jack's charisma.

More recently, the "stretch" concept (sometimes known as BHAG, or Big Hairy Audacious Goal) has been widely misused. I have come across leaders who embody the exact opposite of Nadine, our opening example: they fail to show most of the other transformational leadership behaviors, but they set sky-high goals for the team (often as mandatory budgets), hoping that this alone would electro-shock the team into action. Needless to say, this rarely works.

How do you set high goals if you are, say, a middle manager in finance? After all, your team's goals, hairy or not, cascade from above – they are not of your own creation. But, like your vision that, while serving the CEO's Vision, also has individual meaning for the team, some of your team's goals may be the steps toward that team-oriented vision. Coming back to Monish Patolawala's vision of having the finance team have a seat at the table, a near-term goal representing that vision could be "increase awareness in Operations of the role and value of the finance function".

8. Expresses confidence that goals can be achieved

   Naturally, prodding your team to conquer Mount Everest while you yourself don't think they'll make it beyond base camp is a losing strategy. Especially longtime corporate soldiers will have had their share of BHAGs and may have developed understandable cynicism around the notion. On the other hand, you don't have the option to only set goals that you are 100% confident your team can achieve, since those would hardly qualify as "stretch goals". So how do you set goals that you are, say, 70% sure you can achieve together, while sounding like you are 100% sure, without being inauthentic? The solution cannot be purely reason-based; instead, you need to fill that gap with **emotion**, such as warmth (recognizing the value of each individual in the team), pride (remember when we achieved that incredible feat and no one thought we could?), belonging (we belong to that one team who can do this!), and enthusiasm (can't wait to start!).

At the end of the day, the team needs to sense your absolute conviction that, if the goal can be achieved, this team is the best equipped to achieve it.

Individual consideration. Coaching, not cloning

Individual consideration is about showing your team members that they each matter to you. Here, too, your followers will implicitly rate you on four groups of behaviors:

9. Spends time teaching and coaching
10. Treats me as an individual, and considers my specific needs, abilities, and aspirations
11. Speaks words of affirmation
12. Offers me developmental opportunities

Let's have a look at each of these, when set in a CFO's world.

9. Spends time teaching and coaching
   Teaching is probably something that you, as a finance leader, already like doing. As we have seen, finance leaders tend to keep their expert hat on for a bit longer than most other functions, as they climb through the ranks. This also means that most of us in financial management enjoy sharing that expertise with others. Coaching, on the other hand, may feel less natural to you, as it requires some stepping back and letting the other find their own answers. More uncomfortably, when you are a manager of managers, coaching them will likely have to focus on those ill-defined, ambiguous skills condescendingly qualified as "soft". Yet sometimes this could make all the difference in whether your talented employee stays or goes.

   Sandeep Aujla, CFO of Intuit, built his career starting in investment banking and then working for Visa in the Strategy and M&A area. Later on, he was practically forced to join the finance function in the company, and he immediately set to work on leaving it. But his manager changed his whole outlook on finance and how much there was to learn there:

> When I was at Visa, and they put me in the finance organization, I spent nine months trying to get out. But my manager was amazing, and he taught me so much (29).

The more immediate issue with teaching and coaching, though, will be the scarcity of your time and attention. As a finance expert, you are educated to think in terms of allocating resources to those investments that promise the best risk-return profile. Is coaching your head of FP&A, who is hard-working and knowledgeable but does not seem to get momentum with his team, the optimal use of your time? Mara, CFO of a major communications company, didn't think so:

> I had a great person as head of FP&A, but he was just not able to drive change, right? But he was very capable. So I had to let him go. Which was really hard, because I knew he was very good, but not the right fit at the right time.[10]

This sounds like a case where investing in coaching could have been an alternative course of action. Mara's judgment call was that the risk-reward profile of this investment was not attractive enough to justify the resources invested, and she may well have been right. But, by firing a "very good" person, she may have also sent a signal to the many people she leads that she is not into "spending time teaching and coaching", and this signal could take perceptions of her as a transformational leader down a notch.

The takeaway regarding this Individual Consideration behavior is not "teach and coach everyone who needs it, irrespective of how long it takes and how difficult it may be". It is rather that, when you make your **cost-benefit analysis** for deciding whether or not to invest in coaching someone, you should also take into account the benefit (or cost) of this decision in how you are perceived as a leader.

10. Treats me as an individual and considers my specific needs, abilities, and aspirations

    We are, each of us, quietly convinced of our own uniqueness. And when someone else recognizes even a fragment of that uniqueness, it feels like validation – proof that we matter. This isn't just a fleeting emotional response; it's a fundamental part of how humans connect.

But here's the puzzle: when you are a senior executive, responsible for hundreds or even thousands of employees, how do you replicate that feeling across an entire organization? Your employees will accept that you can't possibly have a meaningful conversation with everyone, that you can't remember every name. But they will still expect to see you engage with more people, at different levels, than only your direct reports.

This is the rationale behind skip-level meetings, informal breakfasts with finance teams, and dinners with department managers. But unlike the common belief that "showing up is half the battle," in these cases, showing up without genuine engagement can backfire. In fact, it can leave people feeling more invisible than if you'd stayed away entirely.

CASE: DANA'S NOTES[11]

Dana leads a finance team spread across three continents. As her company is gearing up for an IPO, the finance team is undergoing major change in its processes, systems, and ways of working. She realized that, to have these people from very different cultures embrace and champion the change, she needed to physically be with them more often than her introverted self would have preferred.

She began traveling regularly, meeting with employees at all levels. She kept notes on her iPhone. She showed me one: "Priya accounting tall one 2 kids older boy piano good work on new ERP." Before each visit, she reviewed these notes. Doesn't it feel manipulative? "It's funny," she answered. "I've actually become more interested in these people since I started jotting down these little notes."

What started as a strategy to manage information evolved into something authentic. The act of recording details made her more attentive, more curious. It transformed routine check-ins into meaningful interactions.

Showing individual consideration to your team members does not mean a perpetual lovefest. Some of your feedback may be quite tough but will still be received as individual consideration when the other (a) trusts in your ability and right to give it (which will happen if they rate you highly on Idealized Influence), (b) can see that you have really been paying attention, and (c) feels that you truly believe not only that they can improve but that they can soar.

Finally, leadership often defaults to an implicit rule: motivate others as you would have others motivate unto you. But as you climb the ranks and lead bigger teams working in diverse functional areas, this becomes a flawed strategy. The people you lead aren't versions of yourself. They come with different motivations, talents, and insecurities. Effective leadership isn't about projecting *your* experiences onto others; it's about uncovering what drives *them*. In Chapter 7, we unpack individual motivation.

11. Speaks words of affirmation

To speak words of affirmation is to engage in one of the most understated yet profound rituals of leadership: the art of recognizing the value of another. It is not merely about congratulating an employee for an achievement, though this has its rightful place. It is also about acknowledging the potential that quietly resides within them, waiting to be summoned by a well-timed word of encouragement.

Many CFOs I spoke with admit, with a trace of guilt, that they dispense recognition far less often than they know they should. As a CFO, I did the same. The reasons for this are as varied as they are revealing. Sometimes, our minds are tethered **to distant strategic horizons**, leaving little attention for the small but meaningful victories occurring in our "kingdoms". Other times, we find ourselves reluctant to praise accomplishments that we used to perform effortlessly in **our own early careers** – or so we seem to remember. There are also those among us who believe that praise must be dispensed sparingly. We imagine ourselves as **the stern teacher** whose rare nod of approval carries the weight of a thousand wordy commendations. And then there are leaders who, as they ascend the hierarchy, quietly convince themselves that the seasoned managers reporting to them require **no more nurturing** than fully grown trees need watering.

Yet, on reflection, none of these justifications withstands scrutiny. Appreciation is not a currency that devalues with circulation. It is not reserved solely for the monumental, the extraordinary, the groundbreaking. In fact, its true power often lies in the mundane – in noticing the diligence that keeps the lights on, the quiet consistency that forms the backbone of an organization – particularly in finance, where work is often noticed only when something goes wrong. The key is specificity. A vague, habitual "great job" may indeed fade into background noise over time. But when praise is precise – anchored to a particular achievement, tied to a distinct strength – it resonates deeply, leaving little room for cynicism or eye-rolls.

And perhaps the most humbling realization of all: no one ever truly outgrows the need for recognition. As a matter of fact, even the Fortune 500 CEOs I interviewed for a research study mentioned the loneliness at the top, how they missed the occasional pat on the shoulder from a boss, the occasional "well done" (30). Titles and seniority may accumulate, but beneath them beats the same human heart, ever responsive to the simple, enduring power of feeling seen and valued.

12. Offers me developmental opportunities

When we think about developing others, we tend to imagine it as a straightforward transaction: identify talent, provide opportunities, watch growth unfold. For example, Sandeep Aujla, CFO of Intuit, makes it a rule of having leaders in his team rotate into a new role every two years. It is not always a promotion. "It's like rock climbing, sometimes you have to move laterally," he says (31).

But what if the process of developing others is less about structured plans and more about navigating hidden cultural codes and unexpected human dynamics?

CASE: EMILIA AND THE FUTURE CFO

Robert (not his real name) was a program manager I inherited in one of my CFO roles, who coordinated a sprawling, politically charged "finance transformation" program across 12 countries. Every week, we'd sit down for updates, and every week, we'd fail to meet each other's expectations.

I wanted crisp summaries, strategic takeaways. Robert gave me sprawling narratives – who said what, who disagreed, who was quietly undermining the process. It was like we were speaking different languages. When mid-year career conversations rolled around, Robert surprised me. He said he wanted to be a CFO. My reaction? I pointed out – in retrospect maybe too bluntly – what he lacked of the requirements for the role. In his version of the story, I told him he'd never be a CFO. Twelve years later, he's CFO for a sizeable medical equipment company. When we reconnected, he delighted in reminding me of my prediction.

We sometimes fail to see the growth potential in people around us, and instead we tend to see them stay where they are, as if framed on the wall. Helping someone grow is also about recognizing that growth is not linear. If I'd been wiser, I would have encouraged Robert's ambition, not because I thought he was ready but because ambition itself often shapes readiness. Maybe I could have framed his development goal around learning to synthesize strategic insights – a skill he clearly eventually acquired, despite my skepticism.

And when their talents do stretch beyond what seems possible, there's another factor at play: what Ruth Porat, CFO of Alphabet, calls "senior air cover":

> I worked for somebody [at Morgan Stanley] who eventually became the head of equity sales and trading. And when I was asked to run technology, equity capital markets, which is a joint venture between Banking and Sales & Trading, he called me into his office, and he said, I think you're gonna soar. But if you slip, I'm here to backstop you, I will be your senior air cover. And I just thought that that was such an important phrase, like we all need senior air cover, and we all need to be senior air cover for someone (32).

The people who grow the most aren't always the ones who are most prepared. They're the ones who know that if they fall, someone will be there to catch them.

Intellectual Stimulation. Making minds do squats

Intellectual Stimulation is about stretching thinking beyond comfort zones, to spark growth, curiosity, and innovative problem-solving. It entails four groups of behaviors:

13. Questions critical assumptions
14. Seeks differing perspectives when solving problems
15. Suggests new ways of looking at old problems
16. Challenges me to think creatively

Did this pique your intellectual curiosity? Let's examine each behavior in more detail.

13. Questions critical assumptions

    Are you asking the right questions – especially when it comes to challenging the status quo? They are often about taking on the "sacred cows," those deeply ingrained assumptions that go unexamined simply because they have long been accepted as truths. When a group converges rapidly toward a decision, pause and ask: What assumptions are we making, perhaps without even realizing it? What beliefs are we treating as indisputable facts, and why?

CASE: KHALID MANSOUR AT EVERGUARD[12]

Consider the experience of Khalid, now the CFO of EverGuard, a major financial organization. Earlier in his career, while serving as a country CFO, Khalid meticulously crafted a business case for launching a new product line, together with his country manager. However, when they presented it to the regional CEO, he listened impatiently and dismissed it with a "Stay away from this product; it never works." They complied, only to witness their main competitor successfully launch a nearly identical product soon after.

The root of this costly misstep? The regional CEO's unexamined assumption, born from a disastrous past experience of his with a similar product – but in an entirely different market context. Besides realizing that he and his boss had made the rookie mistake of not investigating the sentiment around their intended proposal before putting it on the table, Khalid learned another valuable lesson: sacred cows often hide in the minds of those at the top. Failing to identify and challenge them can stifle innovation and strategic growth. Ironically, the regional CEO remained undeterred in his belief about the product's risks, convinced that the competitor would see those risks hidden in the product eventually materialize.

Crucially, this introspection must extend beyond the team to the leader's own beliefs.

The challenge lies in distinguishing between fixed ideas and useful heuristics – the rules of thumb refined over time that genuinely aid decision-making.[13] Leaders must cultivate the discipline to ask, "Is this belief grounded in current evidence and context, or is it an outdated relic of past experiences?"

Remember, as with everything transformational leadership, the act of questioning assumptions must be visible to have its full impact. It's not enough to privately reflect on your own sacred cows. When others witness your willingness to challenge deeply held beliefs, including your own, it fosters a culture of intellectual curiosity and critical thinking.

14. Seeks differing perspectives when solving problems

Alfred P. Sloan, the iconic chairman of General Motors, is said to have once presided over a meeting where every executive nodded in agreement on a major decision. Sloan paused, then said, "Gentlemen, I take it we are all in complete agreement. Then, I propose we table this decision for now. *We can't make a decision of this magnitude without dissent*."

What Sloan understood – and what transformational leaders consistently practice – is the value of seeking differing perspectives when solving problems.

For example, Ruth Porat, CFO of Alphabet and Google, makes it a rule to *ask for the opinions of the most junior people in the room first*, to make sure that they are not intimidated into silence or agreement by the more senior people present (35).

I asked Nathan, a CFO for a major pharmaceutical company, what he had recently changed about how he leads. He said:

> I've only recently come to fully realize the impact that I have on the room. When you take a very senior role, people start reading into your most minute gestures, your most matter-of-fact remarks. So now I make sure that, when I go into a room expecting to reach a decision with the team, that I not only refrain from sharing my opinion, but that I try hard to not have a strong opinion at the outset, because it will somehow permeate the whole meeting.[14]

In environments where differing perspectives are actively sought, psychological safety flourishes. People feel empowered to voice unconventional ideas without fear of reprisal. Leaders who foster this culture don't just ask, "Do you agree?" They ask, "What might we be missing? Where could this go wrong?" They invite the devil's advocate to the table, not as a disruptor but as a catalyst for deeper understanding.

15. Suggests new ways of looking at old problems
    If you think of some of the most inspiring leaders you had, chances are that they had an uncanny, Seinfeld-like talent for reframing a familiar situation to make you see it in a whole new light.

CASE: EMILIA AND THE COO

In one of my earlier CFO roles, I kept getting in conflict with the COO during our top management team meetings. I was unhappy with this situation, and so was he. Mike (not his real name), the CEO, decided he had to intervene. Most leaders would approach such an issue by mediating, finding compromises, or addressing the specific points of disagreement. But Mike reframed the problem entirely. In one-on-one conversations with each of us he asked, "What if this conflict isn't about the disagreement itself, but about how each of you defines success?"

Indeed, while the COO valued speed and efficiency, pushing for quick decisions, I prioritized depth and thoroughness, believing that careful analysis led to better outcomes. Our conflict wasn't personal – it was rooted in fundamentally different views on what "doing great work" meant. This shift in perspective did not make us disagree less, but it made us see our differences not as obstacles but as assets. The atmosphere in the boardroom improved, and the quality of our decision-making improved with it.

16. Challenges me to think creatively
This last behavior in the Intellectual Stimulation toolbox is essential and often what one remembers first about a great leader they worked with. Dan (not his real name), head of Investor Relations for a major organization, recollects about a leader he had in one of his first finance roles:

> I would come to him with a problem, and he would first ask me "what would you do?" and after I made a first attempt at an answer he would sort of poke me with questions and there was an implicit "I know you can do better than this" in those questions, and he always showed real delight when I arrived at an answer, or at least at a new way of looking at the problem.[15]

This behavior of (to borrow an expression used by Jensen Huang, CEO of Nvidia) "torturing them into greatness" is also fascinating because it combines all four dimensions of transformational leadership, now at a smaller scale, as if it had a fractal structure. To be able to really challenge your talented employee to think creatively, first you need to have them believe in your right to do so, to see you as a model (hence Idealized Influence), then you have to set sky-high goals for their creativity while showing absolute confidence that they can achieve these goals (Inspirational Motivation but also Individual Consideration, knowing the strengths of the person), and finally you need to reframe the issue at hand to give them space for creativity (Intellectual Stimulation).

CROSSROADS LIFE: HOW HENK LOST THE ROOM

Henk is the CEO of Crossroads Life Europe – and Clara's new boss. It doesn't take long to realize: Henk is no transformational leader.

On the surface, he seems to embody *Inspirational Motivation*, one of the four pillars of transformational leadership. He paints a bold and vivid vision for Crossroads in the region. He's animated, passionate, and visibly convinced that the ambitious goal – "Crossroads in every home" – is entirely achievable.

So why does his inspiration fall flat? Why is Clara unmoved, even visibly disengaged?

Because Henk fails at the other three core dimensions of transformational leadership:

- **Idealized influence**. As shown in Figure 3.2 above, a leader lacking self-transcendence – concern for others beyond oneself – won't inspire followership, no matter how compelling their vision. Henk doesn't seem to care about people. Not out of malice, but because he's wholly task-focused. He leads with goals, not empathy.
- **Individualized consideration**. Clara isn't a partner in Henk's eyes – she's a means to an end. Her growth, her needs, even her presence in the room seem irrelevant to him. For much of the scene, she could be invisible.
- **Intellectual stimulation**. Henk's vision might have potential – if it didn't feel like a monologue. He's clearly delivered this speech before, and Clara's restrained frustration tells us she's heard it more than once. Though he ends with "that's where I need your help," you won't be surprised to hear that what follows (in the full film) is an order, not a consultation with the CFO. There's no curiosity, no space for ideas or challenge – just a scripted performance. In short, he fails to respect the intellectual capital in the room.

Together, these shortcomings explain why Henk's "inspirational" pitch doesn't land. He doesn't lose the room because he lacks vision. He loses it because he's the only one in it.

Watch the selected scene at: https://www.ed.movie/henk (or scan the QR code).

What if my organization prescribes different leadership behaviors?

Many organizations have defined a list of ideal behaviors, or sometimes competencies, that they expect from their leaders. If your company has such a list, it may, at first sight, look quite different from the 16 transformational leadership behaviors we've discussed. However, most of the differences are due to two easily identifiable (and interrelated) reasons. First, your organization probably defines "leadership" more broadly than we (in alignment with research) do in this book, so that it includes, for example, decision-making processes, operational excellence, or strategic thinking. Second, it likely conflates behaviors and skills and therefore might include skills such as emotional intelligence, influencing skills, or communication abilities alongside desired leader behaviors. In this book, we separate effective leader behaviors (as per the transformational leadership model) from the skills that can support these behaviors (detailed in Part 2, "The finance leadership toolbox").

Once you have excluded non-leadership-related items and those items that reflect skills rather than behaviors, you will likely be left with a list that broadly maps onto the transformational leadership structure we have discussed. There are, however, a couple of transformational leadership behaviors that often tend to be left out of corporations' "ideal leadership" lists. These are "displays a sense of **power** and confidence", "puts the **team before self**", and "**represents the team**".

It is easy to see why power is ignored when companies depict their ideal leader: most organizations tend to gloss over the fact that getting, and having, power are essential ingredients of leadership. All the same, you need to be perceived as having power and confidence in order to lead effectively.

As for the team-focused behaviors, they are probably left out because otherwise they could encourage some leaders to practice the age-old "us vs. them" approach. There is a reason why silos are so pervasive in organizations: nothing unites a team more than having a common enemy. Moreover, from an evolutionary viewpoint, humans are conditioned to feel allegiance to a close-knit community – their village, at most their tribe – and to be suspicious of outsiders. It is therefore tempting for managers in various areas of a large organization to lead their teams by encouraging a silo, "I'll look out for you against everyone else" mentality. Organizations attempt to counterbalance this propensity by mandating leader behaviors such as "collaborate across boundaries: break down silos and encourage cross-functional teamwork globally", or what research calls "organizational citizenship".

Nevertheless, while your team might come to appreciate (if not right away, at least in the longer run) your organizational citizenship, it still needs to see you put the team before self and represent the team so it follows you as a transformational leader. Your art is therefore in **delivering these behaviors without giving in to the silo temptation**.

Transformational leadership: What you can do next

Now that we have unpacked each behavior comprising transformational leadership, it is time to **ask yourself** what your team, your peers, and your boss would answer if questioned whether you display these behaviors consistently. If the answer is a mixed bag, you have your work cut out for you – but you are far from alone.

There are very good reasons why you might not exhibit transformational leadership as often as you'd like. For one thing, transformational leadership feeds on your **personal energy**. We used to think that, when you are an inspiring leader, you get energized by your team. There are certainly many energizing moments in the interaction of a transformational leader with their team. Nevertheless, research shows that, overall, consistently maintaining transformational leadership behaviors day in, day out, is **energy-draining** for the leader (36). To be a transformational leader, you need to be intentional about conserving and growing your energy resources (more about this in Chapter 11, "Leading yourself").

Another factor that may cramp your leadership style could be different expectations from your followers or a difficult environment. (We address each of these in Chapters 4 and 5, respectively.)

Nevertheless, whether you are pushing against a strong wind or enjoying a friendly breeze, you can still work toward becoming a more transformational leader. Therefore:

Keep a checklist with the transformational leadership behaviors and periodically verify how you are doing against it. You may want to do this separately for each constituency whose perception of your leadership is important: your team, of course; your boss; and probably some of your peers.

Prioritize those behaviors that you naturally seem to shy away from. This is not one of those "focus on your strengths" situations. As mentioned, the four I's of transformational leadership are significantly more effective when they are all present than when you have some in spades but almost entirely ignore some others. Granted, Steve Jobs could afford to ignore the Individual Consideration part of transformational leadership and still be seen as the quintessential transformational leader, due to his off-the-charts Inspirational Motivation and Intellectual Stimulation behaviors. But unless you too score at above-human levels in some of the I's, you want to consistently practice all four of them together.

By using all the feedback you can get, **course-correct your own perceptions** about how you lead. If your organization practices regular 360-degree evaluations, that is a great gift. It is harder to get genuine feedback on your leadership informally, but sometimes it might bubble up somewhere in another functional area. If you have a peer whom you fully trust, they could convey what they hear about you from their own teams. Exit interviews can also be useful, although most employees have learned that it's best to always leave an open door, so they may be less than candid in their feedback.

Charismatic leadership: A subset of transformational leadership behaviors

Charismatic leadership, defined as "values-based, symbolic, and emotion-laden leader signaling", is best captured by a subset of transformational leadership behaviors, specifically those listed under Idealized Influence and Inspirational Motivation (18). You might notice that this definition and the associated behaviors do not convey the magic aura that has traditionally surrounded charismatic leaders. There is nothing mysterious about charismatic leadership behaviors such as "puts the team before self" or "has strong values". As we have seen, these and the other Idealized Influence and Inspirational Motivation behaviors can be learned, meaning that charismatic leaders can very well be made, not born.

As mentioned earlier in this chapter, the "signaling school" in leadership research challenged the way transformational leadership (including charismatic leadership) was measured, especially its reliance on questionnaires rather than experiments. In order to capture charismatic leadership behaviors in an experimental setting, they narrowed these behaviors down to a set of rhetorical "charismatic leadership tactics" ("CLTs") that can be applied when delivering a speech (37, 38). For example, the "represents the team" behavior, which, as we discussed, is about shaping, sharing, and communicating the emotions, values, and beliefs of the group, is narrowed down to the rhetorical device of appealing to, or expressing, the "sentiment of the collective", by saying things such as "like all of you, I worry about…" or "we are all in this together".

The benefit of this approach is that the CLTs could be used in experimental settings, wherein they did lead to increased team engagement or productivity, thus establishing a causal relationship (37, 38). By contrast, questionnaires to your real-life followers could at most establish correlation between their perceptions of your charismatic behaviors and their engagement or productivity (leaving open the question of which came first, the perceived charisma or the team engagement). The downside of this new approach is that the behaviors you need to consistently demonstrate in order to be perceived as a charismatic leader represent much more than your use of CLTs when speaking to the team.

Therefore, for our practical purposes, we refer to CLTs as a set of (powerful) rhetorical devices that can support and increase your charismatic leadership but that do not replace charismatic leadership. In Chapter 7, we detail the CLT set, together with tips for maximizing your charismatic tactics as a finance leader.

Final thoughts

This chapter explored the leader–follower dance; the subtle, often unconscious ways in which each molds the other. It is a dynamic that rewards awareness. The best leaders are those who recognize that leadership is not something they do to people but something they do with them.

The lesson here is that leadership requires not only adaptability but also curiosity. Instead of "How should I lead?" perhaps the more revealing question is: "What are my followers drawing out of me?" The leader who understands this interplay does not simply impose a direction but creates a space where leadership emerges organically. And in that space, true influence begins.

Notes

1 These dimensions also roughly coincide with what research calls "consideration" and "initiating structure".
2 Interview with the author.
3 The full "full-range" model also included negative leader behaviors such as "laissez-faire" leadership (abdicating on one's leadership role) and "management by exception-passive" (waiting for things to go wrong before taking action). The intention was for the model to provide a full view of all possible types of leadership behaviors (both the good and the bad). Nevertheless, as subsequent research abundantly illustrated, there are many varieties of "bad" leadership other than those listed in the "full range" model (e.g., abusive leadership, Machiavellian leadership). For our purposes, I only focus on the positive leadership behaviors included in the "full-range" model.
4 The signaling school's concepts of charismatic leadership and transformational leadership sum up to the traditional concept of transformational leadership.
5 An interesting application in economics is George Akerlof's 1970 paper "The market for 'lemons'" about how information asymmetry can destroy the used car market. Akerlof's paper is one of the most cited in modern economics theory and (as of 2022) the most downloaded economic journal paper of all time https://en.wikipedia.org/wiki/The_Market_for_Lemons.
6 Yes, buying this book and keeping it on your desk counts – though best signals involve greater effort on your part… like reading it.
7 Interviewed CFO, anonymized.
8 Interviewed CFO, anonymized.
9 Real-life case, anonymized.
10 Interviewed CFO, anonymized.
11 Interviewed CFO, anonymized.
12 Interviewed CFO, anonymized.
13 Our focus here is on leadership as an interpersonal process, not on how to improve decision-making. However, if you'd like to dig deeper into heuristics, an interesting strand on research focuses on how managers use them (33,34).
14 Interviewed CFO, anonymized.
15 Interviewed Head of Investor Relations, anonymized.

References

(1) van Dierendonck, D. Servant leadership: A review and synthesis. *Journal of Management* 2011, 37 (4), 1228–1261. DOI: 10.1177/0149206310380462
(2) Schowalter, A. F., & Volmer, J. Are the effects of servant leadership only spurious? The state of research on the causal effects of servant leadership, recommendations, and an illustrative experiment. *Leadership Quarterly* 2023, 34 (6). DOI: 10.1016/j.leaqua.2023.101722
(3) Stanley, A. Developing leaders with Carol Tomé. In *The Andy Stanley Leadership Podcast*, https://www.youtube.com/watch?v=Ddr1Eol_Mr4, 2023.

(4) Sun, P. Y. T., Anderson, M. H., & Gang, H. Y. Determining the hierarchical structure and nature of servant leadership. *Journal of Business and Psychology* 2023. DOI: 10.1007/s10869-023-09904-9

(5) Waytz, A. Beware a culture of busyness organizations must stop conflating anvil with achievement. *Harvard Business Review* 2023, *101* (3–4), 57–67.

(6) Lupu, I., & Rokka, J. "Feeling in control": Optimal busyness and the temporality of organizational controls. *Organization Science* 2022, 33 (4), 1396–1422. DOI: 10.1287/orsc.2021.1486

(7) Avolio, B. J., & Bass, B. M. *The full range leadership development programs: Basic and advanced manuals*. Bass, Avolio & Associates, 1991.

(8) Anni, K., Vainik, U., & Mottus, R. Personality profiles of 263 occupations. *Journal of Applied Psychology* 2024. DOI: 10.1037/apl0001249

(9) Bass, B. From transactional to transformational leadership: Learning to share the vision. *Organizational Dynamics* 1990, *18* (3), 19–31.

(10) Bakker, A., Hetland, J., Olsen, O., & Espevik, R. Daily transformational leadership: A source of inspiration for follower performance? *European Management Journal* 2023, 41 (5), 700–708. DOI: 10.1016/j.emj.2022.04.004

(11) Ng, T. Transformational leadership and performance outcomes: Analyses of multiple mediation pathways. *Leadership Quarterly* 2017, 28 (3), 385–417. DOI: 10.1016/j.leaqua.2016.11.008

(12) Jiang, Y., & Chen, C. Integrating knowledge activities for team innovation: Effects of transformational leadership. *Journal of Management* 2018, 44 (5), 1819–1847. DOI: 10.1177/0149206316628641

(13) McCombs, K., & Williams, E. The resilient effects of transformational leadership on well-being: Examining the moderating effects of anxiety during the COVID-19 crisis. *Leadership & Organization Development Journal* 2021, 42 (8), 1254–1266. DOI: 10.1108/LODJ-02-2021-0092

(14) Zainab, B., Akbar, W., & Siddiqui, F. Impact of transformational leadership and transparent communication on employee openness to change: Mediating role of employee organization trust and moderated role of change-related self-efficacy. *Leadership & Organization Development Journal* 2022, 43 (1), 1–13. DOI: 10.1108/LODJ-08-2020-0355

(15) Kabore, S., Sane, S., & Abo, P. Transformational leadership and success of international development projects (ID projects): Moderating role of the project team size. *Leadership & Organization Development Journal* 2021, 42 (4), 517–530. DOI: 10.1108/LODJ-06-2020-0236

(16) Oh, J., & Chhinzer, N. Is turnover contagious? The impact of transformational leadership and collective turnover on employee turnover decisions. *Leadership & Organization Development Journal* 2021, 42 (7), 1089–1103. DOI: 10.1108/LODJ-12-2020-0548

(17) Stock, G., Banks, G., Voss, E., Tonidandel, S., & Woznyj, H. Putting leader (follower) behavior back into transformational leadership: A theoretical and empirical course correction. *Leadership Quarterly* 2023, 34 (6). DOI: 10.1016/j.leaqua.2022.101632

(18) Banks, G. C., Engemann, K. N., Williams, C. E., Gooty, J., McCauley, K. D., & Medaugh, M. R. A meta-analytic review and future research agenda of charismatic

leadership. *Leadership Quarterly* 2017, 28 (4), 508–529. DOI: 10.1016/j.leaqua.2016.12.003

(19) Bass, B. M., & Avolio, B. J. *Transformational leadership development: Manual for the multifactor leadership questionnaire*: Consulting Psychologists Press, 1990.

(20) Avolio, B., Bass, B., & Jung, D. Re-examining the components of transformational and transactional leadership using the Multifactor Leadership Questionnaire. *Journal of Occupational and Organizational Psychology* 1999, 72, 441–462.

(21) Plato. *Republic* (G. M. A. Grube, Trans., C. D. C. Reeve, Rev.). Hackett Publishing Company, 1992.

(22) Sosik, J. The role of personal values in the charismatic leadership of corporate managers: A model and preliminary field study. *Leadership Quarterly* 2005, 16, 221–244. DOI: 10.1016/j.leaqua.2005.01.002

(23) Banks, G. C., Fischer, T., Gooty, J., & Stock, G. Ethical leadership: Mapping the terrain for concept cleanup and a future research agenda star. *Leadership Quarterly* 2021, 32 (2). DOI: 10.1016/j.leaqua.2020.101471

(24) Fu, P. P., Tsui, A. S., Liu, J., & Li, L. Pursuit of whose happiness? executive leaders' transformational behaviors and personal values. *Administrative Science Quarterly* 2010, 55 (2), 222–254. DOI: 10.2189/asqu.2010.55.2.222

(25) Unknown Richard Galanti, MBA '82 Arjay Miller CFO Award Winner. https://www.youtube.com/watch?v=UXmAPL9WNjE: Stanford Graduate School of Business, 2009.

(26) Wang, L., Owens, B. P., Li, J. C., & Shi, L. H. Exploring the affective impact, boundary conditions, and antecedents of leader humility. *Journal of Applied Psychology* 2018, 103 (9), 1019–1038. DOI: 10.1037/apl0000314

(27) Yang, J., Liu, H., & Gu, J. A multi-level study of servant leadership on creativity The roles of self-efficacy and power distance. *Leadership & Organization Development Journal* 2017, 38 (5), 610–629. DOI: 10.1108/LODJ-10-2015-0229

(28) Patolawala, M. Manage the X to get the Y. *EP Thought Leaders*. https://epthoughtleaders.com/manage-the-x-to-get-the-y/, 2022.

(29) Zaki, A. Accounting is no longer just accounting: Intuit CFO Sandeep Aujla. CFO.com https://www.cfo.com/news/accounting-is-no-longer-just-accounting-intuit-cfo-sandeep-aujla/729433/, 2024.

(30) Bunea, E. "Grace under pressure": How CEOs use serious leisure to cope with the demands of their job. *Frontiers in Psychology* 2020, 11. DOI: 10.3389/fpsyg.2020.01453

(31) Estrada, S. Intuit's CFO moves his employees to new roles every two years: Here's why. *Fortune*. https://fortune.com/2024/07/03/intuit-cfo-moves-employees-new-roles-every-two-years/, 2024.

(32) Haas, B. Dean's speaker series: Ruth Porat, president and chief investment officer, alphabet & Google. Berkeley Haas. https://www.youtube.com/watch?v=5nt61IqoS7g, 2024.

(33) Atanasiu, R., Ruotsalainen, R., & Khapova, S. A simple rule is born: How CEOs distill heuristics. *Journal of Management Studies* 2023, 60 (5), 1064–1104. DOI: 10.1111/joms.12808

(34) Luan, S., Reb, J., & Gigerenzer, G. Ecological rationality: Fast-and-Frugal heuristics for managerial decision making under uncertainty. *Academy of Management Journal* 2019, 62 (6), 1735–1759. DOI: 10.5465/amj.2018.0172

(35) Stanford. *All Else Equal: Ruth Porat, Making a Business Decision*. Stanford Graduate School of Business. https://www.youtube.com/watch?v=FApu_vsRR4A, 2022.
(36) Lin, S. H., Scott, B. A., & Matta, F. K. The dark side of transformational leader behaviors for leaders themselves: A conservation of resources perspective. *Academy of Management Journal* 2019, 62 (5), 1556–1582. DOI: 10.5465/amj.2016.1255
(37) Antonakis, J., Fenley, M., & Liechti, S. Learning charisma. *Harvard Business Review* 2012, 90 (6), 127–130.
(38) Antonakis, J., Fenley, M., & Liechti, S. Can charisma be taught? Tests of two interventions. *Academy of Management Learning & Education* 2011, 10 (3), 374–396. DOI: 10.5465/amle.2010.0012

4

THE FOLLOWERS

In previous chapters, we focused on the first two elements in the LIFE model: the leader and the interaction between leader and followers. Now, let's turn our attention to the third element of LIFE: followers. In leadership, followers are never passive spectators – they bring their own personalities, values, and expectations that shape how they respond to your direction.

This chapter explores how CFOs can elevate their leadership by focusing on followers' characteristics. It incorporates findings from organizational psychology on how leaders' effectiveness is impacted by followers' traits, values, and implicit beliefs about leadership. It draws on research about the characteristics of finance employees. Finally, it provides practical strategies for CFOs to enhance engagement and performance across a diverse finance team.

A necessary disclaimer: in this chapter, and elsewhere in the book, I will mention certain patterns of personality or behavior that, according to research, are statistically associated with certain professions (e.g. accounting) or country cultural differences (e.g. India). Needless to say, individual profiles can and will often be very different from what the statistics show.

DOI: 10.4324/9781003581734-6

Are finance employees different?

It's tempting to assume that finance employees form a single, homogeneous group. Yet reality is more nuanced. Accounting specialists differ from FP&A analysts, who in turn are different from Investor Relations professionals. Many CFOs I spoke with describe a divide between "more conservative, dependable" types and "more curious, growth-oriented" types in their finance functions.

Occupational stereotypes and self-fulfilling prophecies

A key reason for these differences can be traced to the "attraction–selection–attrition" cycle, coupled with an internal socialization process:

- **Attraction**: Individuals choose fields they believe align with their personalities and preferences, often shaped by occupational stereotypes (e.g., "accountants are conservative and dependable").
- **Selection**: Recruiters in each domain tend to hire people who match these stereotypical traits.
- **Attrition**: If new hires discover the role is a poor fit, they leave, reinforcing the homogeneity of the group that remains.
- **Socialization**: Norms and culture in each sub-function then further shape employees' behaviors, values, and self-concepts.

Hence, it's no surprise that accounting departments often draw together employees who are, on average, more risk-averse, diligent, and precise, whereas FP&A or Investor Relations may attract people who value analytical problem-solving.

The changing face of finance

However, this landscape may change dramatically. With rapid advancements in artificial intelligence, routine transaction work will be increasingly automated. As Katie Rooney, CFO of Alight, points out (1), the finance function is shifting from a majority of process-focused roles to a majority of analytical and advisory roles. In other words, tomorrow's finance teams may resemble data-driven "think tanks," staffed by employees who are comfortable with technology, capable of deeper business insights, and potentially more open to innovative thinking.

For CFOs, this shift creates two distinct leadership challenges:

- leading a new profile: As the nature of finance work evolves, the personality profile may become unfamiliar (e.g., more akin to software developers: more open to experience, more introverted).
- leading a diverse mix: For at least a transitional period, your team will be a blend of "old" and "new" profiles, requiring different leadership approaches to engage everyone effectively.

Tailoring your leadership to followers' characteristics

To lead effectively, you need to understand how your followers' personalities and values shape their preferences and behaviors.

Follower personalities

Highly conscientious, lower openness to experience

Many accounting professionals exhibit this combination of traits: diligent, dutiful, precise, but often less open to new experiences or taking risks (2, 3). Research shows that these personalities prefer **task-oriented** leadership behaviors (4). Do not think this gets you off the hook regarding the need for people-oriented leadership, though. As discussed in Chapter 3, task-oriented and people-oriented behaviors do not exclude each other, and the most effective leaders engage in both at very high levels.

Further, these personality profiles do not deal well with **ambiguity**. If you are the kind of leader who fires up their employees' imagination with a compelling vision and then lets them figure out the details for how to get there, it might feel inspiring and empowering to you. But to your accounting team it could feel just vague and frustrating. Instead, you will want to be specific, breaking down your bigger vision for the team in measurable deliverables and milestones.

For example, an accounting manager who is very conscientious and not very open to experience will appreciate a CFO who communicates **deadlines well in advance**, offers **step-by-step** guidance for new compliance requirements, and recognizes the importance of accuracy. These employees respond well to leaders who are **reliable and fair**. They want to see that the CFO honors commitments (like review meetings, approvals) and applies rules evenly. Micromanagement is usually not needed (conscientious folks often self-manage meticulously), but they do want the CFO to take their detailed work seriously. Regular acknowledgment of their accuracy and thoroughness can go a long way in motivating them – it signals that the CFO understands and values their careful work that often happens behind the scenes. When introducing change to such employees (say a new accounting system), you should appeal to their **sense of logic and order**: provide training manuals and emphasize how the change will improve reliability or control.

Employees who hate taking risks often avoid **asking for clarification or feedback** from management. This is visible in a study of young accounting professionals in New Zealand, whose employers rate them, on average, as "only sometimes" asking for clarification or feedback, despite the high importance assigned by management to this behavior (5). Now, New Zealand culture is quite low in power distance, with a score of 22. Add the same risk-averse personalities to a culture high in power distance (e.g., India, with a 77 score) and your accounting employees may never open their mouths in your presence. I once had an Indian team work on an accounting process improvement project. It took some missed deadlines for me to realize that, when asking if everything was clear, I shouldn't have taken "yes" for an answer.

Evolving profiles: More openness, more introversion

Interestingly, accounting professionals, as a group, are **only slightly introverted**, contrary to the stereotype (6). However, as accounting profiles morph into a more data-driven, analyst profile, you may soon find a considerable part of your accounting and finance department displaying personality profiles closer to those of software developers: significantly **more open to experience but also more introverted** than the average accounting employee.

The good news is that employees who are open to experience will welcome a less prescriptive leadership style and can be **more proactive**, and ask more clarifying questions, if motivated. However, motivating serious introverts may be harder. Research indicates that introverts are less inclined to perceive a leader as transformational (7). Yet when they do, they can become deeply committed and go above and beyond (8). Think of it like of a deep well: it's more laborious to dig, but once it's there, it provides a lasting source of commitment.

Follower values

Values alignment between leader and followers is another powerful factor. When employees feel that their personal values align with their leader's or organization's values, they respond with greater engagement, satisfaction, and loyalty. For instance, an employee who highly values integrity and transparency will be more committed to a CFO who champions ethical practices and open communication.

On the flip side, a sharp values mismatch can undermine a CFO's leadership. Consider a finance employee who believes in work–life balance and fairness: if they perceive the CFO pushing relentlessly for results at the expense of employee well-being, they may disengage or even leave. Likewise, a team member who values innovation and learning might feel stifled under a CFO who emphasizes only procedures and compliance.

Understanding what motivates each team member – what they care about, what they find meaningful – allows a CFO to tap into those drivers. (We dive deeper into understanding and working with individual motivation in Chapter 7.) Sometimes this might mean *tailoring the "pitch"* of an initiative differently: for example, framing a new automation project as an opportunity to learn cutting-edge skills and free up time for analytical work can excite those who value personal growth, whereas emphasizing error reduction and control might appeal more to those who prioritize accuracy and risk management. In both cases, the project is the same, but the *why* is communicated in alignment with the audience's values.

Over time, teams converge toward a set of shared values, because of the attraction-selection-attrition-socialization process described in "Occupational stereotypes" above.

You might not agree with the team's value hierarchy. For example, you might inherit a team that is highly competitive (high in "self-enhancement" values as per Schwartz's circle of basic human values introduced in Chapter 2) to the detriment of collaboration. Or a team that excessively prizes harmony and helping others (high in "self-transcendence" values), de-emphasizing performance. In such cases, the question is: how should you go about changing your team's values?

Three steps to influencing your followers' values

- **Check for alignment** with your own values. If you're advocating for something that you don't personally espouse, your attempts to reshape the team's values will ring hollow. You might objectively diagnose, for example, the need for more collaboration in your team. But if you yourself are fiercely competitive by nature, preaching about how there is no "I" in "team" will not make your employees any keener to labor for the betterment of the collective.
- **Use charismatic leadership**. If you authentically believe in the values you want to instill, you can tap into charismatic leadership to inspire a values shift. Charismatic leadership (representing, as seen in Chapter 3, the Idealized Influence and Inspirational Motivation subset of transformational leadership behaviors) is particularly effective for shifting a team's value system closer to your own. This is true for when your top values (as per Schwartz's model) revolve around self-transcendence (caring about others) but also when they are dominated by self-enhancement (aiming for achievement and success) (9). However, remember our caveat from Chapter 2: if your top values revolve around self-enhancement, you still need a minimum of self-transcendence in your value system (i.e. caring about something else than yourself) for others to follow you.
- **Respect tradition**. While attempting to motivate your employees to believe in and embrace a specific change, be cautious about signaling *openness to change* as your top value. Paradoxically, of the four quadrants in Schwartz's circle of human values, openness to change, when it is the top value of a leader, is the least likely to fire up their employees (10), making them least receptive to change. Leaders are most successful in driving change when they concomitantly emphasize respect for continuity and tradition. Franklin Roosevelt achieved acceptance of his "New Deal", an unprecedented expansion of the government's role in the economy, by tying its radical shifts in policy to traditional American values. In the mid-20th century, Pope John XXIII led some

of the most sweeping changes in Catholic practices in centuries while framing them as rooted in the Church's long-standing mission. Even when changes are dramatic, embracing a narrative of continuity helps reassure followers that their core identity remains intact.

When strong values backfire

You have inspired your team to adhere to a strong, shared value system, that you champion and model yourself. This is excellent for your team's cohesion and performance. Yet it can also be a combustible situation. Remember Martin, the talented employee who resigned because of what he saw as values betrayal by his leader? The more your employees are inspired by your charismatic leadership, and the more they adopt your strongly held values, the higher the chances that they start holding you to an impossibly high standard and perceive any real-life adaptation you make as an unforgivable compromise. Sometimes your "fall from grace" in their eyes could be due to their misinterpreting a decision you take as contrary to your values, usually because they do not have the full picture.

Other times, your team may unwittingly engage in "value expansion": reading more than you had intended into your communicated values, as in the real-life case of an advertising startup, as studied by Sandra Cha and Amy Edmondson, at Harvard (11):

CASE: JOHN BRYANT AT MAVERICK[1]

John Bryant was the charismatic founder and leader of Maverick, an advertising startup. His vision contained the idea of a new kind of advertising agency. He communicated values such as unpretentiousness (being a hardworking, not-so-glamorous firm, unlike competitors), community (belonging, having fun together), and employee growth. On the send–receive continuum of communication, these were the values "sent" by John.

However, the values "received" by employees were significantly "expanded" to include meanings that the founder had not intended. For example, when John communicated "unpretentiousness" and "community", employees heard "equality", meaning no privilege or rank regardless of employees' differing levels of experience or tenure, and "family", meaning intimate, close ties between all members.

This mismatch became painfully evident when, capitalizing on early success, John decided to grow the company, more than doubling the number of employees and taking on proportionally as many new projects. Employees took this as a sign that John was greedy and willing to sacrifice Maverick's "family" values, which could thrive only in a small, tight-knit firm. Then, as John decided to award shares to a few employees who had been with the firm for many years, his decision was seen as violating the "equality" values that employees thought the firm lived by. Accusations of hypocrisy started flying and soon got a life of their own, with (as the authors note) "limited potential for correction".

This is a heart-rending account of how a charismatic leader who had good intentions and who made significant efforts (even bringing academics to the rescue!) was nevertheless unable to prevent employee disenchantment. All because his employees read more into the values he promoted than could realistically be achieved.

In Crossroads Life, we find another illustration of how good leaders risk losing the hearts of their best people.

CROSSROADS LIFE: DISAPPOINTING LAURA

Laura, a young analyst on Clara's team, has always looked up to her. Even when Clara struggled to adapt to the culture at headquarters, wrestled with regional politics, or failed to fully engage her team, Laura admired her unwavering professionalism, fierce independence, and relentless work ethic.

Ironically, it is *after* Clara grows into a more seasoned senior leader – more politically astute, more strategically aware – that Laura feels let down. In this scene, Laura asks Clara to advocate at the upcoming executive board meeting for the Spanish subsidiary, which has been unfairly restricted from investing in Spanish bonds. Though quite risky at the time these events unfold, these bonds are a natural fit for that market

– more so than for any other subsidiary. Clara refuses. She explains that staying silent is the politically prudent move – better for the region as a whole, even if unfair to one country.

Laura listens and seems to understand. But it's clear she's disappointed. To her, Clara – the role model who once stood firm for her principles – has compromised. In Laura's eyes, the leader she believed in has made a political calculation at the expense of her values.

Clara, now more emotionally attuned, senses the shift. She invites Laura for a coffee, hoping to repair the relationship and realign expectations. But the damage is done. Laura's admiration, once unshakable, has cracked – and may never fully return.

This moment lands near the end of the film, a quiet dissonance in an otherwise triumphant arc. Clara's star is rising. The viewer wants to cheer for her and declare that she has "achieved transformational leadership" as one would achieve Nirvana. But this scene reminds us: **It's followers who decide whether you are truly transformational – and their decision is never permanent, even when you believe you're doing the right thing.**

Watch the selected scene at: https://www.ed.movie/laura or scan the QR code.

Let's distil a few **lessons** for mitigating the risk of values backfiring.
How to prevent values from backfiring

- **Communicate** frequently and openly. As we already saw in Chapter 3, your actions are stronger signals of your values than empty words. Yet don't assume that actions speak for themselves. Explain the reasoning behind your decisions, especially when the stakes are high, or decisions are easily misunderstood. Do not forget that your followers often do not have the whole picture, and from where they stand, your motivations might look very different from what they really are. This is what Clara plans to do at the "coffee at Belmondo's" chat with Laura.

- **Double-check what they hear**. Ask questions to ensure that the values you "send" match the values they "receive." You might say "We value teamwork," but your team might interpret that as radical egalitarianism – an unintended leap.
- **Think ahead**. You might, for example, be someone who genuinely values conservation (stability, security, maintaining the traditions and identity of the team). Yet, if looming budget cuts may force layoffs, it might not be the best time to publicly champion this personal value. Honor your values but also exercise foresight about how your future actions may be perceived in relation to your values.

Implicit Leadership Theories: The boss blueprint your followers don't know they use

Employees unconsciously hold mental templates – implicit leadership theories (ILTs) – of what a "real leader" should look and act like. These templates derive from personal experiences but are strongly influenced by cultural, group, and societal values and norms. For example, during a 30-year period, ILTs broadly shared by North American people have consistently included leader characteristics such as "sensitive", "dedicated", and "strong" (12).

In practice, this means that, if a leader **doesn't match the prototype** of leadership that employees expect, they might initially judge the leader as less competent or inspiring, regardless of his or her actual abilities. For example, if team members subconsciously believe a strong leader must be very charismatic and outgoing, a more introverted CFO could be underrated by those employees – unless the CFO proactively demonstrates other qualities that reshape those perceptions. Similarly, if employees' ILTs hold that a leader should always have the final say, a highly collaborative CFO who delegates decisions might be puzzling to them.

CFOs should be aware of these implicit expectations. By recognizing the leadership image that followers have, a CFO can either align with positive expectations or deliberately challenge and discuss misconceptions.

Sometimes, having an open conversation about leadership approach can help – for instance, a CFO who leads through quiet empowerment might explain this approach to a team used to more top-down directives, helping them appreciate a different style. Over time, good performance and trust can override initial biases in implicit theories, but the CFO must navigate that initial period carefully.

If you've spent much of your career in the same organization, you likely share its ILTs. But if you're an external hire – like 44% of Fortune 500 CFOs (13), you may not immediately align with those expectations. In this case, you will need to **tease out** the ILTs your stakeholders have (your own team but also your peers and your boss).

One way to do this is to listen to your co-workers' **stories about past leaders** whose legacy continues to be revered in the organization. Often the culture of an organization or a team has been heavily influenced by one particularly charismatic leader, who becomes the standard against which all new leaders are measured (14). Notice recurring themes in these stories – for example, humility, directness, or informality – that might differ from your natural style.

CASE: WEI LI AT NEXACHEM[2]

When Wei became CFO for NexaChem, a chemicals producer, coming from a big finance consultancy, he brought with him over 20 years of senior experience and the confidence that he had the ability to inspire and develop those around him.

Yet his team initially had a tepid response to his vision-driven, value-based leadership approach. Then, helped by a coach, Wei invested more time in informal chats with some of the longest-serving members in his team, probing their ideas about what made a "true" leader.

It turned out that much of the blueprint they had in mind was modeled after one person, Jan, who had been CFO earlier on in the life of the company. In contrast with Wei, whose speech and demeanor were polished, Jan had had a down-to-earth, almost peasant-like personal style that made everyone feel instantly at ease. "Jan stories" kept being passed on, from the older to the younger members of the team.

In one such story, Jan was recruiting for a key position and interviewed an applicant (who ended up getting the position) while heartily biting into an apple. This threw the applicant, who was on his best, professional behavior, a little off-balance. Noticing the moment of confusion, Jan paused for a moment, then asked "Would you like a bite?"

Wei got the message: to get through to his new team, he would be best served by a more direct, less sophisticated demeanor. He made subtle adjustments while staying himself rather than trying to turn into "Jan 2.0", and he was happy to notice a step change in his team's engagement with his direction and values.

Once you understand your team's ILTs, make thoughtful adjustments where it feels natural.

Some leaders resist adjusting to their teams' ILTs, citing authenticity. However, authenticity shouldn't be a barrier to growth. As a transformational leader, you can encourage your team to broaden their assumptions while evolving your own style (15). As we underlined in Chapter 2, values are not habits. In other words, you can remain true to your core values while adopting new behaviors that resonate with your followers.

When they decide to trust you

Trust is a curious thing. We use the word in contexts as varied as "I trust my friend to keep this secret" and "I trust the neighbor's ladder to hold me." But in both cases, trust means an act of vulnerability. It is the decision to rely on someone or something, exposing ourselves to the possibility of disappointment.

In leadership, trust is not a passive verdict handed down by followers; it is an active, risky decision. When an employee trusts a leader, they open themselves to the leader's influence. They take the leader's word for it, adopt their worldview, and follow where they are led.

> Trust represents a psychological state comprising the intention to **accept vulnerability** based upon positive expectations of the intentions or behaviors of another (16).

If I asked you why others trust you as a leader, you would probably first think of things such as being accountable, being fair, or making good on your promises. These are all necessary but insufficient conditions for earning your employees' trust. Trust in the leader depends on the leader's characteristics and behaviors but also on followers' predispositions (17). Let's examine each in turn.

What is it about you, that makes them trust you? The "Three Cs" of the trustee

Employees will trust their leader if *all* of three conditions are met: the leader shows competence, care, and character.

- **Competence**. Do you have the skills and knowledge to set direction and put in place the necessary structure for the team to achieve its goals?
- **Care**. Do you genuinely care? Research shows that full-range leadership behaviors (transformational + transactional leadership, as learned in Chapter 3) fulfil this "caring" requirement (17).
- **Character**. Do you exhibit integrity through fairness, accountability, and adherence to ethical principles?

If any one of these "**Three Cs**" is missing, trust falters. Imagine Tom, a newly promoted Investor Relations manager. He is caring and morally irreproachable but visibly in over his head in handling the multiple stakeholders of his new job. His moral integrity and personal warmth might win him friendships, but without demonstrated **competence**, his leadership will be questioned. Or consider Mary in FP&A, whose management efficiency and moral code are impeccable but who seems emotionally detached. Without perceived **care**, trust struggles to take root. And then there's Sam, a knowledgeable and warm-hearted accounting manager, who opts for **ethically questionable** accounting in the genuine hope that it will save jobs in the company. True trust will elude him, shadowed by doubt.

However, even if you master the "Three Cs," trust is not guaranteed. Followers come with their own predispositions, shaped by life experience and personal temperament.

What is it about them, that makes them trust you? The "Three Ps" of the trustor

Followers' trust in the leader is impacted by their propensity to trust, the leader prototype they have in mind, and their prior history.

- **Propensity to trust**. Some people are naturally more trusting than others, often shaped by early life experiences.
- **Prototype of a leader**. Each person has an internalized image of what a trustworthy leader looks like, influenced by culture, past experiences, and personal values.
- **Prior history**. Previous interactions with leaders shape expectations. A history of betrayal or disappointment can harden even the most open-hearted employee.

We have already discussed ILTs, and the prototype for a trusted leader falls in this category. You can also easily imagine how and why prior history would play a role. Let's spend a bit of time on propensity to trust and how it looks for finance professionals.

Propensity to trust. Each individual is naturally more or less inclined to trust others. Propensity to trust is shaped in early life and quite hard to change later. Individuals high in propensity to trust would readily agree with statements such as "most people do not cheat" and "most people can generally be relied on to keep their promises", whereas those low on propensity to trust would find "strongly disagree" too mild for such nonsense (18).

In finance roles, where precision and skepticism are prized, team members may naturally lean toward low trust. Here are three tips for winning over your less trusting employees:

1. **Understand each individual's propensity to trust**. Be patient with those who may be slow to trust, and create safe spaces for dialogue.
2. **Evaluate their "trustworthy leader" prototype**. Tease out (as per our "Implicit Leadership Theories" section above) the "blueprint" they might have in mind for what makes a trustworthy leader and decide how much you can and want to match it. Explicitly discuss your own style and invite feedback. Let people know what they can expect from you, reducing ambiguity.

3. **Acknowledge past wounds**. If your organization has a history of broken trust, don't ignore it. Address it openly and describe how things will be different.

Bringing it all together

Leading effectively isn't just about checking all the transformational leadership boxes; it's about how your leadership resonates with the diverse personalities, values, and unconscious expectations of your team. As CFO, you can use this four-step plan for conquering the F in LIFE:

1. **Understand** whom you're leading.
   - Identify the distinct personalities and values in your finance organization.
   - Recognize evolving finance roles and the shift toward data-centric, analytical profiles that may require new engagement strategies.
   - Be aware of ILTs and propensity to trust that shape how followers judge and respond to your behavior.
2. **Tailor** your leadership.
   - Provide clarity and structure for those who thrive on predictability.
   - Offer autonomy and creative space for those energized by innovation.
3. **Shift** followers' values.
   - Use charismatic leadership – that is, the Idealized Influence and Inspirational Motivation subset of transformational leadership behaviors – to align values and rally your team around a shared purpose.
   - Mind the importance of continuity as a team value while driving change.
4. **Adapt** your own position.
   - Accept that, to some extent, your team's values could influence your own.
   - See if you can adjust your behaviors to be closer to followers' ILTs as long as it feels like personal growth, not like inauthentic pandering.

Ultimately, leadership is a dynamic interaction between you and your followers. By tuning in to who they are and how they operate, you can more effectively steer your finance function toward innovation, collaboration, and growth. Think of it not as changing yourself to please your team but as co-creating a healthy, high-performing environment where each member's strengths, values, and goals can flourish – allowing you, and them, to rethink, adapt, and excel together.

Notes

1 Anonymized by the study authors.
2 Interviewed CFO, anonymized.

References

(1) Workday interview with Alight Solutions' CFO. https://www.youtube.com/watch?v=3X910X98Q4I: Workday, 2021.
(2) Burton, H., Daugherty, B., Dickins, D., & Schisler, D. Dominant personality types in public accounting: Selection bias or indoctrinated? *Accounting Education* 2016, 25 (2), 167–184. DOI: 10.1080/09639284.2015.1127768
(3) Kerckhofs, L., Hardies, K., Vandenhaute, M. L., & Ceustermans, S. Starting your career at an accounting firm: The role of personality in explaining career starts. *Accounting Horizons* 2021, 35 (1), 105–131. DOI: 10.2308/horizons-2020-001
(4) Breevaart, K., & de Vries, R. E. Followers' HEXACO personality traits and preference for charismatic, relationship-oriented, and task-oriented leadership. *Journal of Business and Psychology* 2021, 36 (2), 253–265. DOI: 10.1007/s10869-019-09671-6
(5) Gray, F. Specific oral communication skills desired in new accountancy graduates. *Business and Professional Communication Quarterly* 2010, 73 (1), 40–67. DOI: 10.1177/1080569909356350
(6) Anni, K., Vainik, U., & Mottus, R. Personality Profiles of 263 Occupations. *Journal of Applied Psychology* 2024. DOI: 10.1037/apl0001249
(7) Felfe, J., & Schyns, B. Followers' personality and the perception of transformational leadership: Further evidence for the similarity hypothesis. *British Journal of Management* 2010, 21 (2), 393–410. DOI: 10.1111/j.1467-8551.2009.00649.x
(8) Guay, R., & Choi, D. To whom does transformational leadership matter more? An examination of neurotic and introverted followers and their organizational citizenship behavior. *Leadership Quarterly* 2015, 26 (5), 851–862. DOI: 10.1016/j.leaqua.2015.06.005
(9) Brown, M., & Treviño, L. Leader-follower values congruence: Are socialized charismatic leaders better able to achieve it? *Journal of Applied Psychology* 2009, 94, 478–490. DOI: 10.1037/a0014069
(10) Sosik, J. The role of personal values in the charismatic leadership of corporate managers: A model and preliminary field study. *Leadership Quarterly* 2005, 16, 221–244. DOI: 10.1016/j.leaqua.2005.01.002

(11) Cha, S., & Edmondson, A. When values backfire: Leadership, attribution, and disenchantment in a values-driven organization. *Leadership Quarterly* 2006, *17*, 57–78. DOI: 10.1016/j.leaqua.2005.10.006

(12) Offermann, L. R., & Coats, M. R. Implicit theories of leadership: Stability and change over two decades. *Leadership Quarterly* 2018, *29* (4), 513–522. DOI: 10.1016/j.leaqua.2017.12.003

(13) Cristkolder Volatility Report: https://www.cristkolder.com/volatility-report, 2024.

(14) Bednar, J., & Brown, J. Organizational ghosts: How "ghostly encounters" enable former leaders to influence current organizational members. *Academy of Management Journal* 2024, *67* (3), 737–766. DOI: 10.5465/amj.2022.0622

(15) Billsberry, J., & O'Callaghan, S. The social construction of leadership, implicit leadership theories, leader development, and the challenge of authenticity. *Journal of Leadership Studies* 2024. DOI: 10.1002/jls.21886

(16) Rousseau, D. M., Sitkin, S. B., Burt, R. S., & Camerer, C. Not so different after all: A cross-discipline view of trust. *Academy of Management Review*, 1998, 23, 393–404.

(17) Burke, C. S., Sims, D. E., Lazzara, E. H., & Salas, E. Trust in leadership: A multi-level review and integration. *Leadership Quarterly* 2007, *18* (6), 606–632. DOI: 10.1016/j.leaqua.2007.09.006

(18) Tan, H., Schoorman, F., Sharma, K., & Mayer, R. Towards a psychometrically sound and culturally invariant measure of propensity to trust. *Journal of Business and Psychology* 2025. DOI: 10.1007/s10869-025-10006-x

5

THE ENVIRONMENT

So far, we have unpacked the Leader, Interaction, and Followers components of the LIFE model of leadership. It is time to look at the last element in the model: the Environment.

In this chapter, we will explore how the environment can interfere with leadership, and we will discuss practical ways for CFOs to assess and navigate it successfully.

The environment can change everything

There is an "environment deficit" in leadership books and courses and even in leadership research (1). Not that context is completely ignored, but it typically gets only a minor, supporting role in the drama of leadership. Most leadership development offerings – books, seminars, and corporate trainings – tend to portray the environment as an annoying barrier that exceptional leaders can bend to their iron will.

DOI: 10.4324/9781003581734-7

It's understandable why this happens. Imagine you're taking a senior leadership course at a prestigious business school. You want to leave feeling fired up, ready to move mountains – so that you can, in turn, inspire your team to mountain-moving greatness. You are less inclined to sit through a course explaining why some mountains simply can't be moved and why, in some cases, it might even be wiser to turn on your heel and accept defeat. After all, Napoleon famously said "Circumstances? What circumstances? I *make* circumstances!" *That's* the sort of leader you want to be.

Only, it turns out that Napoleon never really said that. The phrase was added by later, starry-eyed biographers. The truth is, the environment can radically affect how, and even whether, you lead. Glossing over this fact in leadership development is like teaching a mountain climbing course with the motto "The bigger the storm, the bigger the victory!"

This chapter has three goals:

1. To offer you tools for assessing and navigating various environments.
2. To help you be kinder with yourself if you fail in a leadership endeavor largely because of the environment. If you gave it your best, be forgiving of the rest.
3. To prevent excessive smugness when your success was mostly due to the environment. If you conquered Kilimanjaro in exceptionally clement weather, don't leave your goggles and gloves behind when you set out for Mont Blanc.

We will focus on three aspects of the environment: power, culture, and the business context.

Power and leadership

Power in organizations is largely a social construction. To a great extent, you are powerful if others perceive you as such (and therefore adjust their beliefs, intentions, and actions accordingly). As we have already seen, projecting power and confidence is part of transformational leadership.

Power and leadership **feed each other**: having power is a necessary (though not sufficient) condition for exercising leadership, while demonstrating leadership abilities is itself a form of power.

Yet you are unlikely to see leadership gurus deliver an inspiring talk on how to **acquire and maintain** power in organizations. When they do talk about your power as a leader, they usually urge you to minimize or share it. The underlying assumption is that taking a senior role automatically brings heaps of power, so your priority should be to prevent that mass of power from wreaking havoc – hence the many cautionary tales of abusive behaviors, overconfidence, or progressive corrosion of the soul. You are urged to bring your own power down by engaging in status-leveling, power-minimizing behaviors.

Indeed, research shows that leaders who engage in **power-lowering** behaviors inspire and motivate their teams. However, there is a critical condition: the leader must first have considerable power! This "power first" rule applies to servant leadership (2), showing downward deference – recognizing your employees' superior knowledge or experience (3), empowering leadership (4), humble leadership (5), and even self-deprecating leader humor (6).

The real-life experience of most leaders in today's organizations is very different from the stereotype of a dictator wielding enormous power. Global trends in work values, matrix organizations, labor laws, and a highly competitive fight for talent have all chipped away at positional power in many companies. Younger generations worldwide show less deference to authority than their parents or grandparents did (7).

Matrix structures often give employees two and sometimes three or even four bosses, diluting each boss's authority. In many countries, firing an employee can be a two-year, slow-motion ordeal (involving performance appraisals, improvement plans, monitoring, etc.). Meanwhile, companies seeking top-tier talent cannot afford to be seen as overly hierarchical or authoritarian.

A simple litmus test of this decline in position power is that you're much less likely to get away with "just do it" as a managerial request than you might have been 20 years ago.

Of course, your position is not the only source of power you have. Organizational leaders can draw on four types of power: **position, expert, personal**, and **political** power[1]. Let's take a look at each and what they mean for CFOs.

Position power

Your position bestows three forms of power:

1. Reward power (e.g., the ability to grant bonuses or promotions)
2. Coercive power (threat of punishment)
3. Legitimate power (employees deferring to your authority simply because you're the boss).

Reward power

As CFO, you can approve salary increases, bonuses, and promotions for your employees or reward stellar performance with baseball tickets or a night at the opera. Nevertheless, you probably use this power sparingly, not only because all leaders must be mindful of costs and avoid title inflation but also because, as CFO, you hold yourself to a higher standard in this respect.

John Murphy, CFO of Coca-Cola, puts it this way:

> We hold ourselves accountable first. Whether it's governance, compliance, or cost-effectiveness, our finance organization works to exemplify best practices so that the rest of the enterprise follows suit (8).

Because of this, you should always keep an eye out for other, non-material rewards that you can offer your team members. Examples are visibility (e.g., allowing them to present to the Board), exposure (involving them in senior-level or creditor meetings), or sponsorship when they want to apply for a role in another area of the organization. For some finance colleagues, a valuable reward might be representing the company externally (e.g., in industry-level working groups).

The key is to respond to each employee's unique aspirations instead of assuming that everyone wants the same thing. An opportunity to network at an industry event might be seen as a prize by one person and a chore by another. Likewise, visibility to senior leadership might thrill one colleague but create unnecessary anxiety for another.

Coercive power

This includes withholding promotions, giving negative performance evaluations, or even terminating employment. You already know you should use such force minimally. What gives you coercive power is the ability to punish, not the frequency with which you actually do it. If, for example, you are only a "dotted line" boss whose formal feedback about a finance manager can be brushed aside without consequence, then your position power over that manager is effectively low – no matter what your title says.

Legitimate power

This type of power stems from how much employees respect your title, even in the absence of considerable reward or coercive power. It correlates with the cultural dimension called "power distance," which measures how much a society accepts unequal distributions of power. In high power distance cultures, such as China or Mexico, employees might follow your directives simply because you are the boss. In low power distance cultures, like The Netherlands, employees will not budge if your only justification is "because I said so."

Another big factor in legitimate power is how much your position allows you to represent and protect your team's interests. Even in companies with healthy, collaborative cultures, team members appreciate having a leader who can choose whether (or not) to sacrifice the team's immediate interests for the greater good – rather than having that decision forced by someone higher up. The evolution of the CFO role at JCPenney illustrates this.

CASE: JCPENNEY AND THE SHIFTING CFO ROLE

When Ken Hannah joined JCPenney as CFO in mid-2012, the company had just initiated a sharp strategic shift. Its new CEO, Ron Johnson, came from Apple, where he had developed the dazzling Apple retail stores. Johnson started a complete repositioning of JCPenney's marketing (most famously abandoning long-standing promotional strategies in favor of "everyday low pricing") while emulating Steve Jobs's notorious disdain for market testing.

Johnson recruited an all-star executive team, including Apple alum Michael Kramer, who became COO. At the same time, JCPenney parted ways with its long-serving CFO and EVP, Michael Dastugue, and effectively "demoted" the CFO role by making it report to the COO instead of the CEO. Ken Hannah stepped into this downgraded position.

Less than two years later, when Johnson's strategy had largely failed (leading to his and Kramer's departures), Hannah was replaced by Ed Record and the CFO seat was upgraded again to report directly to the CEO.

Some finance employees who experienced the transition from Dastugue to Hannah reported upheaval in the finance department after the CFO change, caused by abrupt policy changes. They perceived Hannah's leadership style as top-down, with little involvement of mid-level finance managers. While this may not reflect everyone's view, it's easy to see how the CFO "demotion" may have played a role in Hannah's acceptance as a leader. Under Dastugue, employees might have seen their CFO at the "grown-ups' table," influencing decisions that impacted finance. Under Hannah, the CFO role seemed less powerful, leaving finance employees feeling they had less protection or representation.

It's also possible that Hannah's top-down leadership approach was shaped by the lower power of his position rather than purely by personal style. If he was often presented with decisions already made by the COO and CEO, there would be limited opportunity for bottom-up consultation in the finance area.

In sum, when taking a new finance leadership role, be sure to gauge the actual position power of the job, as well as any expectations your team might have, from prior leadership. You may still decide to accept a job with modest position power, especially if you trust your ability to draw from other sources of power, such as expert or personal power. Let's explore those next.

Expert power

CFOs have expert power when people perceive them as possessing senior-level financial expertise. However, the general rule in management is that as you move up, you become less of a specialist and more of a generalist. Still, many CFOs maintain a deep reservoir of expert power even while adding more generalist skill sets. Naturally, as your area of responsibility widens, your expertise evolves from detailed knowledge of, say, accounting standards to recognizing broader patterns, having the ability to ask the right questions, and combining financial acumen with business and strategic skills.

Well-known CFOs like Luca Maestri (Apple) or Greg Smith (Boeing) earned tremendous respect inside and outside their organizations by exemplifying two pillars of expertise: control (having thorough knowledge of financial workings) and support (offering strategic guidance to the business).

Expertise benefits your leadership of the finance team in more ways than you might expect. Certainly, it allows you to engage in "spending time teaching and coaching," a dimension of Individual Consideration within transformational leadership. But there's more. When your expertise is recognized and admired beyond the finance area, even junior staff in remote branches of the organization feel proud to be on your team. That translates into greater Idealized Influence, another key dimension of transformational leadership, as in Greg Smith's case.

CASE: GREG SMITH AT BOEING

Greg Smith served as CFO during Boeing's biggest crisis period, beginning with the 737 MAX disaster (two fatal crashes, groundings, halted deliveries) and followed by the COVID-19 pandemic. The company's survival was at stake, morale was shattered, and employees' pride in the organization took a severe hit.

Yet Smith – who had solid connections with the investment community and a sterling reputation – secured billions in debt financing, saving Boeing from collapse. Boeing's rattled investors never stopped trusting Smith, seeing him as the de facto leader of the company during the crisis (9). Despite inevitable job cuts, many at Boeing, across functions and levels, continued to respect Smith. Much of that respect was attributed to Smith's impressive expertise, not only in all things finance but also in operational aspects of the business (10).

As a result, even in the midst of a Boeing identity crisis, its finance employees took pride in being part of Smith's team and followed his lead, illustrating how seasoned expertise can enhance a CFO's power.

Personal power

Personal power comes from your traits, values, and interpersonal skills. Your appearance confers a certain amount of power (all other things being equal, taller and healthier-looking people command more power). Charisma represents a form of power. Interpersonal abilities and leadership skills can make a big difference in the amount of power you command.

One does not often hear the words "charismatic" and "CFO" in the same sentence. This may be because CFOs can feel pressured to tone down overt enthusiasm or charm (see our section on the CFO personality paradox in Chapter 2). Nonetheless, when CFOs do exhibit charisma, it can be a powerful asset. A notorious example is Andrew Fastow at Enron, described as "charming and charismatic, brilliant and quick-witted". Fastow's persuasive powers arguably enabled the intricate financial schemes that contributed to Enron's collapse.

Obviously, charisma isn't always used unethically. Jeremy Barnum at JPMorgan Chase is a very different example of a charismatic CFO, not only because – to the best of my fallible knowledge – he seems to have the right ethical compass but also because he has a special brand of charisma.

CASE: JEREMY BARNUM AT JPMORGAN CHASE

Barnum's charisma draws less on quick wit and sparkle and more on a combination of being different from, yet also similar to, those he leads. He has an unusual background – a chemistry degree and an odd way of speaking "like a movie actor from the 30s" apparently coming from growing up in Barcelona. According to those close to him, he is "a real intellectual" who probably did not plan on a career in finance while being brought up by his pianist mother and participating in "anarcho-syndicalist" debates (11).

These differences could easily have isolated Barnum from those he leads, could have made him seem aloof or elitist. Instead, they contribute to his charisma because they are balanced by his widely recognized congeniality. He is known to walk around the floor, sit down next to a junior staffer, and happily delve into their Excel files, side by side. Opinions are divided whether this inspires or terrifies the respective employee, but there is little doubt that sharing in the minutiae of his team's work makes Barnum feel like "one of us", an essential ingredient of charismatic leadership. We will discuss tactics for projecting charisma in Chapter 7, "Inspiring and motivating others".

Political power

Political power arises from social capital – your networks, affiliations, and relationships – and from political skill: your ability to navigate organizational politics effectively.

Other forms of power can feed into political power. For example, personal power might make you likable in influential circles, while positional power grants you access to certain networks. However, you can also develop political power independently – perhaps because you've been with the same company for decades or because a colleague who likes you just became CEO at another firm and invites you to hop over.

This scenario is not unusual for CFOs. When newly appointed CEOs shift companies, they sometimes bring their trusted finance partner with them. For instance, Mike Santomassimo followed his boss Charles Scharf from BNY Mellon to Wells Fargo, becoming CFO there in 2020, as part of a management reshuffle aiming at cleaning the bank's spotted ethics record. Being seen as the new CEO's "lieutenant" (12) can provide you with significant political power, but it also requires skillful maneuvering to avoid looking like a mere "yes man" without antagonizing the CEO.

Politics are part of organizational life everywhere – except perhaps in mom-and-pop businesses, though even they may have their war stories to tell. If you think your workplace is free of politics, it likely means one of two things: you're new enough to be adorable or powerful enough that the politics now orbit around *you* like moons around Jupiter.

However, **you do not want to go all the way to the other extreme** and see every C-suite as a nest of vipers or every senior executive as an axe-grinding psychopath. This is for two practical reasons:

1. **It's probably not true.** As with the evening news, murderous conflicts at work get retold more, which makes them seem more frequent than they really are. It is quite unlikely that there is a colleague of yours out there who gets up in the morning with the thought "I'm going to get [insert your name] today". Most people think of themselves as good and try to act accordingly. The notion of "corporate psychopathy", much touted in recent years as endemic, actually has no basis; there is no solid research showing that psychopaths are more prevalent in corporations than elsewhere, nor that there are more psychopaths among executives (13).

2. **It is not good for you.** You are better off trusting that others have good intentions (until proven otherwise) than assuming that they don't (until proven innocent). As we will see in Chapter 8 on influencing, trusting that the other is a potential ally is a condition for trying to influence them. Moreover, humans are naturally drawn to other humans who are trusting and open. Of course, trusting does not mean naïve: it's good to add some wisdom to the mix, knowing that all humans – including you – have their foibles, their egos, and their desires.

CFOs are well aware of the power of politics in their organizations. When surveyed about decisions on capital allocation among divisions, one in four CFOs of U.S. companies and one in three CFOs of non-U.S. companies **rated corporate politics as "important" or "very important"** in the decision-making process. And when asked about the role of a division manager's *reputation* in the decision-making process (reputation, of course, partly relies on politics), two out of three CFOs called it critical (14).

The political maturity curve

As leaders grow, their approach to organizational politics often evolves from a naïve to a coping and finally to a "leveraging" stage (15).

- **Naïve stage**: "Politics? What politics? I just work hard and do my best." These are the wide-eyed, usually junior leaders.
- **Coping stage**: "Politics is an evil to endure." These are the disillusioned middle managers, who know that the best idea doesn't always win, but still hope it might on a good day.
- **Leveraging stage**: "Politics is part of how things get done." These are the seasoned executives who understand that politics isn't a distraction from work – it *is* the work, at least part of it.

But here's the twist: recognizing the reality of politics doesn't mean surrendering to it. In fact, *the job of a senior leader is to contain political behavior in their own area*, like a gardener relentlessly pulling out those weeds before they take over the whole garden.

How to minimize the mess

1. **Design matters**. Organizations with too many rules become jungles of workarounds. Too few rules and subjectivity starts ruling instead. The sweet spot is structure that's clear, transparent, and just permissive enough to allow for creativity without creating a free-for-all.
2. **Set the tone at the top**. Imagine this: you leave a leadership team meeting where, ostensibly, a decision was made. Then you tell your team, "Well, the COO only agreed because it helps her bonus, the CHRO is not to be trusted, and by the way, I'm not really going along with it." Congratulations – you've just invited everyone to the great *Game of Thrones* reenactment that is your company culture. Want to minimize politics? Then disagreements need to be expressed and sorted out behind the boardroom door.
3. **Remove the political animals**. Some people aren't just *in* politics. They *are* politics. If someone on your team consistently creates tension, manipulates alliances, or treats every meeting like a Cold War conference, it might be time for a gentle (or not-so-gentle) parting. Political mindsets are usually correlated with low propensity to trust, which, as discussed in Chapter 4, is resistant to change.

Pro-social vs. anti-social politics

Not all politics are bad. Social information gathering, issue selling, influencing, and networking: these can all be examples of pro-social political behavior. At the other end of the spectrum, manipulating, attributing to self the work of others, throwing blame, and vicious gossip are all anti-social political behaviors. The problem is that the examples in the first category could still prove anti-social: were networking and influencing part of creating an alliance against another colleague? Was issue selling about having the person's idea take precedence over someone else's?

There's a litmus test. Ask

Does the person engage in this to advance their work agenda for what they believe ultimately benefits the organization?

Or

Does the person engage in this for their personal benefit, to the detriment of the organization?

The answer, when it's about one instance of political behavior, may not be clear-cut; however, when examples accumulate around one individual, they usually tell you everything you need to know.

We'll delve deeper into political skill – including influencing tactics and networking – in Chapter 8.

Organizational culture

Organizational culture is the system of shared values and norms that define appropriate attitudes and behaviors for organizational members – in other words, "how we do things around here". It is shaped gradually, **as a firm learns** by solving its problems of internal integration and external adaptation (16).

As CFO, you are doubly interested in understanding, and potentially helping change, the culture of your organization. First, as any leader, you will be more or less successful depending on the degree of "fit" between how you lead and the organization's culture.

Second, specifically as CFO, you want to maximize the value of your company, and there is growing evidence that a strong culture is a key asset for today's organizations. In a recent study of U.S. CEOs and CFOs, *over half of them ranked culture as a top 3 driver of firm value and an additional 25% put it in the top 5* (17).

But what culture is best for a company? From the financial literature, we have only indirect evidence: for example, Luigi Guiso and colleagues (2015) study the effects of employee perceptions of management's integrity. They find that this leads to higher productivity and profitability, even after controlling for "halo" effects from things such as better pay or increased work safety. This correlation between perceived managerial integrity and profitability is less intuitive than it might seem at first sight: integrity includes foregoing profit that could be made, for example, at the expense of customers. Unsurprisingly, advertised company values bear no connection with ratings of integrity or with companies' short- or long-term performance. Interestingly, CEO compensation is positively associated with employee perceptions of managerial integrity (18).

A recent study compiled a measure of corporate culture as the average rating for five values: innovation, teamwork, quality, respect, and integrity. It found that companies in the top quartile as per this measure have higher stock liquidity and future stock returns (19).

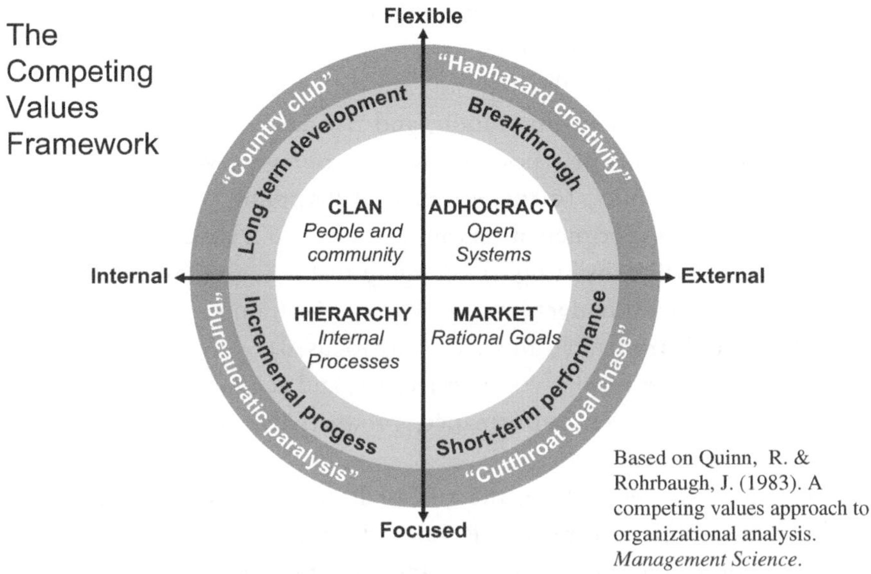

Figure 5.1 The Competing Values Framework.
Based on Cameron & Quinn, 1999 (20)

One of the measures of corporate value most used by researchers and companies alike is the Competing Values Framework ("CVF") (20). As illustrated in Figure 5.1, the CVF clusters organizational cultures into four primary types, arranged along two axes:

- **Flexibility vs. Stability**: How much an organization values adaptability and change versus order and predictability.
- **Internal vs. External Focus**: Whether the organization's primary attention is on internal efficiency and cohesion or on external positioning and competitiveness.

These axes intersect to create four culture quadrants:

1. **Clan culture** (flexible and internally focused)
    - Emphasizes collaboration, teamwork, and a family-like atmosphere. Leaders are viewed as mentors or coaches.
    - As a CFO in a clan culture, you might find it easier to champion initiatives that rely on strong relationships and open communication,

but you may face challenges enforcing strict financial targets if they conflict with maintaining harmony.

2. **Adhocracy culture** (flexible and externally focused)
   - Values creativity, innovation, and risk-taking. Leaders are seen as entrepreneurs or visionaries who encourage new ideas.
   - For CFOs here, balancing financial discipline with a culture that glorifies experimentation can be tricky. You'll need to support bold moves (like investing in emerging technologies) while keeping a close eye on budgets and regulatory constraints.
3. **Market culture** (stable and externally focused)
   - Focuses on results, competitiveness, and achieving targets. Leaders often push for performance, productivity, and winning in the marketplace.
   - In a market culture, the CFO's drive for cost-effectiveness and strong financial metrics is generally well aligned with the organization's focus on achieving tangible outcomes. However, you may need to remind your team (and yourself) that people matter, too, and pure results orientation can lead to burnout if not balanced with employee well-being.
4. **Hierarchy culture** (stable and internally focused)
   - Prioritizes order, structure, and formal processes. Leaders are often administrators or coordinators who ensure that policies and procedures are followed.
   - CFOs frequently feel at home in a hierarchy culture because of the emphasis on control, compliance, and clear rules – elements that align closely with the traditional finance function. That said, you might struggle when swift adaptation is required, and you'll need to push for flexibility if the business context demands agility.

Organizational cultures are usually a blend of the four quadrants above, with one or two dominating. Very often, when corporations decide to measure and work on their culture, they conclude that they would like to have less "hierarchy" and more "adhocracy". Yet there is no universal "best" culture that would fit all environments in which firms operate.

For example, companies with hierarchy-dominated cultures fared best during the 2008–2009 crisis, with fewer layoffs, less negative asset growth, and increased access to debt financing (21). From a financial reporting viewpoint, companies that have predominantly a collaboration-oriented, "clan" culture, tend to have lower financial reporting quality, evidenced by more frequent internal control weaknesses, while competition-oriented, "market" cultures act as a disciplining mechanism, leading to higher reporting quality (22).

As you would expect, getting extreme ratings in any of the four culture quadrants is not good news for the health of your company's culture. Too much adhocracy brings chaos, with great ideas but no structure for delivering and controlling quality; too much "market" and it's all short-term results and no concern for people; too much "hierarchy" and work gets bogged in bureaucracy; finally, too much "clan" and you might as well move the headquarters to a beach club.

A company's culture can be remarkably **stubborn**. Changing it demands herculean efforts, pushing back against the overwhelming inertia of "how things are done around here." In the public eye, the CEO is usually cast as the main hero on this mission, and many believe CEOs shape their companies in their own image. However, research suggests that might be too idealized: for instance, CEOs of S&P 1500 firms seem to have, on average, limited influence on changes in their organizations' cultures (16).

Look at the culture shift that began in 2009 under CEO Piyush Gupta at DBS, the Asian bank. Gupta, who was "raised" in Citibank's strong, competitive culture, discovered that DBS was far more traditional and internally oriented, dominated by clan and hierarchy values. Determined to change course, he launched a multi-year program to make DBS more externally driven – leaning toward market and adhocracy values – and even referred to the revamped company as "a 26,000-person startup." The transformation became an award-winning model of cultural change and is now taught in MBA programs. Yet for all that success, remnants of the old, bureaucratic culture still lingered as late as 2016, when employees on Glassdoor described middle management as "old-school," "political," and "hierarchical."

This isn't meant to discourage you from trying to shift your company's culture – assuming it actually needs shifting. Leaders who hold strong values and work to shape the culture around those values are practicing a key transformational leadership behavior. So rather than give up, celebrate every small, incremental step toward the culture you envision.

While doing so, be aware of how your previous experiences with company culture may have shaped your own value system. While *leaders can change culture, strong cultures also definitely change leaders.* If you've ever worked for a company with a strong culture, you might not even realize how much it influenced your own values and perspectives until you've left, as illustrated by Daria's story.

CASE: DARIA WALTER AT EVERIANT[2]

Daria had been with a major, public company in the tech equipment industry for over a decade, in several finance management roles, when she decided to accept the CFO role at Everiant, a rapidly growing, venture capital-backed software company. She had braced for a cultural shock and was not too surprised to find out that her new organization was, as she put it, "a rebellious teenager with zero discipline". She was ready to pull her sleeves up and put the house in order, in preparation for an (IPO). However, she had not anticipated how different the mindsets of the CEO and the board (representing the venture funds) would be from the risk-aware, structured, public company management and board she had left behind. As she put it:

> You didn't have your typical public governance board members. That's sort of like my language. That's the language I speak. It was just VCs, who have a whole different sort of motive.

In CVF terms, Everiant's culture, as created by the visionary entrepreneur who had started the company and was now the CEO, was dominated by adhocracy (valuing innovation and risk-taking unconstrained by rules). Everiant's board members, representing the venture funds, came with their own, industry-specific culture, in which the "market" quadrant dominated, fiercely competitive and exclusively interested in results. This combination of externally focused cultures was diametrically opposed to the culture Daria had been "raised" in, at her previous company, which was primarily internally focused, with the "hierarchy" quadrant dominating, followed by the "clan" one.

Daria was a seasoned finance professional: she had the ability to dispassionately diagnose a losing investment and cut her losses early on. She quit her new CFO role less than a year after joining and was enthusiastically welcomed back by her previous employer. Several years later, she was promoted to CFO.

A similar case of a former, strong culture influencing the CFO's values and leadership style is that of Jason Child, former CFO of Groupon.

CASE: JASON CHILD AT GROUPON

Jason Child spent 12 years at Amazon, steadily advancing in finance roles, before becoming CFO at Groupon and later at Splunk and ARM. He admits that only "five jobs since" Amazon did he fully grasp how unique Amazon's culture really was and how deeply it shaped his leadership style; as he says, "it mutated my cultural DNA" (23).

For example, Amazon would put every shortlisted candidate through a "bar raising" process involving people other than the candidate's future boss, who had veto power if they did not see a fit with the company's values and standards of excellence.

This major determinant of Amazon's culture – its rigorous, highly selective recruitment process – probably wasn't something Child could replicate at Groupon, especially given Groupon's rapid growth during Child's tenure, when it was declared "the fastest growing company ever" (24).

Groupon was growing so fast it didn't have the luxury to sift talent quite so carefully. Within a year of joining, Child had built Groupon's finance team across 48 countries *and* had taken the company public – only to face a series of high-profile accounting restatements and material weaknesses in internal controls. Groupon's stock soon plummeted to a quarter of its IPO price (25). In fall 2012, one last restatement broke the camel's back. Andrew Mason, the CEO, recalls:

> Me and my CFO were in Barcelona meeting with some investors when we get a call from our controller in France. They had forgotten to accrue a profit-sharing tax, and we had just lost $10 million. So that was it. We missed our numbers (25).

Could Child's Amazon-shaped cultural DNA have contributed to these troubles? The manner in which he describes his preferred leadership style, inspired by Amazon, could be summarized as "hire people smarter than you and let them run with it" (26).

Such an approach worked at Amazon, where excellence, empowerment, and individual responsibility were second nature. But a newly assembled finance team, uncertain about "how we do things around here," might bring assumptions from all sorts of different corporate cultures, creating a mismatch between the leadership style and the team's readiness. Tellingly, within two years, none of Child's direct reports were the same individuals as at the time of the IPO (27).

As Daria's and Jason's examples show, a strong culture you experienced early in your career can shape a value-based leadership style that's highly effective – until you try to apply the same approach in a new, very different environment and find the results disappointing.

This was also Clara's experience in her new role.

CROSSROADS LIFE: CLARA AND THE "BRING YOUR HOBBIES TO WORK" CULTURE

Clara arrives at Crossroads headquarters in Amsterdam from a regional subsidiary – and, before that, from the high-pressure world of investment banking. To her, the culture at HQ feels jarringly relaxed. Her colleagues seem to enjoy a generous work–life balance, and many openly integrate their hobbies into the workplace. Ruben, the Chief Risk Officer, changes into running gear at the office to train for marathons. Oliver, the Group Head of Tax, breaks into opera mid-conversation and organizes full-scale rehearsals for a performance at the company Christmas party.

Clara sees all of this through a critical lens. Out in the field, where she had come from, people work long hours to win and retain customers. Meanwhile, she sees headquarters staff – those responsible for strategy, policy, and support – milling about, seemingly disconnected from the pressures of the front lines. To Clara, it looks like indulgence at the expense of the business.

But the truth, as she gradually learns, is more complex. Dutch work culture places a higher value on work–life balance and personal fulfillment and less on status or overwork, especially compared with the more achievement-driven cultures in Crossroads Europe's subsidiaries.

What Clara begins to understand – through experience and, eventually, painful lessons – is that these hobbies aren't just distractions. They are a social currency. Her colleagues use them to build trust, forge connections, and exchange information that never makes it into official reports or slide decks. And in a political, interconnected environment like regional leadership, that informal network can be more powerful than hours spent alone chasing "objective truth" in spreadsheets and PowerPoints.

Watch the scene selection at: https://www.ed.movie/hobbies or scan the QR code.

Country culture

The environment in which you exercise leadership and the culture of the organization are also colored by country culture, especially when you lead in a global organization.

Geert Hofstede's cultural dimensions framework is a widely used tool to understand how country culture shapes workplace behaviors, including leadership. Hofstede identified six dimensions of national culture: **power distance**, **uncertainty avoidance**, **individualism vs. collectivism**, **masculinity vs. femininity**, **long-term vs. short-term orientation**, and **indulgence vs. restraint** (28). Each dimension represents a value continuum in societal culture. These cultural values act as a "collective programming of the mind" that shapes organizational behavior and leadership expectations in each country. In practice, Hofstede's dimensions provide a framework to anticipate differences in leadership norms from one culture to another. You can access a free country comparison tool that uses Hofstede's dimensions here[3].

For our practical purposes, I will focus on two of Hofstede's dimensions: power distance and individualism – collectivism, which are especially relevant for your leadership success.

Power Distance

Power distance is the extent to which a society accepts the fact that power in institutions and organizations is distributed unequally. In high power distance cultures, hierarchy is respected and inequalities are accepted as normal; in low power distance cultures, people expect power to be distributed more equally and leaders to be approachable.

High vs. Low Power Distance Cultures

In high power distance societies, leaders are expected to be authoritative and directive, often taking a paternalistic, "I know what's best for you" approach. In such societies, superiors are less accessible and decision-making is centralized at the top. Subordinates rarely challenge authority and instead expect clear direction from their leaders. Moreover, expatriates from high power distance countries tend to respond better to paternalistic leadership behaviors (29).

CASE: JIM SCHELL AT CELEROVA[4]

Jim is CFO for a global logistics company and has a finance team organized in several "hubs" over three continents. As the company has been growing rapidly, Jim has that rare luxury that would make him the envy of many leaders: a team he handpicked himself. He is proud of his team and takes great satisfaction in seeing them grow.

To signal that career development for all members of the finance area was taken seriously, he introduced formal, annual career development discussions, separate from the performance appraisal cycle. He had a clear mental image of how these career development discussions should go, shaped by his longtime experience with U.S.-based organizations. In his view, ambitious professionals articulate their goals with precision, laying out medium- and long-term plans as if drafting a business proposal.

But when he tried this approach with managers from his company's Indian finance hub, he hit a wall. They were evasive, reluctant to spell out their aspirations. It wasn't until much later that he realized he'd missed something fundamental: in cultures with high power distance (India's power distance index is 77, compared with only 40 for the United States), ambition isn't something you broadcast. It's something you entrust to your superiors to recognize on your behalf.

Jim was not planning on doing his employees' career thinking for them. What he did was to abandon the formal route and instead to rely on informal interactions and indirect signals to form an image of each individual's ambition.

Jim's assumption – that ambition is universally self-declared – turned out to be culturally specific, not universal.

Interestingly, in high power distance cultures, you can be more appreciated as a leader, compared with low power distance ones, not only when displaying authoritarian or paternalistic leadership but also when displaying transformational, consultative, empowering, or humble leadership (30, 31). It doesn't take much – maybe walking around, chatting to employees, showing a human face – for a new leader to impress and inspire employees when they are used to leaders behaving as kings or father figures.

Does this mean that **leaders have it easier** in high power distance cultures: admired if they dictate but also admired if they empower and consult? Not so fast. The **reverse of the medal** is employees' ability to take initiative and responsibility. In low power distance cultures, employees will feel more comfortable taking the ball and running with it, compared with those in high power distance environments, who see decision-making as something reserved to the exalted leader only.

In short, employees in high power distance countries may love and admire you more as a leader, may even be more motivated, but they will wait for your instructions at every step, whereas employees in low power distance countries may be less starry-eyed about you and the company but are more likely to figure out what needs to be done without waiting for your instructions.

Individualism – Collectivism

This dimension concerns the degree to which people in a culture prioritize individual rights and goals versus group cohesion and loyalty. In a highly individualistic culture, people are expected to take care of themselves and their immediate families only. In a strongly collectivist culture, people are integrated into groups or communities that protect them in exchange for loyalty, and individuals place the interests of the group above their own.

In individualistic cultures, leaders are effective when they emphasize individual **initiative, autonomy**, and **personal achievement**. Leaders often delegate authority and encourage employees to make their own decisions or innovate independently. Rewards and recognition are given to individual accomplishments. Because people in individualist societies value independence, leaders must respect autonomy – micromanaging or paternalistic behaviors may be resented as intrusions.

In collectivist cultures, leadership is most effective when group-oriented and relationship-focused. Leaders are expected to **care for their team like a family**, sometimes taking a paternalistic stance, guiding and protecting subordinates in both work and personal matters.

Leaders emphasize team achievements and loyalty; they may reward group performance and foster strong unity. This style can generate high trust and commitment – for example, paternalistic leaders in collectivist cultures have been found to increase follower job satisfaction and reduce turnover intentions, by virtue of the personalized care and loyalty they cultivate. Likewise, employees in collectivist settings often readily accept influence from leaders they perceive as looking out for the group's welfare.

Sometimes a misconception appears, that employees in collectivist cultures are more engaged when decisions are taken by wider consultation, collaboratively. In fact, the opposite is true. **Collectivism is quite correlated with high power distance**, so that employees in collectivist environments will expect the leader of the group to know what is best and decide accordingly. Because they have pledged allegiance to the group, they do not need their individual voice to be heard but will be content with what has been decided. This does not automatically mean that they will follow the decision taken, but if they deviate they will typically do it surreptitiously while claiming to comply. On the contrary, it is the highly individualistic cultures, especially when coupled with low power distance, that demand leadership by consensus. For example, countries in Northern Europe, well known for their participative, distributed leadership, all rate in the top quartile in individualism and in the bottom tercile in power distance.

These cultural dimensions shape how decisions are made (top-down vs. consensus) and how followers respond to their leaders' actions. Ultimately, effective leadership requires cultural intelligence – adapting one's style to fit the cultural expectations of followers. Leaders who align with their culture's values can motivate teams more successfully and make decisions that gain acceptance, leading to better organizational outcomes.

The business context

When a company isn't doing well or when a big change project fails, things get harder for leaders. This is especially true for CEOs, who usually get more credit than they deserve when things go right – and more blame when they don't. But all C-suite executives share some responsibility for the organization's performance. The CFO's position is unique: on one hand, a struggling company can call into question their effectiveness as a business partner; on the other hand, it's precisely in tough times – when finances are tight and cost cuts are needed – that the CFO can become the most powerful leader in the room.

In Chapter 1, we briefly mentioned David Gibbs (former CFO, now CEO of Yum! Brands) and his advice to CFOs about personal branding: find ways to be known as "the finance guy who says yes" or "the growth finance guy." This approach worked for David, but would it have worked if he had been CFO during a very tough time, when the company needed drastic cost cuts across the board? Marie Myers, CFO at Hewlett Packard Enterprise, needed to take a different approach.

CASE: MARIE MYERS AT HEWLETT PACKARD ENTERPRISE[5]

Marie Myers is currently the CFO of Hewlett Packard Enterprise, a role she assumed in early 2024 after serving as CFO of HP Inc. When the original Hewlett Packard split into two separate companies in 2015 – HP Inc. (focused on printers and consumer PCs) and Hewlett Packard Enterprise (focused on enterprise technology infrastructure, software, and services) – Marie initially remained with HP Inc., the printers and PCs side of the business. By the time the split officially took effect, PC sales had declined, leaving HP Inc. with an operating expense budget that was suddenly unsustainable – an issue Marie was tasked with solving.

Marie recalls the CEO telling her, "Marie, you have to cut your budget by 20 percent." At that moment, she considered leaving the company. "I couldn't bear to face these people and tell them what was happening," she said, referring to the finance team she was building, "especially after I'd just hired them."

But she didn't quit. Instead, she empowered her team to search for a way to reduce the impact of those cuts. Their solution: robotic process automation (RPA). By automating routine tasks within the finance organization, Marie was able to not only preserve more jobs in her organization but increase efficiencies and reduce overall costs within that group. With just a year to execute, Marie and her team moved quickly to implement RPA across finance processes. The journey came with challenges – some successes, some failures, and a steep learning curve – but ultimately it worked. The experience revealed to Marie how significant cost pressures can have positive effects, driving innovation and enabling creative problem-solving.

You've probably noticed from your own experience that **constraints can often spark creativity**. But as a CFO, that's only part of the equation. It is just as important to inspire **your team to see opportunity** in adversity, stay positive, and channel their own creativity rather than slipping into cynicism. That is the essence of **transformational leadership** and an important lesson Marie carried with her when she transitioned to become CFO of Hewlett Packard Enterprise.

The environment: Practical takeaways

We have looked at power, company and country culture, and the business context as important environmental forces that can make or break your leadership. Here are six takeaways to guide your CFO leadership approach:

- **Assess your actual power – not just your title**. CFOs often overestimate or underestimate how much influence they truly have. Especially first-time CFOs might overestimate their position power at first, then feel powerless when the position levers they pull turn out to be duds, thus underestimating their personal and political power potential. Examine the real extent of your reward, coercive, legitimate, expert, personal, and political power. This ensures that you know where you can lead effectively and where you need to build more support.

- **Leverage multiple sources of power**. Don't rely solely on your job title. Cultivate *expert* power by showcasing deep financial knowledge, *personal* power by honing interpersonal and communication skills, and *political* power by building strong networks and alliances. Using these in tandem helps offset any dips in positional authority.
- **Adapt leadership to the organizational culture**. Pinpoint which cultural "quadrant" (e.g., clan, adhocracy, market, hierarchy) your organization leans toward. Align your leadership style – whether it's pushing innovation, reinforcing structure, or emphasizing collaboration – with that culture. If change is needed, recognize that it requires massive, sustained effort and that remnants of the old culture will take time to shift.
- **Account for country culture**. When leading across regions, recognize that concepts like ambition, delegation, and feedback vary by cultural norms. High power distance environments may embrace an authoritative approach but also respond strongly to even small gestures of empowerment or humility. In low power distance, highly individualistic cultures, consensus-building and recognizing personal aspirations become more critical. In collectivist, higher power distance settings, employees may expect top-down decisions and paternalistic care. In individualistic, lower power distance settings, consensus-based approaches and individual autonomy matter more. Adjusting your leadership style to these nuanced expectations ensures better buy-in and outcomes across diverse teams.
- **Use constraints as catalysts for creativity**. When business conditions tighten, do not just revert to cutting costs. Communicate optimism, encourage innovation, and keep your team motivated. Challenging circumstances often spark unexpected solutions provided that the leader models resilience and fosters a culture of possibility.
- **Acknowledge that culture is slow to shift**. Organizational culture can be deeply entrenched. Even if you or your CEO launch bold change initiatives, old habits die hard. Measure progress in small wins and recognize that complete transformation requires consistent, long-term effort.

Leaders – and CFOs are no exception – often focus on refining personal skills and team dynamics without recognizing the enormous influence of the environment. By being intentional about diagnosing power structures, understanding organizational culture, and respecting national cultural dimensions, you set the stage for more effective leadership. Remember, the environment can boost or block your influence. Successful CFOs don't fight the current; they surf it, blending adaptability with a sharp lookout for the tidal forces in their organizations.

Notes

1 This classification is a modified version of French and Raven's (1958) widely used model of sources of power in organizations (that included position and personal power, with personal power further divided into expert and referent power). I add the category of political power based on recent work on political capital (8). I also rename "referent" as "personal" to make the model more intuitive to practitioners.
2 Interviewed CFO, anonymized.
3 https://www.theculturefactor.com/country-comparison-tool.
4 Interviewed CFO, anonymized.
5 Interview with the author.

References

(1) Johns, G. The context deficit in leadership research. *Leadership Quarterly* 2024, 35 (1). DOI: 10.1016/j.leaqua.2023.101755

(2) Yang, J., Liu, H., & Gu, J. A multi-level study of servant leadership on creativity The roles of self-efficacy and power distance. *Leadership & Organization Development Journal* 2017, 38 (5), 610–629. DOI: 10.1108/LODJ-10-2015-0229

(3) Neeley, T., & Reiche, B. How global leaders gain power through downward deference and reduction of social distance. *Academy of Management Journal* 2022, 65 (1), 11–34. DOI: 10.5465/amj.2019.0531

(4) Tang, G., Chen, Y., van Knippenberg, D., & Yu, B. Antecedents and consequences of empowering leadership: Leader power distance, leader perception of team capability, and team innovation. *Journal of Organizational Behavior* 2020, 41 (6), 551–566. DOI: 10.1002/job.2449

(5) Wang, L., Owens, B. P., Li, J. C., & Shi, L. H. Exploring the Affective Impact, Boundary Conditions, and Antecedents of Leader Humility. *Journal of Applied Psychology* 2018, 103 (9), 1019–1038. DOI: 10.1037/apl0000314

(6) Hoption, C., Barling, J., & Turner, N. "It's not you, it's me": transformational leadership and self-deprecating humor. *Leadership & Organization Development Journal* 2013, 34 (1), 4–19. DOI: 10.1108/01437731311289947

(7) Beugelsdijk, S., Maseland, R., & van Hoorn, A. Are scores on Hofstede's dimensions of national culture stable over time? A cohort analysis. *Global Strategy Journal* 2015, 5 (3), 223–240. DOI: 10.1002/gsj.1098
(8) Coca-Cola Q1 2022 Earnings Call. https://www.fool.com/earnings/call-transcripts/2022/04/25/coca-cola-ko-q1-2022-earnings-call-transcript/: Thomson Reuters transcript, 2022.
(9) Trentmann, N., & Tangel, A. Boeing CFO guided aircraft maker through 737 Max crisis. In *The Wall Street Journal*, https://www.wsj.com/articles/boeing-cfo-guided-aircraft-maker-through-737-max-crisis-11618958115, 2021.
(10) Sonnenfeld, J., & Tian, S. Who is the leader to put Boeing back on course? https://insights.som.yale.edu/insights/who-is-the-leader-to-put-boeing-back-on-course: Yale Insights, 2024.
(11) Dilts-Marshall, E., & Herbst-Bayliss, S. JPMorgan's new CFO described as pensive Excel expert with a knack for mentoring. https://www.reuters.com/business/jpmorgans-new-cfo-described-pensive-excel-expert-with-knack-mentoring-2021-05-21/: Reuters, 2021.
(12) Wells Fargo cross-selling scandal. Wikipedia, Ed., https://en.wikipedia.org/wiki/Wells_Fargo_cross-selling_scandal
(13) Bunea, E. The truth about corporate psychopaths. In *To Manage is Human*, https://www.psychologytoday.com/us/blog/to-manage-is-human/202305/the-truth-about-corporate-psychopaths?amp: Psychology Today, 2023.
(14) Graham, J., Harvey, C., & Puri, M. Capital allocation and delegation of decision-making authority within firms. *Journal of Financial Economics* 2015, *115* (3), 449–470. DOI: 10.1016/j.jfineco.2014.10.011
(15) Doldor, E. From Politically Naive to Politically Mature: Conceptualizing Leaders' Political Maturation Journey. *British Journal of Management* 2017, 28 (4), 666–686. DOI: 10.1111/1467-8551.12219
(16) Li, X., Chen, G., & Shen, R. Steering the Intangible Wheel: Chief Executive Officer Effect on Corporate Cultural Change. *Organization Science* 2024, 35 (5), 1770–1794. DOI: 10.1287/orsc.2022.17210
(17) Graham, J., Grennan, J., Harvey, C., & Rajgopal, S. Corporate culture: The interview evidence. *Journal of Applied Corporate Finance* 2022, 34 (4), 22–41. DOI: 10.1111/jacf.12528
(18) Guiso, L., Sapienza, P., & Zingales, L. The value of corporate culture. *Journal of Financial Economics* 2015, *117* (1), 60–76. DOI: 10.1016/j.jfineco.2014.05.010
(19) Tran, T., Nguyen, H., & Pham, M. Do financial markets value corporate culture? *International Review of Financial Analysis* 2025, 98. DOI: 10.1016/j.irfa.2024.103823
(20) Cameron, K. S., & Quinn, R. E. *Diagnosing and changing organizational culture*. Addison-Wesley, 1999.
(21) Fang, Y., Fiordelisi, F., Hasan, I., Leung, W., & Wong, G. Corporate culture and firm value: Evidence from crisis. *Journal of Banking & Finance* 2023, 146. DOI: 10.1016/j.jbankfin.2022.106710
(22) Bhandari, A., Mammadov, B., Thevenot, M., & Vakilzadeh, H. Corporate Culture and Financial Reporting Quality. *Accounting Horizons* 2022, 36 (1), 1–24. DOI: 10.2308/HORIZONS-19-003

(23) How Jason Child transformed finance forever. https://www.youtube.com/watch?v=Wr6PR1zkURI: The Block and Tackle Show, 2024.
(24) Steiner, C. Meet the fastest growing company ever. In *Forbes*, https://www.forbes.com/forbes/2010/0830/entrepreneurs-groupon-facebook-twitter-next-web-phenom.html, 2010.
(25) Blumberg, A. The Super-Quick Rise and Even Faster Fall of Groupon. Former CEO Andrew Mason on what the roller-coaster ride felt like. In *NY Mag, Intelligencer*, https://nymag.com/intelligencer/2018/10/andrew-mason-on-groupon.html, 2018.
(26) The secret to great leadership: Human Connection. Jason Child, CFO of ARM. Show, T. B. a. T., Ed., https://www.youtube.com/watch?v=gIx5GBkC8g4, 2024.
(27) Banham, R. Thinking Big. In *CFO.com*, https://www.cfo.com/news/thinking-big/665471/, 2014.
(28) Hofstede, G., Neuijen, B., Ohayv, D. D., & Sanders, G. Measuring organizational cultures. A qualitative and quantitative study across 20 cases. *Administrative Science Quarterly* 1990, 35 (2), 286–316. DOI: 10.2307/2393392
(29) Nie, D., & Lämsä, A. Chinese immigrants' occupational well-being in Finland: the role of paternalistic leadership. *Leadership & Organization Development Journal* 2018, 39 (3), 340–352. DOI: 10.1108/LODJ-05-2017-0144
(30) Euwema, M., Wendt, H., & Van Emmerik, H. Leadership styles and group organizational citizenship behavior across cultures. *Journal of Organizational Behavior* 2007, 28 (8), 1035–1057. DOI: 10.1002/job.496
(31) Schaubroeck, J., Lam, S., & Cha, S. Embracing transformational leadership: Team values and the impact of leader behavior on team performance. *Journal of Applied Psychology* 2007, 92 (4), 1020–1030. DOI: 10.1037/0021-9010.92.4.1020

PART 2

THE FINANCE LEADERSHIP TOOLBOX

If Part 1 gave you the blueprint of leadership through the LIFE model – Leader, Interaction, Followers, Environment – then Part 2 is where you reach for the toolbox.

This section is about execution. It's about what happens once you accept that leadership isn't a mystical force but a practice. And as with any practice, it demands tools. Some of these may be counterintuitive. Many will be at least partly familiar, yet you rarely pick them up from the shiny toolbox you acquired some time ago, maybe during an MBA or a leadership course.

We begin with **communication**, because numbers don't speak for themselves – you do. Whether you're persuading a skeptical board member, explaining a strategic pivot to your team, or crafting an investor narrative, communication is your currency of credibility.

Then we explore how to **motivate and inspire**, even when your team thinks in terms of risk mitigation rather than lofty mission statements. Spoiler: it's not about becoming a motivational speaker. It's about knowing how to unlock what already matters to your people.

DOI: 10.4324/9781003581734-8

From there, we tackle the messy and often uncomfortable terrain of **politics and influence**. You may not like politics, but rest assured – it likes you. And it finds you, especially as you climb higher. Learning how to navigate power dynamics without losing your soul is a leadership skill worth cultivating.

Next, we confront the high-stakes responsibility of **talent selection and development**. You will learn how to spot potential beyond the résumé, how to think of diverse teams without slipping into checking boxes, and how to manage succession without wishful thinking.

We then move to the **CFO's critical relationship with the CEO and board**. It's a high-wire act between alignment and independence and a source of both impact and existential frustration. We dissect what makes those relationships work – and what quietly erodes them.

Finally, we turn the mirror inward with **self-leadership**. Because before you can lead anyone else effectively, you must learn to lead yourself – your energy, your mindset, your resilience, your habits.

Part 2 is not a checklist to complete but a set of levers to pull with discernment. Not every tool needs to be wielded at every moment. But knowing when and how to use them – that's the difference between surviving the CFO role and shaping it.

6

COMMUNICATION SKILLS

We live in an age that fetishizes communication skills. Even job ads for entry-level positions deem them indispensable. Still, the finance profession often falls short in this regard. This may be, in part, because we finance folk tend to overestimate our communication prowess. A CFO once confided to me how, early in his career, he decided to sign up for Toastmasters. It did wonders, enabling him to deliver presentations to great applause and acclaim. But when he recommended the same path to colleagues, not one followed his advice. "We already know how to speak," they shrugged.

Yet even accomplished CFOs, like Amazon's Brian Olsavsky, confess that they need to keep sharpening their communication tools:

> I also continue to hone my writing skills. The most effective people are those who can communicate their great ideas well to others (1).

We will not dwell on presentation or writing skills, since there are numerous, self-contained courses and books on the topic. Instead, we turn our

DOI: 10.4324/9781003581734-9

gaze to listening – confirmed by research as the most important communication skill yet often sidelined by business schools (2) – and to explaining and persuading, whose nuances hold particular significance for the CFO.

Listening in Hi-Fi

In the late 1950s, a new kind of sound experience hit the market—high-fidelity audio, or Hi-Fi. It was a revolution, transforming music from something scratchy and distant into something immersive and crisp, where every note and nuance could be heard as if the band were playing in your living room. It turns out that listening to people works the same way. Most of us hear others the way we once listened to music – passively, with interference, missing key frequencies. But research by Guy Itzchakov and colleagues suggests that **high-quality listening** operates like a Hi-Fi system for human conversation, amplifying clarity, reducing noise, and, remarkably, changing how people think (3–6).

High-quality listening has three components: **attention**, **comprehension**, and **acceptance**. Each one plays a role in tuning into the other person with precision.

Attention is what many believe is synonymous with good listening. It's eye contact, leaning in slightly, signaling with subtle cues that you are there and engaged. And it's the absence of distractions – few things kill the perception of attention faster than a sideways glance at a buzzing phone. People are exquisitely attuned to divided focus; they can feel, almost at a visceral level, when someone is only half-listening.

Comprehension is deeper. It's not just understanding the words being said but making the speaker feel understood. It includes nonverbal cues – mirroring expressions, nodding (strategically, not robotically) – but also questions, which can either elevate comprehension or destroy it. Good questions do one of three things:

- **Clarify** meaning: "When you say 'transparency,' what does it mean to you?"
- **Confirm** understanding: "Are you saying you want to lead this project?"
- **Expand** thinking: "If budget weren't a constraint, how would you approach this?"

But here's the secret: the magic of a good question isn't just in the phrasing. It's in the intent. If you think you already know the answer and ask purely as a setup for your own response, the speaker will sense it. The question will seem designed to expose ignorance rather than to explore ideas.

Acceptance is where we falter. We listen, but we also judge – often without realizing it. Judgment leaks out in ways we don't expect: a sigh, a skeptical eyebrow, even a well-intentioned "Why did you do it this way?" (a question that often lands as criticism rather than curiosity). A better approach: "What led to this decision?" The shift is subtle, yet one question corners, the other opens. When you listen to an employee describe an issue, even a well-intended "Have you spoken with Tom about this?" is no longer high-quality listening but advice and can be perceived as judgmental (you don't trust the person to solve the issue without Tom's help).

Here's where it gets really interesting. The experiments by Itzchakov and his colleagues found that when people experienced high-quality listening, they didn't just feel heard. Their attitudes actually **shifted**. Political opinions softened. Workplace complaints became less extreme. People became more willing to see both sides of an issue. And this all happened even though the listener didn't offer any advice, argue any points, or try to change the speaker's mind. Just listening – deeply, openly – was enough.

Think about that. Imagine an employee comes to you, fuming about a policy change. You listen intently, ask open questions, without offering opinions or advice. And by the end of the conversation, they're already moderating their own position, acknowledging some benefits to the new policy. That's the power of Hi-Fi listening. It doesn't just make people feel heard. It makes them hear themselves differently.

Getting to "Now I get it!": Explaining and persuading

As CFO, you will have a good amount of explaining to deliver to various stakeholders. Of these, finance employees are the easiest audience for you, as you speak (largely) the same language. Especially if you have a "teacher" leadership style, you will enjoy explaining intricate topics to them.

Things get trickier when explaining complex financial concepts to a **non-expert** audience. It's not only that they don't have the specialist knowledge; it's also that, even when you explain in simple, everyday words, their eyes glaze over. Most often you will find that, with non-specialist audiences, you cannot separate explaining from persuading and that the combo requires some art: an engaging story, a good analogy[1], or maybe a well-placed joke.

CASE: EMILIA AND THE INFLATION GUARANTEE

I had spent years mastering financial models, convinced that logic always prevails. But here I was, on live television, watching my arguments crumble.

It was 2004, and Romania was preparing to launch private pensions. I was speaking for insurers eager to enter the market, but expectations were wildly unrealistic. The union leader, Mr. Popescu, turned to me with a triumphant smirk. "So, you smart people with fancy degrees want to manage people's money, but you can't even guarantee returns above inflation?" I had pages of analysis in my head, but none of it could counter the simplicity of his attack. Having to provide return guarantees (with an annual true-up) would force asset managers to be overly cautious in their asset allocation and duration strategies, forsaking the extra return that a long-term portfolio such as pensions could afford. Quite a mouthful for a televised interview.

What I should have done was tell a story. I should have asked Mr. Popescu if he had children, then said: "Imagine entrusting them to me. You pay me $500 a month to raise them strong and healthy. But there's a catch: they have to be in perfect health every day, not just at maturity. If they catch a cold or scrape a knee, I must pay you $10,000 every time that happens. What kind of childhood would they have? No playing outside, no risks – just fragile children locked away for safety. That's what a guarantee on pension returns means. Safe, but weak."

Of course, I didn't say any of that. Instead, I stammered something about hedging and long-term risk profile, while Mr. Popescu basked in victory. But in my mind – often at 2 a.m., years later – I replay the scene differently. In that version, I deliver my "raising weaklings" analogy, there is an audience that nods in admiration, and Mr. Popescu leans back and concedes, "You know what, you're absolutely right."

Why don't finance leaders use rhetorical tools, such as stories, analogies, and humor, more often? The obvious difficulty is coming up with them, but this is no longer an excuse, in the age of AI. (As I'm writing this, AI is still making mostly cringeworthy suggestions, but it is already a decent brainstorming partner.) Moreover, for now the bar is low: you do not need to be a poet or a standup comedian; only a bit of creativity can distinguish you from the usual droning of corporate communication.

For example, Jim Cook, CFO of Mozilla, wanted to explain to employees how they could help slash overhead costs. What he did was simply share some quirky "kitchen metrics" such as how many quarts of blueberries or pints of kombucha were consumed each month by Mozillians worldwide. He retells how, months later, people would recall his presentation, and, more importantly, how they became readier to take responsibility in managing expenses.

But another reason why we finance people recoil from using stories or metaphors is that they are, by nature, over-simplifying. They leave out parts of the logical argumentation that we believe are essential. For example, in my personal story above, the child-raising metaphor would not have covered another key issue, namely that there were no inflation hedging instruments available in the market. Or, in Jim Cook's case, there were surely more categories of costs that needed containing, besides kitchen ones. What we do not realize is that the metaphor or story, even if partially covering our message, persuades by engaging emotion and makes our audience more receptive to subsequent, rational clarifications.

In his 1992 letter to Berkshire Hathaway shareholders, Warren Buffett wrote about some companies' inadequate catastrophe risk coverage, as exposed by Hurricane Andrew: "it's only when the tide goes out that you learn who's been swimming naked". The masterful (and funny) metaphor does not fully describe the complex insurance and reinsurance landscape at the time, but it makes the reader more open to accepting an ensuing, much more technical description of outcomes for the company.

Similarly, when Jamie Dimon famously said, in a Senate hearing about the purchase of Bear Stearns by JP Morgan, "buying a house is not the same as buying a house on fire", the metaphor made a lasting

> impact, although it did not perfectly encompass all the factors that had led to lowballing the offer for buying Bear Stearns.

Humor can be an extremely effective tool in explaining and persuading: if you make them laugh, you've likely won them over. I remember how George (not his real name), a CFO I worked with, used it when having to explain why our profitable company still needed to undergo painful cost cuts.

> During an all-hands meeting, employees questioned the newly decided round of cost cuts, given that the company had just announced what to them looked like healthy profits. George started explaining something about expected returns and cost of capital, then stopped mid-sentence, with a frustrated sigh. Finally, he said "Look, the market is grading us on a curve regarding cost efficiency, and right now we are a C minus student compared to our competitors. So we can either do nothing and pray that [competitor's name] suddenly decide to use dollar bills as toilet paper, or we can get to work to trim our own costs."[2]

The joke landed. Laughter cracked the tension. And the conversation changed.

Humor is a surprisingly powerful persuader. Research even finds that attorneys who generate more courtroom laughter are more likely to win their cases (8). If humor works in a courtroom, it certainly works in a boardroom. You will find some tips for developing and using humor in leadership here (9).

In summary:

- Make it **relatable**. Everyone has children, has seen people swimming in the sea, and has at least dreamt about buying a house. Imagine that, instead of the swimming metaphor, Warren Buffett had used a bridge metaphor (after all, he is an avid player): "Only when the trump suit is led do you discover who's been bidding without strength". This metaphor is technically as apt as the swimming one, yet most of his audience would have been lost.
- **Oversimplify**. Do not be afraid to leave some elements of your elaborate argument for later. First, capture imaginations.

- Add some **humor**. It's an indispensable tool for any leader, but it can be particularly disarming when coming from the stereotypically straight, no-nonsense CFO.

Communicating with investors

The story

You've heard it a thousand times: when CFOs present financials, they're not just reading off a bunch of numbers; they're *telling a story*. If you're a CFO yourself, you might nod knowingly, thinking, "Of course, I'm telling a story." Yet many CFOs could still polish up their storytelling skills.

But what exactly do we mean by "story" here? Well, we're not talking about weaving a dramatic saga of good versus evil or the classic "situation-complication-resolution" structure that you might find in a novel or in a management consultant's slide deck. No, in this context, you only need to abide by the three minimum rules of a narrative (10).

- Describes **cause-and-effect** relationships between events
- Refers to a particular **time period**
- Impacts particular **characters**

Let's focus on earnings calls to illustrate the CFO's communication with investors.

A good earnings call isn't just a list of figures; it's about connecting those dots to create a narrative that flows with clarity. In essence, your company is the *protagonist*, navigating through challenges, executing strategies, and driving results. And, yes, just like in many good stories, there may be *supporting characters*. For example, your supply chain team, working overtime to lower costs and delivering visible results, might be the unsung heroes in your quarterly earnings tale, as in Cathy Smith's presentation of Nordstrom's Q3 2024 results (11).

The *time period* here is key, too – stretching at least a year into the past for those handy year-over-year comparisons but also looking ahead, offering guidance on what investors can expect. The heart of the story, though, lies in understanding the *cause-and-effect* relationships between events, which requires non-financial information. This is where your company's strategy comes in.

Three things your earnings call should do

As you craft your earnings call narrative, you've got three major goals:

1. **Explain the "why" behind the "what"** of the numbers and connect it to the company's strategy.
2. **Educate investors** about your business, to reduce information asymmetry.
3. **Align expectations**.

The "why" behind the "what"

Andrew Bonfield, the CFO of Caterpillar (whose portrait, improbably, hangs in the National Portrait Gallery in London), once shared with me the challenges he faced when he took the reins at the company. Early on, his team struggled to present a clear, logical story behind the numbers. Most of them had been with the company for decades; so deeply ingrained in their thinking was the "cause" of the numbers that they assumed it was self-evident to anyone. As a result, they would focus solely on the "effect" – the financial outcomes – without ever explaining the underlying reasons.

This disconnect became particularly clear to Andrew during his first quarter at the company, when he noticed a significant increase in margins. The team's explanation? "Volume." But Andrew found that answer unsatisfactory. It didn't make sense to him, in the context of standard costing. The answer, that he eventually had to figure out by himself, was the combination of LIFO (Last In, First Out) accounting and the fact that no finished goods inventory was being held – factors that the team had assumed were common knowledge but never bothered to explain.

> The first thing I say to people now is, 'What's the story? Don't tell me x equals y because a plus b equals c.'

That's code for: don't get lost in the weeds, and don't assume your audience understands all the granular details the way you do.

There's a lesson here: it's easy to assume that investors are as entrenched in the minutiae of your business as you are. But often, it's better to err on the side of over-explaining, not under-explaining. The goal isn't to overwhelm your audience with jargon but to paint a picture of your company's health, growth trajectory, and strategy in a way that's both digestible and engaging.

Educating investors about your business

Reducing information asymmetry is crucial for fostering a healthy relationship between your company and its investors. Information asymmetry happens when one party (in this case, you – the CFO) has more or better information than the other party (the investor). Remember George Akerlof's Nobel Prize-winning "Market for Lemons" theory, discussed in Chapter 3, on how information asymmetry could cause the market for used cars to completely fail, as buyers, lacking information, may assume that all cars are bad (or "lemons") even when that's not the case? In the context of investing, if investors lack a good enough understanding of your company's financial health, operations, or future prospects, they may take an overly cautious approach. Conversely, you don't want your investors to become overly optimistic based on incomplete data, only to be bitterly disappointed later on.

By educating your investors about the nuances of your business – whether it's the intricacies of your supply chain, the reasoning behind a new product launch, or the drivers of cost reductions – you reduce that asymmetry. This transparency builds trust and reduces the likelihood of significantly mispricing your stock.

The benefits are twofold. First, you encourage more rational investment decisions, where investors' expectations align more closely with the reality of your company's prospects. Second, you help mitigate the risk of excess stock price volatility that can come from market misunderstandings. When investors understand the full picture, including both the upsides and the challenges your company faces, they're less likely to be thrown off by short-term fluctuations, sudden news, or unexpected results.

Aligning investors' expectations with your own

It's tempting to get a bit too enthusiastic when the numbers look good. After all, who doesn't want to put a shiny spin on a successful quarter? Yet here is JPMorgan Chase's Jeremy Barnum wisely protecting investors from getting over-excited:

> Don't assume all of this is CIB [Corporate and Investment Banking] as you look forward because there are some versions of the world where the markets and fee, well, it goes one way, and AUM [Assets Under Management] goes the opposite way (12).

Nobody likes a bad surprise. But even positive surprises might send the wrong message: Are you in control, or did you just get lucky? Manage expectations, for now and the future, so investors know what's realistic.

What your story says about you

Your earnings call story should reconfirm three key abilities of management:

1. **We are in control**. If something goes wrong, we'll deal with it swiftly (like adjusting costs).
2. **We're executing on our strategy** consistently while staying alert to shifts in the environment that may require recalibrating our direction.
3. **We are trustworthy**. We don't embellish. We deliver. And we're your long-term partner.

Consistency may be the hardest to communicate, in the fast-changing environment that companies face these days, yet it is essential. A CFO I spoke with, who has a background in investment banking or asset management, shared his perspective from the other side of the table: he saw many small and sometimes not-so-small companies reinvent themselves on the fly, chasing the next latest and greatest thing, be it blockchain or AI. Constantly changing your message and shifting the goalposts often erode your investors' confidence.

Jeremy Barnum's communication around AI illustrates this point:

> There's clearly some very significant opportunities. At the same time, we're not going to be chasing shiny objects here in AI (13).

Let's see how Andrew Bonfield achieves consistency in communication, even when the results have disappointed.

CASE: CATERPILLAR'S Q3 2019 RESULTS

Less than a year into Andrew's tenure at Caterpillar, the company had to lower its guidance, as dealers unexpectedly chose to reduce the level of inventory they were holding.

Rather than dodging the issue or sugar-coating it, Andrew states the uncomfortable truth: "Obviously, it's very disappointing to reduce our guidance for the year."

He then explains what went wrong, but instead of pointing fingers, he takes responsibility.

He doesn't dwell on the negativity; instead, he focuses on the actions the company is taking: closely monitor end-user demand going forward (as a proxy for dealer behavior) and cut general and administrative costs. "We're working on the competitiveness of our cost structure, and a relentless execution of the operating and execution model remains at the center of everything we do".

He concludes with positive, reassuring information: dividend is 20% higher, signaling strong cash flow resilience.

He reaffirms commitment: "We remain very much committed to our strategy of profitable growth and deployment of capital back to shareholders through a growing dividend and consistent share repurchases".

By the end of the call, investors are reassured: strategy is intact, management is on top of it, and the company's commitment to profitable growth remains unwavering (14).

And, yes, it's a lesson that stuck: to this day, Andrew continues to monitor those end-user demand metrics.

The language of the 'story'

Now, although you're telling a story, this is not the time for grandiose rhetoric. Your language should be clear, concise, factual, without hyperbole. As Delfin Rueda, former CFO of NN Group, says: "I keep telling my people: 'if this indicator has grown 11%, it has grown 11%, not double-digit'".[3]

Metaphors in earnings calls

In CFOs' communication within the company, whether to finance employees or to non-experts in other areas, metaphors are most always a powerful tool, but in communication with investors, metaphors are best left behind.

A study of CEOs' language during earnings calls found that, *the more metaphorical* the CEO's presentation, *the less favorable* were analysts' assessments (15). We can assume this would hold even more for CFOs, who are expected to be the rational, down-to-earth counterpart to the CEO's more ebullient persona.

Naturally, the above note of caution refers to full-blown, original metaphors, such as the one used by Chiron's CEO during a Q3 2005 earnings call, when describing a restructuring process: "it's a little bit like breaking in a new Maserati. The first thousand miles, you are not going to step on the gas too hard." This did not go down well with analysts on the call (15).

By contrast, there are metaphors that have become **part of the jargon** of the investments industry: they are typically short (one to two words) and act as useful shorthand. Think of "color" to mean additional detail underlying the numbers or of "headwinds" and "tailwinds" to describe outside factors positively/negatively influencing the company's performance. As CFO, you are expected to demonstrate familiarity with this jargon, also to signal that you are closely in touch with the investor community.

Let's have a look at two very seasoned CFOs and their "story style".

CASE: CATHY SMITH AND JEREMY BARNUM: MASTERS OF FINANCIAL STORYTELLING

We introduced Jeremy Barnum, the charismatic CFO of JPMorgan Chase, in Chapter 5. Jeremy's "real intellectual" aura would suggest he is at home with metaphors. Yet he stays away from metaphors in earnings calls (except for those metaphors already well established as part of the jargon, such as "headwinds" and "cross-currents"). He adds little "color" to the pure financials unless specifically asked to provide more.

Or take Cathy Smith, recently appointed CFO of Starbucks. Cathy has a truly formidable resumé, having been CFO for Nordstrom, Target, Walmart, GameStop, Textron, and Raytheon. Cathy uses plenty of metaphors, but they are still the jargon kind, already familiar to the investment community:

> On the Rack stores, the return profile, it's **kind of a new muscle.** [...] We'll take the learnings from both of those into this year as we continue to **evolve a little bit around the edges**. [...] Maybe **I'll dish off** a little bit (11).

She even sprinkles a bit of self-deprecating humor:

> Q4 is always promotional for retailers. I think we'd like to pretend that it's not, but it is (11).

Both Jeremy and Cathy emphasize **consistency** in execution of the strategy, and **delivering on promises**, while keeping investors closely informed:

Jeremy Barnum:	"I'll touch on the drivers of the year-on-year change, which you'll note are **very consistent** with what you've been hearing from us recently" (12).
Cathy Smith:	"This evolution will support **continued** outstanding after-tax returns on invested capital, something that's **been a strength of this company for a very long time**" (11).

Earlier on, after her company (at the time, Target) announces a big strategic shift, Cathy masterfully outlined the financial implications while underscoring continuity and strength:

> With the changes we're making to our business model, we **expect our financial model to evolve** as well. [...] we expect our business will generate somewhat higher asset turns and somewhat lower operating margins than we've seen historically. [...] In fact, **if you think back in our history, this isn't the first time** our business model and financial model have changed in service of an evolving consumer. Remember, **our company began over 100 years ago** as a traditional department store. It had a business model that generated higher margin rates and lower asset turns compared with Target stores,

> yet even as we completely transformed our business model from department stores to Target stores, our company has generated **strong returns on capital for decades** (16).

Cathy and Jeremy are both keenly aware of the importance of the relationship with the analysts. As research confirms, "financial communication is still largely a people's business" (17). Their responses to analysts often suggest a long history of such interactions based on mutual **trust**:

> Longer term **as we've talked many times, Peter**, we do see that inventory loads, as we move product exactly where we need it when we need it, will continue to come down (16).
>
> Good question, **John**, and **welcome back**, by the way (12).

To maintain trust, these experienced CFOs are also quick to admit when they don't know something:

> (in response to a question on industry data): "That's fascinating, Gerard. I'll have to take a look at that data. I don't actually recognize those numbers" (12).
>
> (in response to a question about an indicator disclosed by the company earlier on): "So, first off, I didn't know that we actually supplied that information in 2015. So, thank you for the information there" (11).

And if they occasionally slip into verbal tics (Jeremy's tic is "at the margin" and Cathy's is "a little bit"), well, it only humanizes them.

In the end, your earnings call story is not just a recounting of financial data – it's a strategic narrative that builds trust, aligns expectations, and ultimately reinforces the long-term vision of your company.

The same broad principles that apply to the story of earnings calls also apply to presenting numbers to senior management. Whether you are a country CFO presenting your country's performance to the regional CEO and CFO or a finance manager reporting on the financial performance of a large project, your story should still (a) explain the "why" behind the "what", (b) educate senior management about your specific segment, and (c) align expectations to avoid unpleasant surprises. Similarly, those three key messages that should transpire from any earnings call ("we are in control", "we are executing on our strategy", and "we are trustworthy") should be the subtext of your presentation.

CROSSROADS LIFE: WHERE'S THE STORY?

Clara's background in banking has taught her the critical importance of storytelling when it comes to presenting financial results. Numbers alone don't persuade – narratives do. Yet, in her new role as regional CFO, she struggles to instill this mindset in her analyst team. We see her frustration mounting as she repeats, for what feels like the hundredth time, that a quarterly report cannot be just a dump of figures. But the team, entrenched in old habits, shows little enthusiasm for change. Her tone – more scolding than inspiring – doesn't help. (Chapter 7 explores more effective ways to motivate and engage.)

Later, after Clara's leadership evolution, we see a striking contrast. She presents the quarterly results to the group CEO and top executives – not just with clarity but with authority and grace. The numbers now tell a story, one distilled through layers of insight and synthesis. Clara and her team have clearly aligned, producing not just data but meaning. And in this moment, we understand: Clara has succeeded in transforming not only how results are reported but how they are understood.

Watch the scene selection at: https://www.ed.movie/presenting-numbers or scan the QR code.

Communicating with creditors

Your CEO's messaging is directed mostly to equity holders, but, as CFO, you speak to the entire capital structure of the company. Unlike equity investors, who are often drawn to the potential for growth and upside optionality, banks or bondholders are far more focused on **ensuring the security** of their investment and how they will get their money back.

For banks, the primary concern is liquidity. They want to ensure that the company has enough cash flow to service debt, meet interest payments, and repay principal when it becomes due. Your communication should emphasize the company's cash position, the stability of its revenue streams, and its ability to generate predictable, reliable cash flows. Be transparent about any potential risks that could affect liquidity, such as fluctuations in market conditions, changes in regulations, or operational challenges, and explain the strategies you have in place to mitigate those risks.

When speaking to bondholders, the conversation shifts slightly toward the company's long-term creditworthiness. Bondholders want to know that the company will continue to operate efficiently, remain profitable, and maintain a strong balance sheet. Their main concern is the risk of default, so they will expect to hear about the company's debt levels, debt maturity schedule, and the overall health of its financial position. A clear explanation of how the company is managing its leverage and how you plan to manage debt repayment is crucial. If your company is planning any new debt issuance, bondholders will also want to know how this affects the company's capital structure and its ability to meet existing obligations.

One key aspect of communicating with both banks and bondholders is credibility. These stakeholders expect a CFO to present the facts clearly, without excessive optimism. A straightforward, data-driven approach is essential, backed by solid financials, stress tests, and scenario planning. Always be prepared to answer questions regarding debt covenants, the company's ability to navigate economic downturns, and the steps taken to ensure financial stability.

By understanding the specific concerns of banks and bondholders, you can tailor your message to reassure them that the company is taking the right steps to protect their investment and ensure long-term solvency. Your role as CFO is not just to report the numbers but to foster trust, instill confidence, and demonstrate sound financial stewardship.

Communication takeaways: Listening, persuading, and storytelling with numbers

Here are the key takeaways for mastering communication as a CFO:

1. **Be a high-quality listener**. Research shows that the most effective communicators are also the best listeners. This means actively engaging in conversations, asking insightful questions, and avoiding judgment. High-quality listening not only helps you understand your team and stakeholders but also shifts their attitudes and opens the door for more meaningful dialogue.
2. **Explain and persuade with clarity**. The ability to explain complex financial concepts in simple terms is critical, especially when dealing with non-expert audiences. Use stories, analogies, and even humor to make your points relatable and engaging. Your goal is to make the audience understand and trust your direction.
3. **Educate investors and align expectations**. Reducing information asymmetry with investors is essential for fostering a healthy relationship. Be transparent about your company's strengths, challenges, and strategies while managing expectations to avoid surprises. Whether you're presenting earnings or navigating changes, always focus on consistency and the long-term vision of the company.
4. **Build trust through consistency and integrity**. Trust is the foundation of your communication with all stakeholders. Be candid about challenges, avoid overpromising, and focus on the long-term sustainability of the business. Your credibility as a CFO depends on your ability to maintain control, execute strategies, and consistently deliver on promises.
5. **Master the art of storytelling**. Financial data is important, but it's the story behind the numbers that resonates. Your earnings calls, investor presentations, and communications with banks should connect the dots in a clear, engaging narrative. This narrative should convey the company's direction and challenges, reinforcing your role as a strategic leader.

In today's fast-paced business environment, the ability to communicate effectively is more important than ever. As a CFO, your capacity to listen deeply, explain concisely, and persuade thoughtfully will not only strengthen your leadership but also inspire confidence among your stakeholders, ensuring the company's success in the long run.

Notes

1 Throughout this chapter, I use "analogy" and "metaphor" interchangeably. Some style experts would disagree, but the subtle differences are not material for our practical purposes.
2 Interviewed CFO anonymized.
3 Interview with the author.

References

(1) Spring 2020 commencement address by Brian Olsavsky. https://vgradpsu.z20.web.core.windows.net/psu/xxxii/: Penn State Smeal School of Business, 2020.
(2) Brink, K., & Costigan, R. Oral communication skills: Are the priorities of the workplace and AACSB-accredited business programs aligned? *Academy of Management Learning & Education* 2015, 14 (2), 205–221. DOI: 10.5465/amle.2013.0044
(3) Itzchakov, G., Weinstein, N., Leary, M., Saluk, D., & Amar, M. Listening to understand: The role of high-quality listening on speakers' attitude depolarization during disagreements. *Journal of Personality and Social Psychology* 2024, 126 (2), 213–239. DOI: 10.1037/pspa0000366
(4) Itzchakov, G., & Grau, J. High-quality listening in the age of COVID-19: A Key to better dyadic communication for more effective organizations. *Organizational Dynamics* 2020, 51 (2). DOI: 10.1016/j.orgdyn.2020.100820
(5) Itzchakov, G., DeMarree, K., Kluger, A., & Turjeman-Levi, Y. The listener sets the tone: High-quality listening increases attitude clarity and behavior-intention consequences. *Personality and Social Psychology Bulletin* 2018, 44 (5), 762–778. DOI: 10.1177/0146167217747874
(6) Itzchakov, G., Kluger, A., & Castro, D. I am aware of my inconsistencies but can tolerate them: The effect of high quality listening on speakers' attitude ambivalence. *Personality and Social Psychology Bulletin* 2017, 43 (1), 105–120. DOI: 10.1177/0146167216675339
(7) Cook, J. (2024). CFO as storyteller. *Cook's PlayBooks*, https://www.cooksplaybooks.com/p/cfo-as-storyteller
(8) Li, S., & Pryor, T. Humor and persuasion: The effects of laughter during US supreme court's oral arguments. *Law & Policy* 2020, 42 (2), 162–185. DOI: 10.1111/lapo.12145
(9) Bunea, E. Can humor make you a better leader? In *Psychology Today*, https://www.psychologytoday.com/us/blog/to-manage-is-human/202211/can-humor-make-you-a-better-leader, 2022.

(10) Dahlstrom, M. F. Using narratives and storytelling to communicate science with nonexpert audiences. *Proceedings of the National Academy of Sciences* 2014, *111* (4), 13614–13620. DOI: https://doi.org/10.1073/pnas. 1320645111
(11) Nordstrom Q3 2024 earnings conference call. https://investor.nordstrom.com/events/event-details/q3-2024-nordstrom-earnings-conference-call, 2024.
(12) JPMorgan Chase 4Q24 earnings call transcript. https://www.jpmorganchase.com/content/dam/jpmc/jpmorgan-chase-and-co/investor-relations/documents/quarterly-earnings/2024/4th-quarter/4q24-earnings-transcript.pdf, 2025.
(13) JPMorgan Chase 4Q23 earnings call transcript. https://www.jpmorganchase.com/content/dam/jpmc/jpmorgan-chase-and-co/investor-relations/documents/quarterly-earnings/2023/4th-quarter/jpm-4q23-earnings-call-transcript.pdf, 2024.
(14) Caterpillar Q3 2019 earnings call transcript. https://s25.q4cdn.com/358376879/files/doc_events/3Q19-Earnings-Final-Edited-Transcript.pdf: Thompson Reuters, 2019.
(15) König, A., Mammen, J., Luger, J., Fehn, A., & Enders, A. Silver bullet or ricochet? CEO's use of metaphorical communication and infomediaries' evaluations *Academy of Management Journal* 2018, *61* (4), 1196–1230. DOI: 10.5465/amj.2016.0626
(16) Target Corporation Q4 2017 earnings conference call transcript. https://www.fool.com/earnings/call-transcripts/2018/03/06/target-corporation-tgt-q4-2017-earnings-conference.aspx, 2018.
(17) Hoffmann, C. Investor relations as strategic communication: Insights from evolutionary psychology. *International Journal of Strategic Communication* 2023, *17* (3), 213–227. DOI: 10.1080/1553118X.2023.2230575

7

TOOLS TO INSPIRE AND MOTIVATE

In Chapter 3, we discussed in detail Transformational Leadership as a set of 12 behaviors that will inspire and motivate your followers. But how does one practice these behaviors successfully? What tools can you use, for example, to "articulate a compelling vision of the future", or how do you determine the "specific needs, abilities, and aspirations" of your team members?

This chapter provides two powerful toolsets for you to use while practicing transformational leadership: Charismatic Leadership Techniques (CLTs) and Motivational Drivers (understanding and working with types of individual motivation). As always, we approach these toolsets from the CFO's perspective.

Charismatic leadership techniques: Firing them up

Imagine this: Dan has just delivered his opening speech at his company's "Top 100 in Finance" meeting. He's laid out his grand vision for the future

DOI: 10.4324/9781003581734-10

of finance. Yet, as the audience quietly begins to filter out for a break, Dan wonders, *Is that the best I can do? How do I make them not just listen but act?*

Meanwhile, Meera walks into a meeting with her project team. She can tell the energy is low. The faces around the table are long, the shoulders slumped. They've hit a major roadblock, and morale is at rock bottom. She knows they need a "pep talk" – but all she can think of are those movie scenes where the coach, or the warrior, gives an impassioned speech, the music swells, and suddenly everything turns around. But here's the problem: she's not in a football locker room, and she's certainly not on a battlefield. So, what's her move?

Then there's Yusuf, who is gearing up to confront Mark, a razor-sharp yet demotivated subordinate. Mark's potential is slipping away, but when Yusuf rehearses what he wants to say, it sounds whiny. It's not the right approach. He can already picture Mark's angry rebuttal.

If you've ever found yourself in a situation like Dan, Meera, or Yusuf, you've likely experienced the frustration of feeling that your leadership is falling short. You want to inspire action and ignite passion, but somehow you're missing the spark. "If only I were more charismatic!" we can almost hear the three CFOs tell themselves. Like many people, including the ancient Greeks, they believe that charisma ("divine favor" in Greek) is a gift that some simply have while others don't.

But here's the good news: charisma, like leadership, is a skill. And, yes, it can be learned. Take Ruth Porat, Alphabet's CFO. In 2014, Ruth was already a highly visible and powerful executive. Yet, if you compare a 2014 interview with Ruth (1) with one from 2025 (2), you'll see a noticeable evolution in her presence, her delivery, and, yes, her charisma. She didn't just wake up one day with it. She worked at it, honed it, and kept leveling up. So, let's put the myth of *natural charisma* to bed, shall we?

CLTs are precisely what they sound like: tools that can help you become a more charismatic leader. A growing stream of research shows that the CLTs ignite greater **engagement**, **productivity**, and **proactive behavior** (3, 4). They work in a wide range of leadership contexts, from political leaders to small team leaders (5) and from face-to-face interaction to online calls, TED Talks, and social media (6–8). Most importantly, they can be learned and practiced.

This brings charisma down from the mystical pedestal it was traditionally placed on, within reach for every leader determined to invest in learning it. It's not easy: like any skill worth pursuing, mastering the CLTs requires deep understanding and consistent practice.

Figure 7.1 presents the 12 CLTs at a glance. They comprise nine verbal tactics and three non-verbal ones. Of the nine verbal techniques, four relate more directly to the substance of your message. These include setting high goals, conveying confidence that the goals can be achieved, expressing the group's sentiments, and projecting strong moral conviction. The other five are rhetorical devices (the "usual suspects" like metaphors and stories) along with three-part lists, contrasts, and rhetorical questions. The three non-verbal tactics aim to convey emotion: animated voice, facial expressions, and gestures. Now let's dive into the techniques that can take your charisma to a whole other level.

Setting high goals and conveying confidence that they can be achieved

In Chapter 3, when reviewing the behaviors that compose transformational leadership, we discussed (a) setting high goals and (b) demonstrating confidence that they can be reached. We talked about the lure of "stretch goals" and the risk of having the team descend into cynicism when those stratospheric goals are repeatedly missed. But don't make the mistake of thinking that your goals always have to be monumental. It could be about a smaller, more immediate goal – perhaps completing a daunting task by the end of the week or helping a team member achieve a significant personal development goal.

Expressing the group's sentiments

Winston Churchill's speeches always connected to what the country was thinking and feeling. For instance, in October 1940, he said: "I see the spirit of the British nation rising through the pain and confusion of the hour" (9).

When you reflect the emotions of your team – especially the tough ones – you're showing that you understand their struggles and that you're *one of them* (which, as you remember from Chapter 3, is part of transformational leadership).

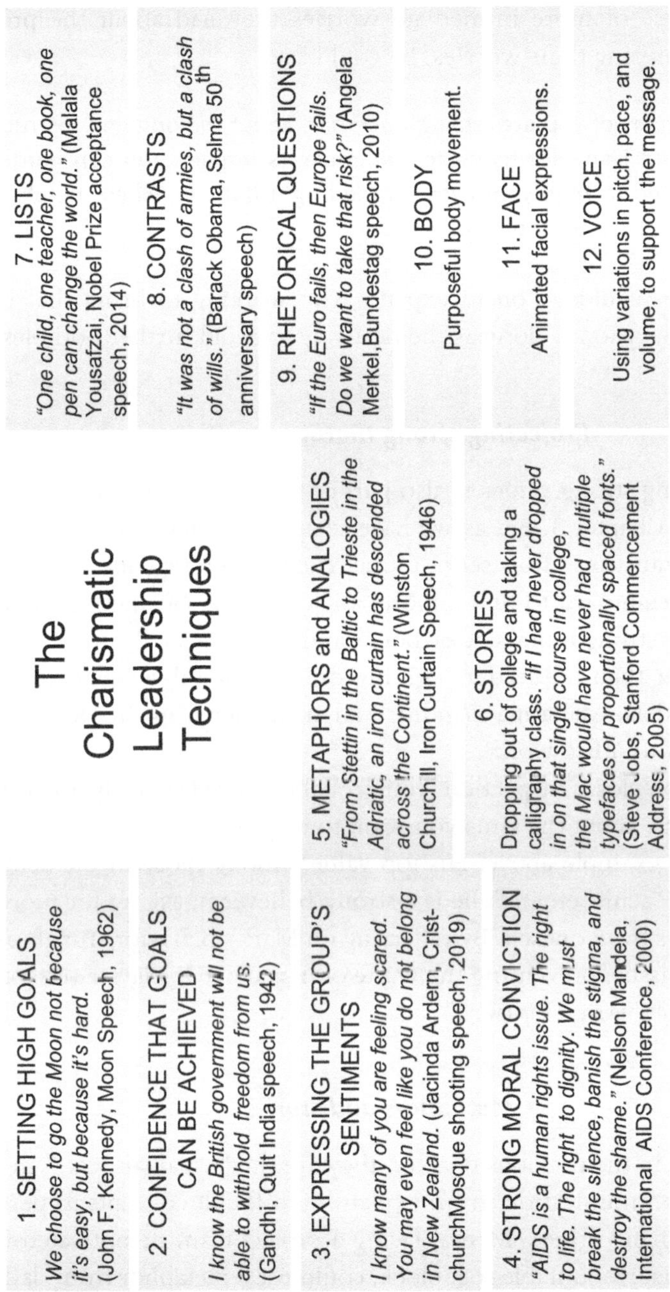

Figure 7.1 The charismatic leadership techniques.

Based on Antonakis et al., 2021 (4).

In Dan's case, maybe the audience was not focusing on his vision of the future because of more immediate worries they had about the present. Instead of ignoring their worries, he could say:

> I know many of you are feeling uncertain about the ongoing restructuring, and I am not trying to minimize its impact. You can hardly be expected to keep your eyes on the bright horizon, when there's a pothole right in front of you.

And then he would go on to explain why working to bring that bright horizon – the vision – closer is the best way to avoid further potholes.

Projecting strong moral conviction

Demonstrating strong values is also part of transformational leadership, as discussed in Chapter 3. But as we have seen in Chapter 2, not every value necessarily translates into a set of moral, right-or-wrong, rules.

It might seem hard to find a moral angle to every business goal. When talking about strong moral codes, books and courses usually provide examples of bigger-than-life leaders fighting dramatic good-versus-evil battles: Nelson Mandela, Mahatma Gandhi, Martin Luther King Jr. How do you translate that to office work?

And yet, on closer inspection, you probably do feel strongly, in "right or wrong" terms, about the aims you want to inspire your followers to reach. Take Yusuf's example above. His top value, among those in the Schwartz hierarchy, is "achievement": he is a strong believer in asking for more and greater things from oneself. By reflecting on Mark's behavior, Yusuf can see it as a moral issue, preventing the waste of his talent: "*I believe in your potential, and I will not stand to see it slip away.*"

Metaphors and stories

As discussed in the previous chapter, they are the "usual suspects" in most leadership communication, from explaining difficult concepts to persuading and inspiring others. Meera, facing a project team demotivated by an apparently insurmountable roadblock, could use a metaphor from daily life to lighten the mood and reestablish optimism. For example:

> You know when you're trying to move a giant couch up a tiny staircase? You get stuck, someone's yelling 'Pivot!' and you're about to give up and just leave it there forever. But eventually, after a lot of shoving and swearing, somehow you find the right angle, and it fits. That's exactly where we are. We're mid-stairwell. It's awkward, it's messy – but we'll figure out the right angle if we work at it together.

Lists

The human brain likes lists. They make listeners subconsciously dial up their perception of the speaker's competence. In speech, three-part lists seem to be most effective, but they can go up to five.

Steve Jobs was a master of this technique. Remember his launching the iPhone? He described it as "an iPod, a phone, and an internet communicator."

Dan, in our opening example, could formulate three conditions for achieving his vision for the finance function: "To get there, we need three things: curiosity, competence, and collegiality." (Yes, you get bonus points for alliterations – having all elements of the list start with the same letter. However, never sacrifice meaning or clarity for the sake of a melodious "3 Cs" list.)

Contrasts

Presenting what something is not has the effect of more vividly painting what it is. Indra Nooyi, former CFO and then CEO of PepsiCo, when explaining the complexity of leading change in a major organization, once said, in a perfect showpiece of using contrasts, metaphors, and lists:

> You always have to be in beta [metaphor]. It sounds wonderful as a set of words, but when you actually have to practice it, it's pretty scary [contrast, wonderful vs. scary]. Because it's not motivating a small group of employees that have the same thinking that you do. We have 260,000 employees [contrast, small group vs. hundreds of thousands]. And when you decide to "zag" instead of "zig" [metaphor], you've got to tell them what you'll be doing, why you're doing it, how it's going to impact them, and why they all have to come along with you on the journey. [four-part list] (10).

Rhetorical questions

The invitation to use rhetorical questions may sound a bit old-fashioned. You immediately picture the beginning of a TED Talk: "Have you ever…?" Yet rhetorical questions, when used in a less heavy-handed manner, are highly effective in engaging your listeners and work as effectively for TED-sized audiences as for just one person. For example, "Do you realize what this means?" or maybe "What would you rather have?" followed by two options presented in stark contrast: the current state of things and your vision.

Non-verbal tactics

You know very well that your **face**, your **body**, the variations in your **voice**, have a lot of weight in how your message is received. I will not spend time on detailing these tactics, since you can find them in self-contained books and videos. Let's just note here an important point: the non-verbal tactics are the most *culturally sensitive and contextual*. What might come across as charismatic in one setting could seem like a complete loss of self-control in another. Take Steve Ballmer's (former Microsoft CEO) infamous "I love this company" performance (11). To my Finnish students, it seems to border on madness; to the Microsoft employees in the room, it was a powerful and uplifting moment.[1]

The key takeaway here is that charisma can be enhanced through a set of techniques – tools that you can learn, practice, and refine. It's about being intentional with your words, your gestures, and your presence. Like any skill worth mastering, becoming a more charismatic leader isn't easy. It takes time. It takes effort. And it takes a deep understanding of the people you're leading.

Motivational drivers: What makes them tick

The Golden Rule does not apply in leadership. "Lead others as you would have them lead you" may feel tempting. After all, it feels honest and relatable. But as we saw back in Chapter 3, transformational leaders don't simply copy and paste their own motivations onto others. One of the core transformational leadership behaviors is this: "considers my specific needs, abilities, and aspirations." Not "our needs." My needs.

This raises an uncomfortable truth for finance leaders: not everyone is wired like you. Not everyone gets a dopamine hit from closing the books three days early or optimizing capital structure over lunch. The real challenge of leadership is not motivating people *in general* but motivating *each* person specifically.

So how do you do that?

The hidden forces: McClelland's three implicit motives

David McClelland, a Harvard psychologist, separated the vague idea of "motivation" into three surprisingly tidy components: **achievement**, **affiliation**, and **power** (12). These motives are socially learned, shaped through childhood experiences and cultural context. People have different hierarchies for the three needs; some want achievement the most, others primarily want affiliation, and yet others desire power above all. This influences how they work, interact with colleagues, and engage with the world around them.

Let's unpack each one, with one foot in science and the other firmly planted in the CFO's patent leather shoe.

Need for achievement: The hunger for the next big win

Picture this: a senior analyst on your team sets a goal to reduce report turnaround time by 20% – not because anyone asked but because she *can*. She's not chasing recognition or a raise (although she won't object to them either). She's chasing the high that comes from checking a box that no one else thought to draw.

This is the **achievement-motivated** employee: fueled not by rewards but by the thrill of the stretch goal. While they're a dream to manage in roles that demand problem-solving and drive – think treasury, investor relations, FP&A – they come with three fine-print warnings:

1. They get **bored**. Fast. Repetitive work is to them what sand is to an engine: grinding, frustrating, and eventually destructive. You will have to constantly present them with new challenges. The problem is that corporate life cannot constantly offer an Indiana Jones level of discovery and excitement in any job. The solution? Gamify. Invent levels. Set a

target even for a repetitive task (e.g., "10% faster") and make it sound like "Level 3 Boss Fight."

2. They're **lone wolves**. Collaboration is fine – as long as credit is clearly divisible, which is rarely doable. So, when you need them to play with others, frame teamwork as a more advanced form of achievement. "You've mastered the individual quest. Now comes the group challenge." Recognize their ability to work in a team as a new, valuable addition to their skillset.
3. They're **perfectionists**. This means they're prone to burnout – especially if promoted too quickly, which is something you may be tempted to offer, given their boredom propensity. Suddenly, their success depends not just on their own effort but on the team they manage. Cue existential crisis. They will work increasingly longer hours trying to untangle all knots by themselves and will spiral into burnout. The fix? Don't rush the promotion ladder. Add intermediate rungs, where possible. Coach early for a **learning-oriented** mindset. Reframe setbacks as part of the growth track, not as derailments.

Need for power: The thrill of shaping outcomes

People with a strong power motive have the desire to **impact** and **influence** others and to demonstrate **reputation** and **prestige**. They want to feel strong and in control.

It might seem like this is not a need you would openly confess to at parties, yet the motives of power-driven people can be laudable: wanting to **guide** and **support** others, wanting to make **a positive difference**. At the other end of the spectrum, you can have power-driven individuals primarily wanting to be **feared** or **blindly obeyed**.

Unsurprisingly, people with a strong power motive are more likely to attain leadership positions (13). This is tricky though: people tend to dislike a leader who badly wants the leadership role. Plato famously said, "The best man is he who *is least like a ruler*, and *is unwilling to rule*, but who, in spite of his unwillingness, *is forced to rule*" (14).

For the second time in this book, I have to disagree with Plato. Good leadership is a profession, requiring learning and hours of practice as much as any other demanding occupation out there. Imagine applying Plato's decree to any other occupation: "he's the best surgeon, because he would really rather be anywhere else than in the surgery room". Not quite what you'd want to hear before going under the knife. Leadership doesn't just happen to people, it needs intentional effort, and therefore it needs to be wanted.

So the real question isn't: "Do they want power?" It's: "Do they want it for the right reasons?" These reasons should include **pro-social** aims, wanting to inspire and guide others toward making a difference. How do you identify this? This may take some extra work on your part because destructive power-driven individuals are usually also adept at manipulating others, including their boss. Try to gather information from their peers and (if they are managers) from their direct reports. In Chapter 8, we discuss how to get information from "the ranks" without looking like you're developing a spy network.

Once you have established – as much as possible – that your power-driven employee has their heart in the right place, here's how you can motivate them:

- **Map their career path**. Don't hand out shortcuts but do show them the route. Power-motivated folks are marathoners – they need to know where the finish line is.
- **Hand them the mic**. Visibility matters. Invite them to present to higher-ups, even if it's just one slide. They'll rise to the occasion and probably polish your deck while they're at it.
- **Give them a sandbox**. A small team, a pilot project, a taskforce. Let them lead, fail, recalibrate, and try again. It's practice with guardrails.

Also, forgive them if their earliest vision of leadership looked more like Steve Jobs on a stage than Jacinda Ardern checking in with her staff. We've all been there. Help them evolve their image of power from *command* to *stewardship*. Teach them to appreciate the value of soft power, responsibility, and generosity. You could tell them something like "I see people start to look up to you more, and I think it's mostly because of the way you show concern, you model collegiality, they respect that." Or: "You are emerging as a leader of the group: so, you have a responsibility for keeping the group together, helping them perform even better."

Need for affiliation: The terror of being left out

Now we come to the most underestimated – and often misunderstood – driver: affiliation. These are your harmony-seekers, the ones who care deeply about how the team is doing. Not in a vague, HR-speak way – but in a *please-don't-let-there-be-tension-at-the-all-hands* kind of way.

This need is often driven less by the joy of connection and more by the **fear of rejection** (15). It's less "I love the group" and more "please don't let me be the one who's left out of the group chat." Individuals strongly motivated by affiliation tend to develop **more contacts** (16) and to **avoid conflict** (17).

Many of the CFOs I spoke with, when asked what makes their accounting employees tick, said that it was all about being accepted and respected by the team. Often, though not always, employees primarily motivated by affiliation may come across as "lacking ambition". They are happy to put in the required work hours but no more, will not step forward for a promotion, and do not look forward to change. How do you motivate such employees to keep up with, and ideally ride, the wave of change that is sweeping all over our workplaces nowadays?

Here's what they need: **to see success as group-preserving**. That a new skill, a new project, or even a new title isn't a threat to the group but something that keeps the group strong. Use tools like the Belbin team roles exercise[2] to help them and their teammates see how everyone contributes to the bigger picture. Emphasize that their growth matters not just for them but for the cohesion of the group.

And watch out for **groupthink**. Affiliation-heavy teams are at risk of nodding in agreement when what they really need is productive disagreement. Introduce the idea of "obligation to dissent" (long known to McKinsey associates). The key here is to help develop an identity *for the whole team* as one that encourages constructive argument. During your team identity work (more about that in Chapter 9), introduce the aim for the team to have a "brand image" that includes healthy disagreements: "Those [team name] guys, they really go at each other! But it's all in good spirit, just how they do things, because they are actually a very tight knit group". You might also want to assign a "chief dissenter" role, to be played by each team member in turn, in each meeting. Make constructive conflict a team norm – not a social risk.

CROSSROADS LIFE: MOTIVATING JOEP

Joep, senior finance analyst at headquarters, effectively led the team during Clara's predecessor's hands-off tenure, managing complex, manual reporting in the absence of a unified ERP. The team may have not produced the most insightful reports, but Joep took pride in keeping the boat afloat and in his role as de facto leader.

Clara, coming from a high–power distance culture and with low regard for the HQ team's past output, took a hands-on approach from the start, which clashes with Joep's self-image. She aims to raise the team's game, starting with a high-stakes project: replacing the simplistic cost-cutting allocation method with a tailored analysis across 12 business units – while assessing the murky impact of Project ACE, a delayed cross-border Ops-IT program promising savings but provoking political tension.

Joep dismisses the task as "impossible". Clara's appeal to the project's strategic value and the finance team's transformation into "business partners" for the business units falls flat – she even manages to offend Joep by dismissing his team's current status as "bean counters".

Clara wrongly assumes that Joep shares her achievement-driven motivation. In reality, his primary driver is power – status, influence, and visibility with the upper layers. Her wish to better serve the country CEOs and CFOs does not check any of these boxes, especially since, after years of complaints, Joep has grown cynical regarding the possibility of ever satisfying the business unit management.

Years later, we see a more seasoned Clara finally tapping into the power of individualized motivation. When the Group CEO expresses appreciation for a new analysis included in the quarterly report, Clara grabs the opportunity to give Joep (who is not in the room but will undoubtedly hear about it) what he really values: exposure and recognition. She offers to "lend" him to the Benelux CEO for a similar analysis – which would thrill Joep, given that the Benelux is a more powerful, "big brother" to the smaller "Europe" business segment.

Sometimes, what looks like insurmountable resistance is really a mismatch of motivations.

Watch the scene selection at: https://www.ed.movie/motivating-joep or scan the QR code.

Conclusion: Motivation as a custom build

There's no such thing as a one-size-fits-all motivator – no silver bonus, no magic medal. What works wonders for one team member might leave another cold or even stressed.

McClelland's genius was in turning the question of "what motivates people?" into "what motivates *this* person?" His theory offers a practical, nuanced framework for leaders – certainly including CFOs – who manage teams that run on different fuel. Achievement. Affiliation. Power. Three invisible engines under the hood of every team.

The most effective leaders listen closely enough to hear what really makes each person tick – and lead accordingly. Like a good orchestra conductor, they don't just hear music; they hear individuals, each playing their part in a symphony. Your job isn't to change the notes. It's to help them play as an ensemble.

Notes

1 https://www.youtube.com/watch?v=f__n8084YAE.
2 https://www.belbin.com.

References

(1) Porat, Ruth. Executive Vice President and Chief Financial Officer, Morgan Stanley. https://www.youtube.com/watch?v=ick47mQNAsw: Yale School of Management, 2014.

(2) Alphabet's Porat: US lead on AI not a forgone conclusion. https://www.bloomberg.com/news/videos/2025-01-21/alphabet-s-porat-us-ai-lead-not-a-foregone-conclusion-video: Bloomberg, 2025.
(3) Maran, T. Developing and validating the charismatic leadership tactics scale: evidence from multi-source questionnaire studies, cognitive and behavioral assessments and a leadership training evaluation. *Review of Managerial Science* 2024. DOI: 10.1007/s11846-024-00782-w
(4) Antonakis, J., D'Adda, G., Weber, R. A., & Zehnder, C. "Just words? Just speeches?" On the economic value of charismatic leadership. *Management Science* 2021. DOI: 10.1287/mnsc.2021.4219
(5) Jensen, U., Rohner, D., Bornet, O., Carron, D., Garner, P., Loupi, D., & Antonakis, J. Combating COVID-19 with charisma: Evidence on governor speeches in the United States. *Leadership Quarterly* 2023, 34 (6). DOI: 10.1016/j.leaqua.2023.101702
(6) Ernst, B. A., Banks, G. C., Loignon, A. C., Frear, K. A., Williams, C. E., Arciniega, L. M., Gupta, R. K., Kodydek, G., & Subramanian, D. Virtual charismatic leadership and signaling theory: A prospective meta-analysis in five countries. *Leadership Quarterly* 2022, 33 (5). DOI: 10.1016/j.leaqua.2021.101541
(7) Nieken, P. Charisma in the gig economy: The impact of digital leadership and communication channels on performance. *Leadership Quarterly* 2023, 34 (6). DOI: 10.1016/j.leaqua.2022.101631
(8) Tur, B., Harstad, J., & Antonakis, J. Effect of charismatic signaling in social media settings: Evidence from TED and Twitter. *Leadership Quarterly* 2022, 33 (5). DOI: 10.1016/j.leaqua.2020.101476
(9) Churchill, W. Broadcast to the nation. 1940.
(10) Nooyi, Indra. PepsiCo chairman and CEO. https://www.youtube.com/watch?v=xl32J4TCS0E: Stanford Graduate School of Business, 2016.
(11) Ballmer, Steve. I Love this company! https://www.youtube.com/watch?v=f__n8084YAE, 2000.
(12) McClelland, D. C. How motives, skills, and values determine what people do. *American Psychologist* 1985, 40 (7), 812–825. DOI: https://doi.org/10.1037/0003-066X.40.7.812
(13) Schueler, J., Baumann, N., Chasiotis, A., Bender, M., & Baum, I. Implicit motives and basic psychological needs. *Journal of Personality* 2019, 87 (1), 37–55. DOI: 10.1111/jopy.12431
(14) Plato. *Republic* (G. M. A. Grube, Trans.; C. D. C. Reeve, Rev.). Hackett Publishing Company, 1992.
(15) Boyatzis, R. E. Affiliation motivation. In *Human motivation: A book of readings*., General Learning Corporation, 1973; pp 252–276.
(16) Lansing, J. B., & Heyns, R. W. Need affiliation and frequency of 4 types of communication *Journal of Abnormal and Social Psychology* 1959, 58 (3), 365–372. DOI: 10.1037/h0045906
(17) Exline, R. Need affiliation and initial communication behavior in problem-solving groups characterised by low interpersonal visibility *Psychological Reports* 1962, 10 (1), 79–89.

8

POLITICAL SKILL, NETWORKING, AND INFLUENCING

Political skill: Leading between the lines

Back in Chapter 5, we talked about political clout – one of those invisible currencies that CFOs trade in, whether they admit to it or not. Now, let's zero in on the skills needed to play the political game. After all, no organization is a politics-free zone. Politics is as endemic to corporate life as spreadsheets and "World's best boss" coffee cups.

Numerous studies associate leaders' political skills with higher leadership effectiveness. Political skill helps leaders tend to their teams, craft a vision, and – this is the magic part – *sell that vision* to the people around them (1). Leaders versed in company politics achieve better relationship quality with their employees (2) and are better at dealing with conflict in the team (3). And just in case you were tempted to chalk all this up to good old management skills, political skill explains leadership effectiveness over and above other managerial competencies (4).

DOI: 10.4324/9781003581734-11

Political skill even plays a role in the last place you would look for it: authenticity. While leaders who practice self-regulated attention – basically, mindfulness in a tailored suit – are seen as more authentic, that effect is *amplified* when the leader is politically skilled (5).

How politically skilled are you? Take the questionnaire in Appendix 2 to find out

In a study of senior British managers, the vast majority declared political behavior a workplace necessity. Yet the vast majority of them had never been trained in it. They were essentially asked to dance without ever learning the steps. According to them, the most common moves on the political dance floor were networking, aligning with key players, befriending power brokers, bending rules, and, of course, a self-promotion pirouette or two (6).

So what does this elusive "political skill" actually look like? Research distills it into four abilities (1):

1. **Social astuteness**. The ability to read a room. These are the people who intuitively know how to present themselves, who sense the motivations and hidden agendas of others, and who know the right thing to say or do.
2. **Networking ability**. The ability to call on a wide web of colleagues, to mobilize resources, to form alliances. Think of it as knowing how to lay political infrastructure.
3. **Interpersonal influence**. Finding it easy to develop rapport with most people, putting people at ease, communicating effortlessly, and – without trying too hard – being genuinely likable.
4. **Perceived sincerity**. And here's the curveball. Political skill isn't about being slick – it works only if others see you as sincere. I'm going to assume that you are not interested in the dark arts of manipulation: if you were, you wouldn't have reached this point in the book. In this case, this dimension of political skill means not only appearing but genuinely trying to be interested in others, to speak and behave with authenticity.

Now, you may have scoffed at "intuitively" in social astuteness above. Let's clear something up. This is not some mystical birthright handed down at the cradle. As you've likely guessed by now, very few abilities are locked in the vault of natural talent. Social astuteness – like any other skill we've explored – is built through curiosity, practice, and attention. Remember all that terrain we've covered together, about personalities, values, emotional intelligence, implicit leadership theories, cultural nuance, propensity to trust, and key motivators? That's your groundwork. Social astuteness is the scaffolding you build atop it, through purposeful practice, until it becomes second nature.

Which brings us to the rest of the political skill quartet: networking, influence, and perceived sincerity. In the sections ahead, we'll unpack networking and influence and we will touch on sincerity – exploring the tactics that work, the ones that backfire, and the ever-tricky business of being authentic while, well, trying to appear authentic.

Networking: Capital, connection, and coffee

In the early 2000s, Raytheon, a major electronics company, started adding social capital training to its leadership programs. At the time, this was unusual: employers would rarely admit that networking (a term that suggested political behavior and supplementing inefficient formal channels) was needed in their own organization. But Raytheon management, in the wake of an acquisition spree, realized that it needed to address the problem of its acquired companies turning into silos, hardly ever collaborating.

Even more unusually, Raytheon's senior management allowed the academics conducting the networking training to follow the evolution of managers who had taken it and compare it with that of equally promising managers who did not. Their findings show a startling superiority of graduates of the social capital program in terms of getting job promotions and stellar performance evaluations (7).

Here's an interesting detail: Greg Smith, who later became CFO of Boeing (and whom we commended in Chapter 5 for his universally respected expertise), likely participated in the social capital course when head of investor relations at Raytheon. He probably capitalized on those networking skills in his subsequent roles, adding social acumen to rock-solid expertise to go from VP of FP&A to Corporate Controller to CFO and interim CEO at Boeing.

The hidden power of a CFO's network

A CFO's influence and effectiveness emerge through their web of relationships – with colleagues, stakeholders, mentors, and industry peers – as much as through their technical skills. Extensive studies show that top managers' social capital is critical for a variety of outcomes, from supply chain gains (8) access to critical resources (9) and even increasing due diligence speed (10).

For CFOs, outside networking pays off in hard numbers. Firms with CFOs who are highly connected in executive networks secure **bank loans** on more favorable terms – notably with lower interest spreads and fewer restrictive covenants (11). They can also afford to hold thinner **cash cushions**: when the CFO is replaced with a new CFO with finance industry connections, the proportion of assets held in cash by the firm decreases on average by seven percentage points (12). A well-networked CFO serves as a credibility signal to lenders: their connections imply access to better information and oversight, reducing the lender's risk. It is telling that personal networks afford such power that it becomes inebriating to some: CFOs who have powerful outside networks are also more likely to engage in financial misreporting (13) and in aggressive tax avoidance practices (14).

As you already know (and as the Raytheon experiment reminds us), networking also correlates with personal career gains (15). For CFOs with eyes on eventual CEO roles or board positions, this is even more compelling.

As a matter of fact, nurturing a network – inside and outside your company – is so valuable that it can even affect your decisions to take, or extend, international assignments, despite the obvious learning and cultural acumen benefits they offer. An intriguing study finds that international experience is beneficial for CFOs… up to a point (16). According to this paper, that turning point seems to be around 11 years (with diminishing returns to scale before then). Why? Because as time passes, the "absent" CFO's social capital in, and around, the "mother ship" diminishes and weakens, and those ties are critical for your career.

Networking where you need it most

How well you are connected is measured by your "**centrality**" in your network. Centrality aggregates four measures (13):

1. **Betweenness**. How many of the shortest paths between two individuals in your network go through you.
2. **Closeness**. How short are, on average, the paths from you to all other individuals in the network.
3. **Degree**. How many direct connections to other individuals you have.
4. **Eigenvector**. How important are the individuals that you have direct connections with.

CFOs of large US public firms tend to be highly central compared with other executives: the median centrality of a CFO in a large US public firm is above the 72nd percentile among all executives and directors of large US public companies (11). This makes sense, since many of the major company CFOs are recruited externally rather than promoted from inside (17) and often come from other industries (consulting and investments); therefore, they bring with them considerable networks to add to the company's own environment. Once in their role, they often also sit on other companies' boards and continue to build their external networks, while internally they tend to be an unchallenged strategic business partner to the CEO and the rest of the business, ideally positioned at the center of the organization.

Things may be different, though, for CFOs of smaller companies, who might still be struggling to establish finance as a business partner in their company as well as for finance leaders below the CFO. They would therefore most benefit from a purposeful, systematic approach to networking externally and internally. There are numerous books and courses dedicated to diagnosing the centrality of your social network, identifying where more work is needed, and targeting those areas (e.g., *Never Eat Alone* (18), *The 20-Minute Networking Meeting* (19), or *How to Talk to Anyone* (20)).

Yet, as research discovered, there is a catch: *not everybody benefits from every type of networking*, and even worse, we tend to find it easier to engage in *the type of networking that least benefits us!* (21) Let me explain:

> Individuals belong to two categories, depending on their cognitive style: *adaptors* and *innovators*. Adaptors are great at implementing, rather than generating, new ideas and enjoy stable work interactions. Innovators come up with creative breakthroughs and are bored easily.

Now, adaptors would be most valuable when networking across **structural holes** (between parties that otherwise are not in contact with each other) taking in a diversity of perspectives and information and fitting it all together, like a many-dimensional puzzle. But guess what? They *hate* that kind of networking. It goes against their preference for well-regulated and consensus-based working relationships. Instead, they are often comfortable with networking inside a dense relationship group (e.g., inside the finance function or, in the CFO's case, with the rest of the top management team), further deepening their connections there.

Conversely, innovators would perform best when having strong network centrality within established groups, which help them convert that outlandish idea into an innovation that can actually *survive* in a climate of established rules and processes. Yet – you've guessed it – they prefer networking outside of such groups, across structural holes, because it offers more novelty and room for experimentation. The rule that our mothers knew so well: "If you don't like it, it must be good for you", seems to apply here too.

Based on my conversations with finance leaders and supported by personality-based inferencing (since finance people tend to be conscientious and somewhat introverted), I suspect that most of us fall within the "adaptor" rather than the "innovator" category. If you recognize yourself in this category, you are probably more comfortable networking inside your function or with another close-knit team (such as the Top Management Team in our opening story) rather than spanning structural holes. Push against your comfort boundaries and invite those managers from different areas (who rarely talk to each other or to you) for an after-work drink or go meet new people at an industry event: connecting dots that you would otherwise never have seen as part of the same picture.

Overcoming the "networking ick" factor

Despite all these benefits, most CFOs I spoke with admit that they network – especially on "new territory" as discussed above – less than they know they should. If you've ever hesitated to reach out or felt a bit "icky" about schmoozing, you're not alone. When people engage in networking with a purely instrumental mindset (i.e., solely to advance their own professional goals), it can trigger feelings of moral impurity – essentially making them feel "dirty" for doing it (22). Those who feel this way are less likely to continue networking and, consequently, see negative impacts on their work performance. This dynamic can create a vicious cycle: feeling uncomfortable leads to shying away from networking, which in turn limits opportunities and keeps one at a disadvantage, making further interaction more uncomfortable.

So how can CFOs break out of this trap, especially if they're someone who isn't a natural glad hander? The research offers a reassuring insight: the key lies in **reframing your approach**. Networking doesn't have to be a selfish, superficial game of trading favors. In fact, it's most effective when it's approached with authenticity and a broader purpose. When people start seeing networking as an opportunity to learn and to contribute, not just as self-promotion, those negative feelings dissipate (22). In practice, this means shifting your mindset from "What can I get from this interaction?" to "What can I give in this interaction, or learn from it?" For example, attending an industry mixer with the goal of sharing insights about a new fintech trend or genuinely curating new ideas can feel very different – and far more rewarding – than trying to 'work the room' for personal gain. When CFOs focus on curiosity (asking others about their experiences and challenges) and on generosity (offering help or information where they can), networking starts to feel like a natural extension of their leadership rather than an alien chore.

As CFO, you can take small, sincere steps: congratulate a peer on their company's earnings success (with no agenda attached), invite a department head you don't know well to lunch just to hear about their challenges, or volunteer in a finance leaders' association where you can both contribute to the community and meet others. When done in this spirit, networking ceases to be an "extra" task – it becomes an enriching part of your job, one conversation at a time.

Relationship with other departments

If you ever told yourself "My, I don't get how these marketing people think", you were not necessarily overdramatizing. According to research, functional areas each operate in their own "thought worlds": what is different is not only *what* they know (their "fund of knowledge") but also *how* they know it (their "systems of meaning"). One thought world may view another's central issues as "esoteric, if not meaningless" (23).

For example, many CFOs complain that they are not getting the needed support from HR. They often end up taking much of the talent acquisition, retention, and development work onto themselves instead of trying to establish a working relationship with HR and its foreign thought world. Or take IT. Big spender, often with a spotty track record of project success. IT, on the other hand, sees Finance as the party who always says "no". Truth is, for Finance, it's sometimes easier to say "no" than to understand the complexities of IT projects. And, although today's CFOs can rarely get away with having no understanding of IT, and especially of data architecture, your life as CFO would still be so much easier if you could completely trust your company's CIO, which makes building the relationship with them one of the best investments you can make. Marketing is yet another case. Ironically, and my opening example notwithstanding, many of today's marketing chiefs speak the language of the CFO more than their HR or IT counterparts do, because marketing has become a highly quantitative subject and because all marketing wizards now know that they have to build a compelling business case to put their plans into action. Still, this may be quite different in smaller firms, where the marketing person is often wildly creative but not necessarily numbers-minded. In such cases, the CFO may sometimes have to take a (measured) leap of faith and approve this or that idea without much of a financial case behind it, in order to build a trust relationship with the marketing head.

The quality of a CFO's relationships with other functional areas in the firm is so important that it even bubbles up in studies of companies' financial reporting quality: When CFOs have stronger social ties with other senior managers in their firm, there are fewer financial restatements (24).

In short, as Mark Hawkins, former CFO of Salesforce, puts it:

> Your longevity in the CFO role, and your mental health, will directly correlate with the quality of relationships you have with the other people who report into the CEO (25).

CROSSROADS LIFE: CLARA AND THE PROGRAM DIRECTOR

Kevin is the Program Director of Project ACE, a massive cross-country Ops-IT initiative already in full swing when Clara steps into her role as regional CFO. When we first meet him in the film, Kevin is eager to win Clara over as an ally. But their value systems clash. Kevin prioritizes loyalty over competence, takes things personally, and assumes hidden agendas in every C-suite conversation. These traits intensify under pressure, especially as the project falls behind schedule and regional CEOs and CFOs begin to question its business case.

Clara, meanwhile, is uneasy with how the project's financial controls are structured. Technically, she isn't responsible – Kevin has his own finance team, and ACE is accounted for under a separate "special projects" line in the region's financials. Still, as regional CFO, Clara feels accountable for every dollar spent or invested in the region. She also sees a clear conflict of interest: Kevin both runs the project and reports on its finances. So, she asks Henk, the regional CEO, to shift oversight of Kevin's finance team under her control.

When Kevin finds out, he's furious. What Clara views as an obvious fix – a lack of proper oversight – Kevin sees as a personal betrayal.

Was Clara wrong to express anger during the confrontation with Kevin? Not necessarily. Past interactions suggest Kevin underestimated Clara, assuming she was easily swayed and confident in his influence with Henk. A strong response may have been necessary to reassert her authority over regional finances.

Where Clara did misstep – and we see her realizing this in the film scene – is in failing to tell Kevin beforehand about her intent to take control of the financials. He would have pushed back, certainly, but blindsiding him damaged trust and made the move look like a betrayal.

As a CFO, you should expect conflicts with other departments. Your decisions may stem from sound financial logic or risk principles – but others may see them as power grabs or political maneuvers. Different roles bring different perspectives, and bridging that gap requires clarity, communication, and occasionally confrontation.

Watch the scene selection at: https://www.ed.movie/kevin or scan the QR code.

Build connections at multiple levels

In the early 2000s, a curious thing began to happen at a major telecom company in Europe. On the one hand, the executive team – eight people with polished shoes, firm handshakes, and what looked like an enviable camaraderie – were seen regularly having lunch together, joking in meetings, and nodding approvingly as each spoke. From the outside, they looked like a dream team. On the other hand, two layers down, things looked very different.

A war was quietly under way. The heads of departments under those executives rarely spoke to each other. They sent curt emails, played Calendar Tetris to avoid face-to-face meetings, and occasionally redirected blame upward, hoping their bonded bosses wouldn't notice. One leader later described it as "dysfunctional harmony". Harmony at the top, dysfunction below.

This isn't rare. In fact, it's a pattern.

Organizations are complex social systems, and like any social system, they are vulnerable to the illusion of cohesion. Cohesion at one level often masks fragmentation below. Which brings us to an often-overlooked leadership question: **how do you build connection that runs deep – *not just laterally* but *vertically and diagonally*, through the entire organizational matrix?**

For a CFO, this may be particularly difficult. Finance is often viewed – fairly or not – as a gated compound.

One antidote: **cross-pollination**. Encourage your finance team to engage with the rest of the company not only at the top but throughout the hierarchy. Invite a product manager to a finance team meeting. Let a salesperson explain their monthly report face-to-face. Or do what one regional CFO did: have her finance analysts deliver product trainings. It was a clever reversal – numbers people teaching the business, not just analyzing it. It made her team indispensable.

This isn't just a nice-to-have. It's what network theorists would call **boundary spanning**: the act of connecting across formal silos to broker relationships, knowledge, and influence. Boundary spanners are those magical team members who have lunch with engineering on Monday, join a marketing standup on Wednesday, and somehow manage to be liked by both. They're rarely the quietest in the room. They're the ones who ask, "Have we checked with Legal on that?" or "I think Sales might be doing something similar".

And here's the rub: finance managers, conditioned to equate hard work with hard figures, often undervalue these people – especially if their contributions don't look like productivity in the traditional sense.

CASE: ZHANG AND THE BOUNDARY SPANNER

Zhang was the country CFO of a global advisory services firm, known for her precision and steadiness. She wasn't quick to judge, nor easily swayed. But on this particular afternoon, she sat unmoving in front of her screen, cursor hovering over the "Approve" button on the annual performance review summary for her whole area.

One name, one rating, was holding her back: Georgia.

Mark, her head of FP&A, had rated Georgia – a senior analyst – as simply "meets expectations". Not poor. Just average. But Zhang hesitated. Georgia was visible. She volunteered for cross-functional initiatives, seemed at home in conversations outside of finance – and, yes, she had a particular talent for making herself known. Zhang had to admit to herself that part of Georgia's visibility came from her way of showing enthusiasm and, yes, admiration for Zhang's leadership.

Mark, by contrast, was solid. Dependable. Quiet. And increasingly irritated. "She's always chatting with other teams instead of cleaning up her forecast deck", he had complained. "More networking than working". Georgia's measurable results as captured in the performance evaluation did not seem stellar, indeed. But could that partly be because Mark overloaded her with calculation and analysis tasks to keep her "under control"? Did Mark feel eclipsed by Georgia, did he feel like she was somehow taking over the representation of the FP&A department to the outside world?

Eventually, Zhang signed off on the rating. She told herself she was deferring to Mark's direct knowledge, that her own perception might be colored by Georgia's subtle ingratiation with her. Two months later, Georgia resigned.

Six years after that, Georgia was appointed CFO of a rapidly growing brokerage firm. Zhang learned it through a LinkedIn post someone forwarded with the subject line: "Look who's back". And she felt a strange mix of pride and regret.

She later reflected: "Mark saw a distraction. I saw an asset. But I didn't follow my instinct".

As a CFO, you aren't only managing financial capital – you're also fostering social capital at all levels. People in your area who travel between silos might not always look like your top performers on paper. But they're often the glue that holds innovation together. And sometimes they grow into leaders themselves.

Practical next steps: Networking for the numerically inclined

1. **Map your network**. Sketch out your internal and external connections. Identify gaps – who in Marketing, IT, HR, or Product haven't you had a real conversation with this quarter?
2. **Introduce cross-pollination moments**. Invite a non-finance colleague to a finance team meeting – or have your team deliver value-adding sessions to other departments.
3. **Identify and nurture boundary spanners**. Who in your team naturally bridges silos? Acknowledge and protect the time they dedicate to this.
4. **Reframe networking in your mindset**. Don't think "self-promotion". Think "idea exchange" and "problem-solving in new company corners". Enter conversations with curiosity, not a pitch.
5. **Use discomfort as a compass**. If a particular networking opportunity feels awkward or outside your comfort zone, take it as a sign that you may be headed in the right direction.
6. **Recognize the cost of silos**. Remember Zhang and Georgia. Sometimes the person chatting by the coffee machine is brokering your next big cross-departmental project success.

At first glance, networking may seem like something for the extroverts, the marketers, the schmoozers. But the truth is more nuanced: for CFOs, networking is a form of organizational infrastructure. It enables agility, builds credibility, and quietly powers the decisions that charts and models alone cannot make. Whether you are nurturing talent, chasing strategic edge, or simply trying to sleep better at night knowing that IT won't spring a big software write-off on you – building your relationships matters. One coffee chat at a time.

Influencing skills: How to steer without a steering wheel

Imagine a CFO sitting in a high-backed chair, with a line of people outside their office, all waiting to make their case.

This is the fantasy version. In reality, CFOs rarely sit in positions of absolute command. Even at the top of the financial food chain, they often find themselves needing to **influence people they don't control**: the Head of Sales who disagrees with her salespeople filling out a form that would greatly benefit FP&A in the management reporting cycle; the manager of a large-scale change program who conveniently "forgets" to involve finance in the early planning; the regional GM pushing back on operating expense cuts.

Which brings us to a deceptively simple question: **How do you lead, when you are not actually in charge?**

In 1984, two professors – Allan Cohen and David Bradford – started answering that question. Their book, *Influence Without Authority*, offers a **six-step model** (not an edict!) for leading through **exchange**. A model built for cross-functional, consensus-driven, KPI-misaligned reality.

The Cohen–Bradford influencing process

Step 1: Assume all are potential allies.

There's an old joke. A peasant walks to his neighbor's house to ask for a spade. As he walks, he thinks: "What if he's using the spade?" Then, "What if he doesn't *want* to lend it?" Then, "What if he resents me asking?" By the time the neighbor opens the door, the peasant has worked himself into such a froth that he shouts, "You can keep your damn spade!" and storms off.

Finance professionals, trained to anticipate risk, often fall into the same trap. They prepare for rejection before they've even made the ask.

But here's the twist: **cooperation isn't a naïve hope – it's a strategy**. Robert Axelrod's research on the Prisoner's Dilemma (26) showed that mutual benefit can emerge even in cutthroat scenarios. Soldiers in World War I trenches stopped firing during meal hours. Vampire bats share blood with non-relatives. Businesses silently agree not to start price wars.

So start by assuming the party you intend to influence is a potential ally. Yes, they will eventually want to fill that additional form. Yes, they will eventually understand the need to cut their cost further. Every one of the following steps rests on how solid this first one is.

Step 2: Clarify your goals.

Sometimes, in the middle of a negotiation, something shifts. The goal becomes not "get the headcount approved" but "prove I'm right". The numbers fade. The ego takes over.

CFOs aren't immune. Which is why you should write your goal down – literally. A sticky note. A sentence fragment. Not because you'll forget (you're not Dory, the memory-challenged fish) but because your ego will try to hijack the mission mid-flight.

Instead of focusing on achieving the initial goal, we suddenly want to be right, to come on top, to have the last word. If you can get what you want while making the other feel like *they* won, so much the better (although it would be even better if the transaction had a "win-win", not a "win-lose" flavor to it).

Step 3: Diagnose the world of the other person.

Don't barge into someone else's priorities like a gunslinger kicking down the saloon doors.

Do your homework instead. Before you present your case, **step into their world**. What incentives drive their decisions? What constraints do they face? Are they maybe completely absorbed by something else going on right now? A CFO at a SaaS company once told me he made peace with his CMO only after sitting through two weeks of demand-gen planning. "I realized", he said, "her world runs on CAC and leads. Mine runs on EBITDA. We weren't disagreeing. We were mistranslating".

Step 4: Identify relevant currencies.

Cohen and Bradford had a brilliant insight: **not all value is money**. They introduced the notion of *organizational currencies*. These are the things that people value and that you can offer.

At first sight, you might think you don't have much in your pocket that would be valuable to someone else.

Joseph Nelson, CFO of Delta Corp, told me about a presentation he held soon after joining his previous company as Head of Investor Relations:

> I told them 'I'm going to be making a big ask on all of you, drawing on your expertise, asking for information, relying a lot on all of you here. And there's not a whole heck of a lot that I'm going to be able to return. I'm not an operational function. I'm really overhead. So if there is literally anything that I or anybody on my team can do for you, we're willing to do it.' And I really think that's the way to do it, otherwise you just become like this hungry machine that swallows everything and doesn't give anything in return.[1]

This is an excellent approach for setting the stage, putting yourself in the others' shoes, showing humility and collegiality. But here's the thing: Joseph had more to offer his colleagues than it appeared. And so do you. Here are five kinds of "currencies" that drive influence:

1. **Inspiration-related currencies.** These appeal to people's values, ideals, and sense of purpose. They might relate to
   - Vision
   - Excellence
   - Moral/ethical correctness
   - Meaningful work

   For example, you are asking Engineering to implement a new project-costing system. You frame it not as a compliance issue but as part of building a more responsible organization that uses capital wisely – appealing to their pride in doing meaningful, high-impact work. Or, as in one of our earlier examples in Chapter 3, you convince your geographically dispersed finance teams to implement software that tracks how much work each team puts in. The tool appeals to their sense of fairness, as it ensures everyone is measured equally.
2. **Task-related currencies.** These are things that help someone get their job done better, faster, or with less pain. They could include
   - Resources (time, money, personnel)
   - Information
   - Access to data
   - Problem-solving support

   Say that your HR counterpart is overloaded preparing for comp reviews. You offer a finance team member to help model headcount costs, saving them time and increasing accuracy. Or you support the sales team in preparing a client pitch with a compelling financial case.

3. **Position-related currencies**. These deal with enhancing someone's visibility, reputation, or influence within the organization. You might be able to offer
   - Recognition
   - Visibility to senior leadership
   - Enhanced reputation
   - A seat at the table

   Maybe you invite the Marketing Director to co-present at a quarterly business review to showcase ROI improvements on campaigns – giving them exposure to the CEO and board. Or you name-drop a helpful peer in a CFO staff meeting, publicly acknowledging their contribution.
4. **Relationship-related currencies**. These appeal to people's need to feel connected, appreciated, and part of a team. They might be things such as
   - Inclusion
   - Gratitude
   - Personal support
   - Loyalty and trust

   You ask a colleague to join a project team by underlining the "in" status they would get, belonging to a tight-knit, fun-loving group. Or you offer emotional support or a sounding board to a peer going through organizational change – even when it's not strictly "finance business".
5. **Personal currencies**. These are tailored to individual preferences, personalities, and personal goals. This is an opportunity to put to good use what we've talked about in earlier chapters (e.g., personal values and motivational drivers). They might include items such as
   - Autonomy
   - Challenge and learning
   - Sense of importance and power
   - Enjoyment, fun

For example, you tell a colleague who loves a challenge: "This project is a mess. Most people wouldn't touch it. But you could pull it off". Or you ask a colleague who values power to lead a taskforce, making it clear that they would be seen as the full owner of the project.

Step 5: Offer the exchange.

This includes offering the currency or currencies that you feel are most valuable to the other party and asking for what you need. Most of the time, this is not framed as an actual exchange, even in your own mind You are not bartering like a market haggler. You wouldn't say (or think): "I'll listen to your woes for 10 minutes, after which here's what you can do for me". The best exchanges are often asynchronous, looking more like deposits and withdrawals from an "influence bank account" you have with the other party. Maybe you helped them last quarter. Maybe you're depositing now for a future withdrawal.

Step 6: Make it safe to say yes.

People resist not because they're stubborn but because they're afraid – of being wrong, exposed, or blamed. Influence means de-risking the "yes". Make it reversible. Break it into smaller parts, maybe a pilot first. Offer air cover. CFOs, who are usually the guardians of caution, must learn to help others feel safe, too. Make it safe to say yes, and you'll hear it more often than you think.

CROSSROADS LIFE: GETTING OLIVER TO SAY YES

Oliver is the Global Head of Tax – and to Clara, like many at headquarters, he seems to be floating around with too much title and too little to do. So she's genuinely surprised when he curtly declines her request for help. In her view, it's literally his job. She tries to explain why her request matters. Oliver remains unmoved. And then, just to twist the knife, Ruben swings by with a similar request – and Oliver says yes immediately.

Clara is furious. As she storms out, she mentally files Oliver under "useless bureaucrats who play favorites".

But... there might be more to it.

If Clara had used the Cohen–Bradford influence model, she would have taken a moment to understand Oliver's world before making her ask. She might have learned that his team is stretched thin, that he's been vocal about lacking resources, and that he has to ruthlessly prioritize. Ruben gets a yes not because he's a favorite but because he's trusted. He knows Oliver's bandwidth and wouldn't ask unless it really mattered.

Clara, by contrast, is still new. From Oliver's perspective, she may seem like a megaphone for every unfiltered complaint coming out of the business units. Trust hasn't been built yet.

According to Cohen–Bradford, influence is a two-way street – Clara needs to offer something in return. But to do that, she first has to understand what Oliver values. Does he thrive on solving knotty technical problems? Or does he want recognition, control, or visibility? And what about that impromptu opera solo he burst into during a coffee break – maybe a lighthearted compliment on his Puccini impression could open a door?

Sometimes, getting to "yes" starts with understanding what makes someone sing – literally and figuratively.

Watch the scene selection at: https://www.ed.movie/oliver or scan the QR code.

The examples above focused on peers. But the same model is equally valuable when interacting with managers and employees in your own area. After all, we started by defining leadership as a *social influence* process, not a "because I said so" one.

What Cohen and Bradford understood is that influence is transactional, but not in the cold, manipulative sense. You earn trust. You invest in goodwill. You build relationships that yield returns when the ask is big and the time is short. One finance leader I interviewed put it this way:

> I stopped trying to get my way, and started building IOUs. And eventually, the things I cared about... just started happening.[2]

Influence is about how to create value in the currency that others spend – and how to trade in it wisely.

Influence: Practical takeaways

1. **Practice** the Cohen–Bradford model like a craft, not a script. Don't just memorize the six steps – try them. Especially Step 4: get into the habit of asking yourself, *What does this person truly value?* Hint: it's not always more budget.
2. **Be patient**. See each relationship as a bank account with deposits and withdrawals. Do not expect an immediate – or necessarily proportionate – return. Withdraw when it counts. Influence, like interest, compounds over time.
3. **Read** Dale Carnegie, seriously. *How to Win Friends and Influence People* may be a grandfatherly classic, but its lessons remain strikingly aligned with modern psychology. It complements the Cohen–Bradford model, which is mostly about the "what" of influence, with a very useful (and entertaining) "how".

In the end, influence is about being valuable, in a currency the other person actually spends.

Perceived sincerity: The often-overlooked foundation of political skill

When we talked about political skill earlier in this book, we listed four components: social astuteness, networking ability, interpersonal influence – and sincerity.

Sincerity might seem less glamorous. But it's the foundation. Without it, all your attempts at influence risk sounding like spin. If you are *seen* as political, you have failed the political skill test. And as I wrote earlier, I am going to assume that you are not a master of manipulation, meaning that the safest (and sanest) way for you to *appear* sincere is to *be* sincere. Sometimes this may mean reframing some political activities so that they do not contradict your authenticity (as we have seen in the case of networking), and other times it may mean refraining from some political activities altogether (such as praising the boss for what was in fact an appalling speech).

More generally, integrity is required for your networks to hold and for your influencing attempts to deliver. And when it comes to the CFO, the standard of integrity is higher. As Marie Myers, CFO of Hewlett Packard Enterprise, puts it:

> Because you're the CFO, you have a different judicial obligation, meaning people watch how you spend and how you tally up the company's money and resources. It matters, because you set the tone. I think, in a company, everybody's watching a CFO to see, are their words and their actions lined up, or are they inconsistent?[3]

This extends to what you ask from yourself and your team, in relation to what you ask from others. Asking business units to optimize every bit of cash while your own treasury department is sitting on a generous cash cushion, just in case, or demanding heavy cost cuts while you treat yourself and your team to a luxury offsite would make your elaborate influencing constructions crumble.

In the end, influence is about empathy, consistency, and long memory. It's not about having power – it's about being worth listening to.

Notes

1 Interview with the author.
2 Interviewed finance manager, anonymized.
3 Interview with the author.

References

(1) Ferris, G., Treadway, D., Perrewé, P., Brouer, R., Douglas, C., & Lux, S. Political skill in organizations. *Journal of Management* 2007, 33 (3), 290–320. DOI: 10.1177/0149206307300813
(2) Brouer, R., Chiu, C., & Wang, L. Political skill dimensions and transformational leadership in China. *Journal of Managerial Psychology* 2016, 31 (6), 1040–1056. DOI: 10.1108/JMP-05-2014-0166

(3) Tu, Y., & Zhang, L. Relationship between team conflict and performance in green enterprises: A cross-level model moderated by leaders' political skills. *Complexity* 2021, 2021. DOI: 10.1155/2021/6635426
(4) Snell, S., Tonidandel, S., Braddy, P., & Fleenor, J. The relative importance of political skill dimensions for predicting managerial effectiveness. *European Journal of Work and Organizational Psychology* 2014, 23 (6), 915–929. DOI: 10.1080/1359432X.2013.817557
(5) Dietl, E., & Reb, J. A self-regulation model of leader authenticity based on mindful self-regulated attention and political skill. *Human Relations* 2019. DOI: 10.1177/0018726719888260
(6) Buchanan, D. You stab my back, I'll stab yours: Management experience and perceptions of organization political behaviour. *British Journal of Management* 2008, 19 (1), 49–64. DOI: 10.1111/j.1467-8551.2007.00533.x
(7) Burt, R. S. & Ronchi, D. Teaching executives to see social capital: Results from a field experiment. *Social Science Research* 2007, 36 (3), 1156–1183. DOI: 10.1016/j.ssresearch.2006.09.005.
(8) Choi, E., Özer, Ö., & Zheng, Y. Network trust and trust behaviors among executives in supply chain interactions. *Management Science* 2020, 66 (12). DOI: 10.1287/mnsc.2019.3499
(9) Tasselli, S., & Sancino, A. Leaders' networking behaviours in a time of crisis: A qualitative study on the frontline against COVID-19. *Journal of Management Studies* 2023, 60 (1), 120–173. DOI: 10.1111/joms.12884
(10) Popli, M., Li, Y., Wu, L., & Rajwani, T. Due diligence speed in technology acquisitions: The impact of top management team's social capital. *Asia Pacific Journal of Management* 2024. DOI: 10.1007/s10490-024-10002-4
(11) Fogel, K., Jandik, T., & McCumber, W. CFO social capital and private debt. *Journal of Corporate Finance* 2018, 52, 28–52. DOI: 10.1016/j.jcorpfin.2018.07.001
(12) Anderson, C., Wintoki, M., & Xi, Y. CFO social capital, liquidity management, and the market value of cash. *Journal of Banking & Finance* 2024, 163. DOI: 10.1016/j.jbankfin.2024.107163
(13) He, J. Executive network centrality and corporate reporting. *Management Science* 2022, 68 (2), 1512–1536. DOI: 10.1287/mnsc.2020.3924
(14) Liu, C., & Chiu, J. External social networks and tax avoidance. *Review of Quantitative Finance and Accounting* 2024, 62 (4), 1459–1504. DOI: 10.1007/s11156-024-01242-y
(15) Wolff, H., & Moser, K. Effects of networking on career success: A longitudinal study. *Journal of Applied Psychology* 2009, 94 (1), 196–206. DOI: 10.1037/a0013350
(16) Schmid, S., & Altfeld, F. International work experience and compensation: Is more always better for CFOs? *European Management Journal* 2018, 36 (4), 530–543. DOI: 10.1016/j.emj.2017.11.001
(17) Cristkolder Volatility Report: https://www.cristkolder.com/volatility-report, 2024.
(18) Ferrazi, K., & Raz, T. *Never eat alone*; Crown Currency, 2014.
(19) Ballinger, M., & Perez, N. *The 20-minute networking meeting*; Career Innovation Press, 2012.
(20) Lowndes, L. *How to talk to anyone*. McGraw Hill: 2003.

(21) Carnabuci, G., & Quintane, E. When people build networks that hurt their performance: Structural holes, cognitive style, and the unintended consequences of person-network fit *Academy of Management Journal* 2023, 66 (5), 1360–1383. DOI: 10.5465/amj.2021.1227
(22) Casciaro, T., Gino, F., & Kouchaki, M. The contaminating effects of building instrumental ties: How networking can make us feel dirty. *Administrative Science Quarterly* 2014, 59 (4), 705–735. DOI: 10.1177/0001839214554990
(23) Dougherty, D. Interpretive barriers to successful product innovation in large firms. *Organization Science* 1992, 3 (2), 179–202.
(24) Kuang, Y., Liu, X., Paruchuri, S., & Qin, B. CFO social ties to non-CEO senior managers and financial restatements. *Accounting and Business Research* 2022, 52 (2), 115–149. DOI: 10.1080/00014788.2020.1793719
(25) Gustafson, C. J. What I Wish I Knew as a First Year CFO. https://www.mostlymetrics.com/p/what-i-wish-i-knew-as-a-first-year, 2023.
(26) Axelrod, R., & Hamilton, W. D. The evolution of cooperation. *Science* 1981, 211 (4489), 1390–1396.

9

SELECTING AND DEVELOPING TALENT

The author of the "Secret CFO" blog once summed up his leadership "secret sauce" this way: "I hire wonderful people and then I work really hard to keep them" (1).

Not exactly the stuff of TED Talks or leadership bestsellers – but a great reminder that you need to approach the talent topic with humility and patience.

When your next finance star looks like trouble at first glance

Senior leaders universally agree that selection is becoming ever more important. With timelines contracting and performance expectations rising, you cannot afford to make selection mistakes.

When I asked CFOs how they select new hires, most offered a version of this golden trio:

DOI: 10.4324/9781003581734-12

1. "Hire for attitude, train for skill".
2. "Build for the future, not just for the now".
3. "Prioritize diversity".

In reality, things rarely unfold this way in finance departments.

1. Choosing attitude over skills and future over now essentially means accepting that the person you are hiring might not be able to deliver at full capacity anytime soon. This might be a **tradeoff** that you, the CFO, are willing to make. But how does it look to Mark, the head of FP&A (the same Mark from our "boundary spanner" case in Chapter 8)? Mark is the direct boss of the new hire and, after the latest round of headcount cuts, has only 20 FTEs to do the work of 25. To him, hiring someone who cannot hit the ground running does not look like such a great deal. Mark will happily take the skills over the attitude (unless the attitude is truly unusable – think Stanley from *The Office* TV series) and current ability to do the work over the intellectual curiosity and adaptability needed to evolve toward the future shape of the finance function. Moreover, what looks like the right attitude to you might look all wrong to Mark – remember how Mark did not appreciate Georgia's networking and information-gathering behaviors? And, no, the solution is not "fire Mark". There are many competent, hardworking, loyal Marks heading finance departments everywhere, and the fact that they have their nose too close to the ground to see the bigger picture may also partly be your fault (more about this in "The trouble with succession" section below).

   So what do you do, if you, the CFO, really mean to walk the talk and hire attitude and potential, with an eye to cultural and/or functional change in finance? **Be closely involved** in the hiring (and not only in the last phases) and weigh in on the choices of the new hire's direct boss as well as **offer support** afterwards to allow the new hire to survive in the existing structure and culture. This will require a lot of your time but is probably one of the best places to invest it.
2. **You might not have a lot to choose from**. Gartner's report on CFOs' *biggest 2025 challenges* places "ability to hire and retain talent" high up in the list, second only to "slower top line growth" (2).

Sometimes – for example, in some geographies or when your company has an excellent reputation as an employer – this may be less of an issue.

For example, Andrea Burlacu, VP of Global Finance Operations for Coca-Cola, fondly remembers when, earlier in her career, she was tasked with setting up the finance teams for Nokia's Latin American operations. She was able to select from excellent candidates because multinationals in general, and Nokia in particular, had excellent employer brand values in that region.[1]

But if you are a CFO not for a major global brand but, say, for a mid-size manufacturing company, you might not get the pick of the litter. Earlier on, we mentioned the leadership philosophy that Jason Child (former Groupon CFO, now CFO of ARM) abides by: "hire amazing people and let them run with it". This could work if you are at Amazon (where Jason started on his financial management path) and you have excellent candidates queuing up to submit themselves to Amazon's grinding recruitment process. It might not work as well at other companies; at Groupon, where Jason built the finance team from scratch,[2] his hiring track record must have been less stellar, since only two years after Groupon's (IPO) he had changed all of his direct reports (3).

How do you address this challenge? By applying everything in this book, really. If you practice transformational leadership, if you create a people-oriented culture all the way through your finance organization, if you inspire and motivate your team, *word will go out*, and the pool of talent in which you can fish gets bigger. Moreover, in today's connected world, it is increasingly easier for prospective candidates for a job to reach out to the previous incumbent and ask them for *the tea* on management's care for people. What would they say about you and your team?

3. **Diversity** in teams is hard to achieve and hard to maintain. In Chapter 4, we spoke about the attraction-selection-attrition cycle and how it tends to produce homogeneous finance teams. If you are building a whole team from scratch, you might be able to carefully compose a diverse mix and then cross your fingers in the hope that the group won't somehow spit out its more atypical members or fracture along age, gender, or other fault lines. But in most cases, you do not have that luxury, and instead you deal with trying to make a team more diverse by replacing one member at a time. That is an uphill battle.

A CFO for a large multinational told me about his Swedish finance management team that had been all-female for a long while. He had recently personally participated in the recruitment for an opening in that team and eventually selected a man, despite some resistance from the group. When we spoke, the CFO was preparing to fly to Sweden and do some damage control because the finance team there complained that the newest member of the team "was not quite getting it".

If you add diverse new members to an established team, you will likely need to be quite closely involved in the team's dynamics for a while, to **protect** and help integrate the new member. Unless the new member is an informal leader.

CASE: GEORGE AND THE INFORMAL LEADER

George joined Avira, a global consumer goods company, as CFO for its Greece subsidiary. He found what he called "good people in a bad culture". There was deep mistrust; politics – the toxic sort – abounded, and customers were an afterthought. Together with the CEO (who was also new), George started out on the painstaking road to changing the culture. This was going to be hard, as the employees had been conditioned to mistrust top management and second-guess their every word.

But then George recruited, for the risk management team, Nico, a young man who came from George's former company. Nico had a very different mindset: naturally trusting, open to trying new things out, curious. He brought with him, from his (and George's) former company, a strong customer orientation, which was almost comically at odds with how his risk colleagues saw their role. George was so busy with his own "first 90 days" that he could not afford to allocate time to overseeing Nico's integration, and he found himself, now and then, worrying that Nico would be gone before long.

Then something almost magical happened.

George started hearing Nico's name in connection with a host of stories or initiatives all around the company. That park run group that was growing fast, with some entertaining stories about colleagues who had never run before and swore they would never run again, only to be there at the next meet? Nico had started it. That grassroots initiative to smooth out a headache of a process that meandered through four departments? Nico was at its origin. His colleagues found following him, and trying to emulate him, so natural, it felt like it had always been like that.

Within a year, the culture in the company had visibly shifted, and while much of it was due to the CEO's efforts (and, George hoped, his own), Nico's informal leadership might just have been the extra nudge needed for the shift to get traction.

When recruiting talent, it might not always be easy to spot a "Nico". What turns out to be leadership ability might first look to a finance manager as oversized ambition, politicking, or loafing. This could be especially true when the finance manager has quite a different cognitive and motivational profile (say, an introverted, highly conscientious, "Protestant work ethic"-motivated one) and is tempted to recruit individuals similar to themselves.

I recently challenged Pekka, a Finnish CFO, to really reflect on how he selected new talent. To make him visualize it, I described in detail the profile of an individual with a personality quite different from Pekka's. I painted a gregarious young man, with a slightly "loud" sense of humor. I did also specify that he was a team player – actually preferred working in a team rather than by himself – was hard-working and had strong technical skills. Pekka thought for a moment and then said quietly:

> "I would never recruit such a person."

Let's stop here for a moment, and in the spirit of transformational leadership's "questions critical assumptions", ask: *Is it so bad if a nose-to-the-ground finance manager recruits a team similar to themselves?*

After all, there is ample research that shows that people will be more inclined to follow a leader similar to them – personality, cognitive styles, values – as we've shown in Chapters 2–5. So recruiting people like yourself certainly makes your leadership job easier. And yet choosing to take the difficult path and select – especially as your direct report – someone with complementary characteristics can yield the better results in the long run.

CASE: DAN AND THE PEOPLE-ORIENTED MANAGER[3]

Dan, a CFO for a financial services company, confesses preferring content to people, especially in his early CFO days. He would much rather delve into the details of an information memorandum than walk the finance floor or join social events with the team.

When the top position for finance and control (the biggest team in finance) opened up, he surprised everyone by promoting Mike, the head of Strategy. Bets were secretly made on how long Mike would last. He did not have an accounting background and had been with the company for only a little over one year.

What Mike did have, however, was people skills. He proved great not only at motivating his people but also at involving Dan in it: he would sometimes pull a reluctant Dan out of his technical ivory tower and have him deliver a motivating speech to a team that had just completed an important project or have a talk with a team leader who needed putting back on track.

Dan wisely recognized his own limits and selected the right person to expand them.

What about diversity in the team: do you really need to make it a priority? **The business case for diversity in teams is far from clear.** Diversity in personality characteristics, such as propensity to trust (discussed in Chapter 4), does not help team dynamics. When teams are made up of a mix of naturally trusting and mistrusting people, the trusting people grow increasingly frustrated by the perceived differences, which leads to generalized lack of trust and lower performance – more so than when the team is made entirely of mistrusting people! (4). More generally, recent comprehensive reviews of diversity research conclude that diverse teams are better at generating new ideas but worse at execution (5, 6).

This does not mean that you should throw efforts to increase your team's diversity out the window. There are strong ethical reasons to strive for diversity: giving equal chances to all workers is simply the right thing to do. As Alex Edmans, professor of finance at London Business School and a relentless debunker of confirmation bias-based "research", puts it: "It would be a sad world if the only reason firms increased diversity were to obtain higher performance or meet a regulatory target" (7).

However, it should be clear to you (and to others) what your reasons for, and the implications of, pursuing diversity really are. We have seen that leaders who have strong values (in this case, fairness to diverse candidates) are more likely to inspire and motivate their followers, and *that* does translate into a strong business case.

Paying for talent: The counteroffer conundrum

For most of my CFO years, I took a hardline position whenever an employee let us know that they had received a better offer from a competitor: let them go. My arguments were twofold: first, when someone has started searching for another job, even if you temporarily retain them by offering a significant raise, they will still end up leaving the company within the year: this was based on research, or so I thought at the time. (Now, as an academic, I have tried to locate that research without success.) Second, caving in to "pay up or I'll go somewhere else" blackmail sets a dangerous precedent for the whole finance organization.

Things have changed. Most CFOs I've asked about this confessed to taking a case-by-case approach in such situations. The job market has become more transparent and more fluid, and tenures at one single company have decreased. Conversations among workers about their own wages are no longer taboo (8). When your talented employee interviews with a competitor, it's increasingly because they were approached rather than because they were actively searching. Finance people, specifically, have been trained in the comparables valuation method. If invited to an interview, they would take the opportunity to benchmark their comp against the market. So, even if your inner reaction is "How could you?", it would be hard to see this as betrayal or necessarily as a confirmation that they want to leave their current job.

Similarly, you might feel compelled not to hire someone whom you'd otherwise very much want, because their comp level is outside your company's ranges for that position. Just in our previous chapter, we spoke about finance setting an example. One such example is to abide by internal procedures ultimately meant to keep costs from spiraling. This is a trap that several CFOs confessed falling into: they hired their second, or third, choice because they "couldn't afford" their first one. Often, that decision ended up costing them more than the "expensive" hiring option would have.

The trouble with succession (hint: it's you)

We've said it before: transformational leaders grow leaders.

And yet CFOs seem to have a particularly hard time developing credible successors. When my conversations with CFOs turn to "Do you have a potential successor for your job, in your team?", the answer is often a variation on "Not really, they don't have what it takes". Even when they say "not ready yet", further digging suggests that those "successors" will never be ready. Some CFOs admitted that they only go through the motions and perennially list one of their direct reports as "ready in 5 years" in their succession planning. The numbers confirm it: in 2024, over 40% of CFOs of Fortune 500 and S&P 500 companies were externally recruited, an all-time high (9).

Why don't the CFO's direct reports "have what it takes?" The CFOs spoke about their head of controlling, or head of treasury, or the CAO, as experienced, competent… but not someone with a bigger picture, with a strategic view.

Could this be because your head of controlling is caught in a "hamster wheel", the recurring and all-consuming processes in finance? Finance functions in an organization have largely predictable, monthly recurring tasks. They tend to put their nose down and do it, working hard, often putting in overtime during closing periods. You can hardly then expect them to also look further, think bigger, be inspiring.

Why is this a problem? After all, things are working well; not everyone has the ambition to become CFO; and it's an effective division of responsibilities, whereby the CFO mostly looks toward the outside (communicating with, and managing expectations of, internal and external stakeholders) while the next level under the CFO looks toward the inside and holds the fort.

Plus, as a CFO, you don't need to worry about being replaced by one of your direct reports (turns out that CFOs of both sexes can behave like queen bees). An interesting study finds that CEOs who delegate less are less in danger of being forced out, because their boards have less access to information (10). Arguably, this can be the case for the CFO too, possibly more than for other executive team members, because the CEO rarely knows much of what is happening in the CFOs' area – and doesn't want to know much either, as long as the CFO has it under control.

Still, for readers of this book – leaders interested in upping their leadership game – not having credible successors is a serious problem. First, if you feel threatened by promising talents in your area, then you might as well forget about this whole leadership thing. But even assuming that you don't have a "queen bee" syndrome: if you genuinely cannot see a successor among your direct reports, this will sabotage your efforts to motivate the talented, ambitious finance employees, since it means that they are looking at an uninviting career ladder with the top rungs missing.

So you want to give your senior managers a serious shot at the top finance role (or, even earlier on, you want to promote to senior management positions people who not only can do that job well but show promise, and ambition, to go further). To do that

- **Be aware of their workload**. Sounds obvious? Actually, many CFOs do not have a true idea of the operational load of their accounting and finance teams (11).

  This is especially a risk when the CFO comes from a different finance function, such as investor relations or investments, or from an outside role in consulting, audit, or banking. Step out and talk to your people.
- **Have an honest chat with yourself**. Are you pigeonholing your hard-working, effective CAO? Is she really not CFO material, or is it because your imagination cannot reach far enough to see her in a different role, plus it is so convenient to keep her where she is? David Gibbs, CEO of Yum! Brands, recollects how, when working in the finance area at PepsiCo, he was up for a big promotion, only to find out, through back channels, that *his own boss* was blocking it:

  > There's nothing that makes you feel worse than working so hard to help someone succeed and then find out that you're doing such a good job that they don't want to let you go (12).

- **Have a real development plan** for them. Allocate time to coaching your hard-working managers in the loftier matters of strategy, communication, and an overall "bigger picture". Karen Lynch, former CFO of Aetna, then CEO of CVS, told me how important the CFO at her first company was to her career. He became her mentor when she was still a quite junior talent, and he followed her career even after he retired, to the point where, when years later she became president at Magellan and was preparing her first press release, he edited it and sent it back to her![4] Also, expose rising finance stars to the *business* beyond finance. A stint in operations or a project in a regional office can fast-track an internal candidate's growth by expanding their business acumen.

- **Use influence and political skill to champion your talent**. Selecting and promoting the right people means more than rationally picking who's best on paper – it often involves *influencing others' opinions* and navigating organizational politics (remember Chapter 8's lessons on political skill and influencing). As CFO, you usually have a seat at the executive table, but you still may need buy-in from the CEO or other executives to promote one of your protégés or to create a new role for a high-potential employee. This is where your political savvy comes in. If you believe your finance manager is *the* right person to lead a new data analytics initiative, you might "sell" the idea to the COO and CTO informally to get their support before the official decision. Put your rising stars in front of the CEO whenever possible or recommend them for cross-functional task forces where they can shine and build their reputation. The key, as always, is sincerity: Chapter 8 highlighted that true political skill isn't about manipulation; it combines social astuteness, networking ability, interpersonal influence, *and* perceived sincerity. People will support your talent decisions if they trust your judgment and see your advocacy as genuine. One CFO I know made a habit of *informally* updating the CEO on the finance team's "bench strength," framing it as ensuring that the company's future is in good hands. This not only put his people on the CEO's radar in a positive way but also pre-empted any resistance when formal promotion discussions came – a politically skillful move that benefited the individuals and the organization.

Promoting from inside to develop a strong leadership pipeline also makes financial sense. **Internally promoted employees outperform external hires**, despite being paid less. Moreover, external hires take longer to reach comparable performance levels and are more likely to exit the organization prematurely (13). Developing internal candidates therefore is good not only for cultural continuity and motivation but also for performance outcomes and reduced talent churn over time.

Growing leaders extends beyond preparing successors and may sometimes mean having to let them go. Sandeep Aujla, Intuit's CFO, has been in situations where a carefully coached talent ended up leaving Intuit (e.g., to become CFO of a startup). But Aujla saw his job as "working to develop world-class leaders":

> Even if you go outside of Intuit, all that changes is the company name on the W2; our friendship and the relationship continues (14).

Carol Tomé, CEO of UPS, was CFO of Home Depot for 18 years. She proudly counts, among talented individuals who were part of her team there, 16 *current CFOs* of listed companies. And, yes, this includes her successor at Home Depot.

If you spend time nurturing and developing leaders, and they end up leaving the company because you did not have the right next role for them at the right time, they will still always consider themselves "alumni" of your "academy". At one of the companies I worked with, senior management even threw a goodbye party for every talent that left. They go elsewhere, impress others, get promoted. You will get a good name in the market. It's another way to increase your outside network. More importantly, your younger talents will see these positive examples of career paths inside/outside the company as a definite plus for joining/staying with you.

There is even an increasing trend toward re-hiring former employees once they have acquired valuable experience and connections outside your company. These "boomerang" employees statistically outperform purely external hires (15).

Are your finance managers good leaders?

In 1987, Ronald Reagan quoted an old Russian proverb to Mikhail Gorbachev: "Trust, but verify." It's become a cliché since then, but it captures something essential – and profoundly complicated – about managing people who manage other people.

Every CFO believes they know who their best managers are. After all, they see the performance. But performance is a lagging indicator. Which is why insightful finance leaders aren't just looking at department KPI – they're watching body language in conference rooms in Milan, swapping notes with local HR partners in Kuala Lumpur, and gently coaxing truths out of junior analysts over coffee in Rotterdam.

Take Brian, a CFO for a global pharmaceutical company.[5] In a meeting in Spain, he was presenting a new vision for finance. One by one, the local leaders stood up to speak. Eyes were attentive. Heads nodded. Then Julio spoke. The room shifted. Heads dipped, not in reverence, but avoidance. Pens moved across notebooks. Eye contact vanished. "That's when I knew," Brian says. "He had lost them." It wasn't what they said. It was how they *didn't look at him*. That moment, wordless and subtle, said more than any engagement survey could.

Or consider Arun, CFO of a large Dutch insurer. Even in a country famed for its directness – The Netherlands – he found that all-hands often left the real questions unasked. Employees were reluctant to speak out in front of peers. So Arun began holding quiet, one-on-one meetings with every employee in finance (over one hundred in total). Not to interrogate, but to listen. The result? A clearer, truer picture of leadership on the ground, filtered through candor rather than performance theater.[6]

And then there's Joe. Joe runs finance for a sprawling global organization. When he travels, he doesn't just meet with his finance leads. He talks to their peers – the heads of operations, marketing, HR. Not formally. Over lunch. In hallways. In these informal conversations, he picks up on things no dashboard can show: how respected, how trusted, how *followed* his finance leaders really are. It's not easy. You have to listen without prying. You have to notice what's not being said. But when done well, it's a kind of leadership anthropology.

Of course, many CFOs rely on engagement surveys or 360s. And those tools are useful – until your Head of FP&A's scores mysteriously dip after she delivers a tough but fair performance review. Context matters. Timing matters. Interpretation matters.

CROSSROADS LIFE: HOW PETER GATHERED INTEL

Peter steps in as the new regional CEO following Henk's unexpected departure. Warm, personable, and naturally outgoing – everything Henk was not – Peter impresses Clara with the detailed insights he gathered from his first visits to business units. Clara had always found visits to places like Crossroads Poland or Greece exhausting and awkward. She had little rapport with the local finance teams, dreaded the ceremonial dinners with CFOs and their staff at traditional live-music restaurants, and felt frustrated by her own limited ability to support them, given the demands of Project ACE and the stretched resources of her regional team.

Yet Peter returns from the same visits with strikingly specific observations – like the disengagement level of a particular country CFO – all from what he describes as "just sitting on people's desks."

Part of his success lies in his natural ease with people and cultures and his genuine curiosity. But there's another factor: Peter listens sympathetically when local CEOs and CFOs voice frustrations about Project ACE. Clara, by contrast, had avoided these conversations. In her effort to remain objective and professional, she discouraged local complaints – whether about ACE or the ACE team. But this stance, intended to preserve neutrality, ended up cutting her off from meaningful dialogue.

In hindsight, Clara realized she had made a common mistake: confusing listening with agreement. While it's true that allowing complaints can risk bias, skilled leaders know how to listen without endorsing. As we discussed in Chapter 6, true listening isn't passive – it's strategic. And in leadership, it can reveal what metrics and dashboards never will.

Sometimes, the smartest way to verify is simply to invite people to speak – and let them know you're actually listening.

Watch the scene selection at: https://www.ed.movie/peter or scan the QR code.

Leadership is a paradox. To evaluate your managers, you must trust them – *and* verify. You must be supportive – *and* discerning. You must be their ally – *and* their evaluator. You are not the secret police. You're a gardener of potential, trying to figure out which plants need pruning, which need more sunlight, and which might thrive in a different spot altogether.

Notes

1 Interview with the author.
2 According to Mr. Child's LinkedIn profile as of May 2025.
3 Interviewed CFO, anonymized.
4 Interview with the author.
5 Interviewed CFO, anonymized.
6 Interview with the author.

References

(1) The_CFO. Q&A: The SecretCFO tells all. https://the-cfo.io/2024/04/12/qa-the-secretcfo-tells-all/, 2024.
(2) Gartner. Gartner Finance Survey shows slower top line growth and talent issues biggest CFO worries for 2025. 2024-12-10-gartner-finance-survey-shows-slower-top-line-growth-and-talent-issues-biggest-cfo-worries-for-2025, 2024.
(3) Banham, R. Thinking Big. CFO.com: https://www.cfo.com/news/thinking-big/665471/#:~:text=%E2%80%9CNone%20of%20my%20direct%20reports, bring%20in%20people%20with, 2014.
(4) Ferguson, A. J., & Peterson, R. S. Sinking slowly: Diversity in propensity to trust predicts downward trust spirals in small groups. *Journal of Applied Psychology* 2015, 100 (4), 1012–1024. DOI: 10.1037/apl0000007
(5) Sieweke, J., Hentschel, T., Gazdag, B., & Henningsen, L. The business case for demographic diversity in strategic leadership teams: A systematic and critical review of the causal evidence. *Leadership Quarterly* 2025, 36 (1). DOI: 10.1016/j.leaqua.2024.101843
(6) Wallrich, L., Opara, V., Wesolowska, M., Barnoth, D., & Yousefi, S. The relationship between team diversity and team performance: Reconciling promise and reality through a comprehensive meta-analysis registered report. *Journal of Business and Psychology* 2024, 39 (6), 1303–1354. DOI: 10.1007/s10869-024-09977-0
(7) Edmans, A. The business case for diversity: A critical look at the evidence. In *Response to Financial Reporting Council's consultation on the Corporate Governance Code*, https://alexedmans.com/wp-content/uploads/2019/02/Diversity.pdf, 2018.
(8) Zaki, A. Salary transparency's impact on the future of labor. https://www.cfo.com/news/salary-transparencys-impact-on-the-future-of-labor/654695/: CFO.com, 2023.
(9) Cristkolder Volatility Report; https://www.cristkolder.com/volatility-report, 2024.
(10) Oehmichen, J., Schult, A., & Wolff, M. Keeping their cards close to their chests: How non-delegating CEOs avoid forced career ends. *Human Resource Management* 2017, 56 (2), 225–242. DOI: 10.1002/hrm.21732
(11) Noto, G. Yooz Closing the finance strategy perception gap. https://www.cfodive.com/news/yooz-closing-finance-strategy-perception-gap-generativeai-transformation/721113/: CFO Dive, 2024.
(12) Duke_University. https://www.youtube.com/watch?v=WYWkwB5aUGA: Duke University - The Fuqua School of Business, 2022.

(13) Bidwell, M. Paying more to get less: The effects of external hiring versus internal mobility. *Administrative Science Quarterly* 2011, 56 (3), 369–407. DOI: 10.1177/0001839211433562

(14) Estrada, S. Intuit's CFO moves his employees to new roles every two years. https://fortune.com/2024/07/03/intuit-cfo-moves-employees-new-roles-every-two-years/, 2024.

(15) Keller, J., Kehoe, R., Bidwell, M., Collings, D., & Myer, A. In with the old? Examining when boomerang employees outperform new hires. *Academy of Management Journal* 2021, 64 (6), 1654–1684. DOI: 10.5465/amj.2019.1340

10

RELATIONSHIP WITH THE CEO AND THE BOARD

Relationship with the CEO: Alignment, dissent, and everything in between

The most important partnership a CFO has is with the CEO. The chemistry, or lack thereof, between these two individuals can make or break a company's trajectory. But here's the paradox: alignment is vital – and so is dissent.

Research studies almost unanimously mandate **dissent**: the CFO should be quite dissimilar in thinking and personality to the CEO and should vigorously disagree with the top boss.

For example, CFOs who unconsciously mimic their CEO's communication style – what researchers call "language style matching" – are more likely to engage in excessive M&A activity that results in lower announcement stock returns (1). Why? Because the language mimicry is an indicator that the CFO stopped being the sceptic, the devil's advocate.

Other studies also sternly point to the dangers of too much of a CEO–CFO lovefest: for example, when the CEO and CFO are both high in "promotion focus" (chasing goals, seeking opportunities), they are more likely

DOI: 10.4324/9781003581734-13

to engage in IPO fraud (2). By contrast, promotion-focused CEOs perform better when paired with prevention-focused CFOs – those who are risk-aware, detail-oriented, and a little wary of shiny new things (3).

Shi et al. (2019) conclude, in Nurse Ratched style: "CFOs need to be forced to voice dissent, regardless of their true feelings" (p. 407).

Though unusually strong, this prescription makes an important distinction between personal traits and the role to be played. As we briefly discussed in Chapter 2, the most effective CFOs know how to **separate the self from the role**. Dissent doesn't have to mean distrust. You're not disagreeing because you're disagreeable. You're playing the part that needs to be played.

When separating self from role, you are making it easier not only for you to always be the voice of prudence without feeling inauthentic but also for the CEO to accept and appreciate your arguments, knowing that you are on the same side. You want conflict between ideas, not between persons.

As a matter of fact, those same studies that mandate CFO dissent also admit that this dissent is associated with better firm outcomes *only* when the CEO is open to accepting the CFO's advice. That is much easier to achieve if the CEO **trusts and likes you**. How do you get there? Expertise is non-negotiable. But it's not enough. You also need political skill.

CASE: AMALA AND THE IMPORTANCE OF BEING (NOT QUITE SO) EARNEST[1]

Amala is brilliant. She's a CFO at a major manufacturing firm, an honors graduate of a top university, and battle-tested through a fast-paced career in investment banking. She entered a senior leadership team (all of them with long tenure in the company) where she is the youngest – and by far the bluntest.

"I'm very direct," she told me. "People always know where I stand." Her style is all transparency, no subtext.

Did she need to adjust to the new company's culture? Not really. "It was more adjustment for the other people," she says. Her colleagues were a bit taken aback at first but then accepted her bluntness as a personal style. She is the same with the CEO: she challenges him, expresses dissent openly when needed, something that apparently no one else in the executive team had been doing.

How is this working for her? Well, not so great. She confesses to struggling to have the CEO accept that she is doing her – crucial – devil's advocate job, and sometimes he takes it personally.

Could this be different if Amala invested some effort into creating a close relationship with the CEO? Maybe taking some time to compliment him on his latest keynote talk, or choosing when to challenge him in the presence of other TMT members, and when to do it in private? Maybe finding ways to check in with him more frequently outside of formal meetings? These are all tried-and-tested influencing and networking tactics.

Research has even devised a way of measuring one's getting into the graces of the boss: **"the upward networking scale"**. It includes strategies that you might find easy to engage in, such as "*I take the initiative to discuss work-related matters with my supervisor*", "*I proactively consider my supervisor's needs and/or problems at work*", and "*I reach out to my supervisor on a personal level, e.g. a chat, lunch, coffee*". It also includes strategies you might find less palatable, such as "*I proactively attend social events and gatherings outside of work that my supervisor attends*", "*I take an interest in my supervisor's likes and hobbies to get closer*", and even "*I do favors for my supervisor on non-work-related matters to get closer*". If you think that such tactics lay it on too thick, and bosses should see right through them, think again. Recent research confirms that these "upward networking" tactics bring more support from the boss, better performance evaluations, and more promotions (4).

When it comes to the CEO–CFO relationship, the "language mirroring" study also finds that those CFOs who match their CEOs' language tend to get higher pay and more power in the top team (1). This is because *"mirroring" another person's behaviors (physically or verbally) makes that person like us more* (5). And another study on the similarity between the CEO's and the CFO's personality finds that, the more similar the two, the better they communicate and the more freely information flows, which leads to reduced audit risk (6).

So what does this all mean for you?

- If you naturally have a personality that complements that of the CEO (you are Steve Wozniak to the CEO's Steve Jobs or Paul McCartney to his John Lennon,[2]) you will automatically play your "cautious CFO" role well. Do not forget, however, that the dissimilarity will make it less "natural" for the CEO to like you, so put intentional effort into **building a trusting personal relationship**. Choose the level you feel comfortable with, on the "upward networking" scale, remembering that CEOs are human too, and so are not impervious to the right-timed compliment or to trusting people who share their hobbies more. The key here is to remind yourself that, while you are not naïve to the personal benefits that these behaviors may bring you, they are also meant to help the smooth functioning of your organization.

- If, on the other hand, you have a personality quite similar to that of the CEO (both of you are optimistic, promotion-focused, ready to conquer the world together), you will find it easier to build good rapport with your boss, and some of the "upward networking" tactics described above will come to you naturally. However, remember that you also have a key role to play, that of **the risk-aware, conservative CFO**, the one who tests the boss's visionary ideas against reality. As long as you separate self from role, your boss will appreciate being challenged by you and respect your "adult in the room" attitude.

CROSSROADS LIFE: JAN AND CLARA'S PARTNERSHIP

At the start of our story, Clara is CFO of Crossroads Life's Romanian subsidiary. Her CEO, Jan, is a Dutch expatriate who built the business from the ground up into an undisputed market leader. Jan combines entrepreneurial instinct with deep industry know-how and genuine people skills. He's as close as it gets to a textbook transformational leader – demonstrating idealized influence (the team reveres him), inspirational motivation (he raises the bar and rallies people behind bold goals), individualized consideration (he knows everyone by name and takes a real interest in their aspirations), and intellectual stimulation. (As Clara puts it in the opening scenes: "I worked with Jan for four years, and he still surprised me every day. I loved and hated that about him.")

Clara "hates" the surprises because it's her job to apply the brakes when Jan's creativity risks outpacing reality. But she plays her role – the grounded realist – exceptionally well. Their banter reveals the strength of their partnership. When Jan jokes that he can finally "spend to his heart's desire" now that Clara's leaving for the regional CFO post, or tells her to "go boss around some other Dutch people," we see two things clearly: Clara is no pushover, and theirs is a relationship built on deep mutual respect.

Of course, there's a hidden cost to having such a great leader early in your career: you may end up holding every future boss to the same gold standard – and most will come up short.

Still, when the CEO–CFO relationship works like Jan and Clara's, it's more than effective – it's energizing. It becomes a model for what the right blend of vision and realism can achieve.

Watch the scene selection at: https://www.ed.movie/jan or scan the QR code.

Conversely, when the CEO–CFO relationship does not work, there are several recurring patterns in their clashes:

Clash #1: A difference in philosophy

At Airbnb, CFO Laurence Tosi was the adult in the room. A former Blackstone exec, he understood the numbers, the risks, the street. During his three years at Airbnb, he helped make it profitable. CEO Brian Chesky was the visionary – dreaming up experiences, expansions, and reinvention.

Tosi pushed for discipline and a timely IPO. Chesky wanted transformation and "an infinite time horizon". Tosi and Chesky also saw other strategic choices differently: Chesky even wanted to start an airline, while Tosi advocated for a more reasonable solution such as integration with an existing flight-booking platform.

Were Tosi's and Chesky's differences in philosophy accompanied by a clash of personalities? According to insiders, Tosi was "pretty assertive and alpha" in management meetings. He came with Wall Street polish and swagger into an idealistic, founder-centered company culture. Did he push for an early IPO purely because he thought it was the right direction for the company or also because it would have added power to the CFO role?

Was the conflict strategic? Cultural? Personal? Likely all three. In the end, Tosi left, and Airbnb's IPO was delayed. The firm did eventually go public in 2020 – with stronger financials and a broader portfolio (7).

Clash #2: Trying to rein back the CEO

A fierce rift emerged during HP's controversial $11 billion acquisition of Autonomy. CFO Catherine Lesjak vehemently opposed the deal, warning the board of her concerns that CEO Leo Apotheker was about to make a mistake and attempting to cancel the purchase days before the announcement. Apotheker, determined to shift HP into software, was infuriated – he sought board approval to pay a $20 million severance to terminate Lesjak (8).

The fight ended with the board siding against Apotheker; he was fired weeks later, and Lesjak remained at HP. The Autonomy deal was later revealed to be ill advised, validating Lesjak's concerns that the acquisition was not the right move for the company at that time – concerns grounded in her extensive experience at HP and understanding of the company's needs.

In the end, it turned out Lesjak wasn't just counting pennies – she was counting the red flags, and the board finally realized that following the money sometimes means saying no to the CEO.

Clash #3: Fighting for business partner rights

At Snap, CFO Tim Stone – an Amazon veteran – lasted just eight months before abruptly walking out in January 2019.

Snap's CEO, Evan Spiegel, had a dictatorial leadership style, not uncommon among young founder-CEOs (he seems to have mellowed since). Stone, used as he was to the decentralized culture at Amazon and to the authority wielded by the CFO, probably felt de facto demoted in his new CFO role. He tried to regain higher authority by applying for the Chief Strategy Officer job, the No. 2 position in the company. CEO

Spiegel denied the request, apparently irked that his CFO wanted more than the job he had been hired for. Observers spoke about a clash of personalities between the two (9).

Was it ambition? Misalignment? Probably both. But it's a cautionary tale: if you are not seen as a true strategic business partner, you will either get sidelined or part ways.

Clash #4: Cost-cutting as a solo sport

It happens more often than you think. The CFO is brought in, explicitly or implicitly, to "tighten the ship." But once the budget knife starts slicing through beloved headcount or pet projects, the CEO goes quiet – or, worse, sides with the protesting functional heads.

Disney's CFO Christine McCarthy did more than disagree. She went full political operator. When CEO Bob Chapek centralized power in ways that alienated creative leaders and fumbled earnings guidance, McCarthy decided to escalate. She raised concerns to the board and lobbied for his removal. Weeks later, Chapek was out, Iger was back. Ironically, after being instrumental in Iger's reinstatement, McCarthy clashed with Iger too, again over cost cuts, and ended up leaving the company in June 2023 (10).

It's lonely being the cost cutter, especially when your partner is AWOL.

Clash #5: You got the job I wanted

Sometimes, the conflict is deeply human. The CFO had eyes on the top job. They didn't get it. Now, they have to play second fiddle.

It happened at General Electric. Jeff Bornstein, a GE veteran and respected CFO, was passed over in favor of John Flannery for the CEO seat. Just a few months later, Bornstein was out. Officially, it was a "shake-up." Unofficially, it was about power. The CEO wanted his own team. The CFO didn't want to play second string to the man who beat him to the top (11).

No one said it was personal. It never is. But beneath the press releases and "mutual decisions," you can often find bruised egos and unspoken rivalries.

These five stories serve as cautionary tales – and as reminders. Even the most experienced CFOs can find themselves caught in conflict when chemistry, communication, or strategic alignment falters. So how can you avoid repeating their mistakes?

Practical tips for a successful CEO–CFO duo

1. **Challenge** – but wisely. Your role as strategic business partner is to challenge the CEO and put their dreams to the test of reality. But if you think of yourself as someone who is not afraid of conflict, who never compromises, make sure that you don't oppose the CEO just for the sake of staying true to your self-image. Pick your battles.
2. **Separate role from self**. You are not a pessimist. You are playing the pessimist. Build the best personal relationship with the CEO that you can possibly achieve, so that they can see beyond the grumpy "Chief 'No' Officer" stereotype.
3. **Influence to cinch the strategic partnership**. You have the expertise to help shape strategic decisions, but your CEO sees the CFO role as mainly keeping the books in order? Do not ignore influencing and politics (e.g., demonstrating a powerful outside and inside network, making alliances with powerful others, subtle self-promotion) to reposition yourself as a strategic partner.
4. **Clarify the conflict early**. If you sense a strategic divergence – on timeline, risk, or cost – don't let it fester. Don't passive-aggressively "let the numbers speak for themselves." Speak. Set up a private meeting. Put it on the table: "I think we're approaching this from two different angles. Let's map out the implications."
5. **Support in public, challenge in private**. CEOs hate to be blindsided. Disagree early and behind closed doors. (One CFO I know, when she has to disagree with the CEO in meetings, texts the CEO in real-time during the meeting to give a heads-up!) Then, once a decision is made, fall in line. Nothing poisons trust faster than a public reversal or a CFO who starts leaking doubts to the board or the press.
6. **Know when to escalate**. Sometimes, the CEO is wrong – and the board needs to hear about it. But escalation should be the exception, not the strategy. And it works best when your record of loyalty is strong and your motives are unimpeachable.
7. **Be honest about your career motivation**. If you were passed over for CEO, you need to check in with yourself. Can you fully support the person who got the job? If not, it's time to leave. Lingering in bitterness is corrosive – to you, your team, and the company.

In a well-functioning executive duo, the CEO dreams with their head in the clouds, and the CFO walks with their feet on the ground. But they do this while walking arm in arm – and without elbowing each other in the ribs.

Relationship with the Board: A strategic balancing act

The relationship between a CFO and the board is often one of the most daunting aspects of the job – especially for first-time CFOs. A global survey by Egon Zehnder highlights "board interaction" as the top skill gap for new CFOs (12).

Why is board interaction such a universal pain point?

First, let's understand what the board is there for. Corporate boards fulfil two important, and very different, roles: **control** and **advice**.

Why "control"? Because shareholders face something called "*the agency problem*": the risks coming from giving your money/assets/company to someone else to manage. They appoint the board to minimize this agency risk by controlling management's actions and their alignment with shareholders' interests. Moreover, boards have multiple oversight duties mandated by regulators.

Why "advice"? Because corporate directors bring senior experience, knowledge, and connections that can all be very valuable to management.

So it is understandably a bit of a whiplash, if you are a new CFO, to experience a board sternly questioning you, in legalese, on a compliance topic, only to next propose to make an informal, golf-course introduction to a potential creditor. Board members have various roles (e.g., chair, independent director, head of audit committee), various backgrounds (e.g., former CEO, former political figure, former or current CFO), and various personalities (from suspicious to gregarious), so you will get "control" and "advice" firing at you from different directions around the boardroom table.

The **level of detail** board members require may also be different: one director (say, an experienced non-executive) might expect a concise story, abstracted to the level of strategic guidance that the board can offer, while another (say, a former CFO) will forget that they are in a non-executive seat and will want to go deep into the weeds.

Moreover, the CFO is often seen as *somewhat independent from the rest of the company's management*, so after the CEO has delivered their optimistic story, you might get tire-kicking questions, to make sure that no major flaw is overseen. The expectation is that you don't parrot the CEO. However, you also don't want to deflate their story (unless the situation is serious, as in some of our examples from the "Relationship with the CEO" section). This delicate balance is enough to give newer CFOs the jitters.

Earning trust in the boardroom

The key ingredient for a successful CFO–board relationship is trust. Charles Holley, a retired CFO of Walmart, viewed the board – particularly the Audit Committee Chair – as his most important relationship after the CEO. "*No matter how capable I may have been as CFO,*" Holley said, "without the board's trust, I would not have been in a position to command their attention or respect when discussing important company matters" (13).

In other words, and as in other contexts we have discussed in this book, brilliant financial acumen alone isn't enough; the board needs to trust that the CFO is giving them the unvarnished truth and looking out for the company's best interests.

How do CFOs earn that trust? Experienced CFOs and board members consistently emphasize a "**no surprises**" rule. Make it a practice to brief your board on important plans and potential issues in advance, so that nothing comes as a shock in formal meetings.

Another aspect of trust-building is **accountability**. When mistakes happen (and they will), owning up promptly is key. Jonathan Orze, a CFO in the education sector, recounted an incident where a reporting error skewed the company's financial projections. The moment he discovered it, he personally alerted the board, explaining what went wrong and how it would be fixed. He didn't stop at an apology; he outlined a plan to tighten controls so it wouldn't happen again. Far from losing confidence in him, the board praised his proactive response (14).

This kind of accountability signals to board members that the CFO puts the organization's interests above ego or image, further cementing trust.

Trust also grows from **consistent communication**. It's not just about crisis updates or quarterly presentations – it's about an ongoing dialogue. Make a point of keeping the board informed *between* meetings. For example, some CFOs provide **regular interim updates** on key metrics or emerging risks rather than waiting for the formal board meeting. Peter Lai, CFO of a healthcare organization, began sending his board a brief monthly video summary highlighting critical numbers, trends, and any concerns during a period of rapid growth (14).

Board members often serve on multiple boards and have **limited time**, in which case they usually appreciate a CFO who keeps them in the loop succinctly. As Adam Remis, a CFO-turned-board member observed, board members have "an extremely limited focus and attention span", so concise, digestible updates are far more effective than information overload (15).

Crucially, communication should be **two-way**. A wise CFO doesn't just report to the board; they also listen and solicit input. Many successful CFOs will quietly network with directors outside of meetings – a coffee with the Audit Chair, a phone call to a financially savvy board member – both to build rapport and to harvest their insights. Our research with US listed companies' boards indicates that about half of their directors have finance/accounting experience (16). By engaging one on one, a CFO can better understand what issues certain directors care deeply about and tailor communications accordingly. This personal touch helps transform the board from a panel of intimidating overseers into a set of individual partners whom the CFO knows and respects. One US CFO summed it up: "Make time for people and listen well… Different board members have different preferred engagement methods. Meet them where they are comfortable" (17).

Make them like you. As an experienced CFO puts it, "Your opinion matters to the extent that other people are willing to listen to it. So being likeable is an important factor for you to be able to influence people and achieve your goals" (17).

I know, you've heard this from me many times before, but it bears repeating: network, be a good listener, use your influencing skills. Ultimately, trust is the foundation, and it is built brick by brick – through honesty, accountability, proactive communication, and personal connection.

From numbers to narrative

Many CFOs discover that their style of board interaction needs to evolve over time. Early on, new CFOs might stick rigidly to financial facts, "focused on the detailed financial data", as one finance leader admitted about his first board meetings. It's a natural tendency – after all, CFOs are trained to be accurate and thorough. But over time, effective CFOs learn to elevate the conversation. They shift from simply reporting numbers to weaving a narrative around those numbers.

Adam Remis realized that in board discussions "a director's role is more strategic than tactical". In his initial meetings as a new director, Remis caught himself diving into minutiae – only to conclude that such nitty-gritty wasn't adding value at the board level. He learned to "focus on larger issues with strategic implications", leaving the granular details for management to sort out offline (15).

But what do you do if a less experienced board member draws the conversation into the weeds? Usually, the board chair should intervene to bring the conversation back to strategic level; if they don't, you will need to do it yourself (tactfully). The other board members will be grateful for it. Offer to provide the detail after the board meeting, and remember to do some repair work outside the boardroom, to make sure that the director asking for the detail isn't left feeling slighted.

Successful CFOs adapt by **simplifying complexity**. They act as translators of financial jargon into plain business insight. One survey of CFOs found that "reducing complexity" was a top priority when dealing with boards.[3]

A savvy CFO can take a convoluted 50-page budget report and distill its essence into a one-page summary or a compelling story. Every report should tell a story – connecting current performance to long-term goals and decisions ahead (similarly to the storytelling we discussed in "communicating with investors" in Chapter 6). This narrative approach encourages productive discussion. It shifts the board's questions from "What happened in the numbers?" to "What should we do next?", which is exactly where a strategic CFO wants the focus to be.

Another evolution in CFO–board interaction is the development of mutual confidence to challenge each other constructively. Early on, a new CFO might be cautious, deferring to the board's wisdom on all matters. But as trust grows, the dynamic ideally becomes more collegial and candid. Board members come to value the CFO not just as a reporter but as a thinker with a unique perspective.

In fact, a trusted CFO can serve as a crucial "dissenting voice" in the boardroom just as they do in the interaction with the CEO – respectfully pointing out risks or alternative views that others may overlook, backed by data and logic. For example, a board might be exuberantly pushing for an aggressive expansion, but the CFO would tap the brakes by illustrating the strain on cash flows and balance sheet stability. If done with credibility and goodwill, such interventions are immensely valuable.

Over time, boards come to expect and welcome the CFO's candid input. It's telling that in a recent McKinsey survey, **92% of board directors said they needed a good connection with their CFO.**[4]

In turn, board members also become more comfortable giving the CFO direct feedback. A healthy CFO–board relationship is one where issues are surfaced and debated openly, without anyone taking it personally. One board chair interviewed about best practices remarked that it's important that the engagement be "friendly but not chummy" – there's trust and warmth but also the understanding that the board will question and challenge the CFO when required, and the CFO should welcome that scrutiny (18).

In the best cases, CFOs even **seek out this feedback**. They might ask in a private moment, "How did the financial briefing meet your needs? What else would you like to see?" – showing willingness to adapt to the board's style. This openness creates a cycle of continuous improvement in communication.

Finally, as the relationship matures, the CFO begins to **anticipate the board's concerns** and address them proactively. For instance, if the board in prior meetings fretted about liquidity, a savvy CFO will begin the next meeting with a clear update on cash flow and debt status – answering questions before they are asked. This not only saves time but also signals that the CFO is taking the board's concerns seriously.

In summary, the nature of CFO–board interactions often **starts transactional** (reports and queries) **and evolves into a true partnership**. The dialogue shifts from past performance to future strategy, from cautious exchanges to candid conversations. And when that evolution happens, it's a powerful thing – one board member likened a strong CFO–board alliance to having "an extra pair of eyes and ears" guiding the company.

Bridging worlds: A globally relevant narrative

While corporate governance practices differ across the world, the fundamental dynamics of the CFO–board relationship have universal resonance. Whether it's a board in New York or Nairobi, Tokyo, or São Paulo, CFOs often face similar expectations: be truthful, be clear, and add value. Yet context matters, and understanding cultural and structural nuances can help CFOs navigate their particular board environment.

Consider regional governance differences: In the United States, it's common that the CFO (while part of the management team) is not a formal member of the Board of Directors, whereas in many European and Asian companies, the CFO might actually sit on the board as an executive director. In Germany or The Netherlands, for example, a CFO will be on a Management Board reporting to a separate Supervisory Board. In such two-tier systems, the formality can be even greater – supervisory boards meet less frequently and tend to be primarily control-oriented, which requires a different focus for the CFO's presentation.

Theo Brink, ANWB's CFO, recalls his first board meeting:

> I think my first supervisory board,[5] I entered that meeting with a lot of confidence. I just thought that a supervisory board was almost the same as a management board. So the first time I talked a lot about financial performance, expense levels, and so on.
>
> I later learned that the supervisory board is far more interested in risk metrics. What is your biggest risk? What keeps you awake at night? So not just sending out a story, but sharing your dilemmas.
>
> I also learned that sharing dilemmas is good for two reasons: first of all, it helps you as the CFO, there are a lot of experienced people on supervisory boards, which can really help you with your thinking. And secondly, they will appreciate it, because this is where they can add value, so it strengthens your relationship.[6]

In Asia-Pacific, CFOs sometimes contend with boards that have a strong controlling shareholder presence (founders or family owners). A CFO of a family-owned conglomerate in India shared that in his board meetings the patriarch would often dominate discussion, and junior directors stayed reserved. For this CFO, the challenge was to respect hierarchy while still asserting his professional viewpoint. He learned to pre-brief the chairman (the patriarch) on sensitive financial matters one on one, which allowed frank discussion in private and earned him the chairman's backing to speak more freely in the full board meeting. In Japan, by contrast, boards tend to operate by consensus. A Japanese CFO of a multinational noted that board interactions often happened indirectly – board members would relay concerns through the CEO rather than confront the CFO in the meeting. Picking up on those subtle signals was crucial. He made a habit of meeting the CEO right after each board meeting to ask, "What questions or worries did you sense that weren't explicitly stated?" By proactively addressing those, he built credibility as someone who understands the unspoken context.

In emerging markets, the CFO–board relationship can take on additional complexity due to factors like governance reform and investor scrutiny. In Nigeria, for example, a bank CFO described how a few high-profile corporate scandals put all boards on high alert. Her board's audit committee became much more hands-on, asking detailed questions about controls and compliance. Rather than bristling at this as micromanagement, she welcomed it – she provided workshops to educate board members on the bank's risk management framework (bridging a knowledge gap) and in turn gained allies who understood and trusted her processes.

This reflects a global truth: when CFOs treat board members as partners in learning, both sides benefit. As one CFO in South Africa put it, "I see part of my job as educating the board on the economics of our industry, because if they get it, our conversations can be so much richer."

Despite cultural differences, the core challenges and solutions remain remarkably similar. Virtually every CFO, regardless of geography, grapples with communicating complex financial issues in an understandable way, building personal credibility, and navigating the power dynamics of the boardroom. And across the globe, the CFOs who succeed are those who build bridges – of trust, of communication, of understanding. There is comfort in knowing, as you prepare for a board meeting in, say, Johannesburg, that a fellow CFO in Toronto or Singapore likely shares the same butterflies in the stomach and the same determination to get it right.

When you are part of the board

In countries with one-tier boards, sometimes the CFO is part of the board. This does not change the applicability of most of our discussion above – but the dynamic shifts subtly, as the CFO's word has more weight. However, what should change significantly is your mindset. You should not limit yourself to only contributing financial insights to a board discussion. You now wear a different hat, a board member hat, and need to think at that level, on behalf of the organization and its shareholders. CFOs who **joined their company's board expand their mindset beyond the CFO's functional scope**. They report thinking more broadly about strategy, risk, and long-term value rather than focusing only on finance. They also describe developing new skills in the boardroom – from improved communication with directors to a greater emphasis on listening and collaboration – which in turn made them more effective in their executive roles.

Every CFO–board relationship will have its tense presentations, its "aha" moments, and occasionally its rough patches. It's a relationship of continuous negotiation and mutual influence. The finance chief who can confidently walk into the boardroom, engage in rich, story-driven conversations, and come out with the board's respect is not just a number-cruncher – they are a true leader.

Notes

1 Interviewed CFO, anonymized.
2 For an engrossing account of famous creative duos' dynamics, see Joshua Shenk's "Power of Two: How Relationships Drive Creativity", 2015, HarperOne.
3 https://www.linkedin.com/pulse/how-cfos-can-build-value-enhancing-relationship-board-susie-clements-0ohfe/.
4 https://www.linkedin.com/pulse/how-cfos-can-build-value-enhancing-relationship-board-susie-clements-0ohfe/.
5 In European listed companies, boards often follow a two-tier system: A management board (executive members) runs day-to-day operations, and a supervisory board (nonexecutive members) oversees the management board. In the UK and in the US, companies typically use a unitary board composed of executive directors (typically the CEO and sometimes one other) and a majority of non-executive directors.
6 Interview with the author.

References

(1) Shi, W., Zhang, Y., & Hoskisson, R. E. Examination of CEO-CFO social interaction through language style matching: Outcomes for the CFO and the organization. *Academy of Management Journal* 2019, 62 (2), 383–414. DOI: 10.5465/amj.2016.1062
(2) Gong, M. J., Zhang, Z., Yang, X. H., & Jia, M. Birds of a feather flock together: How and when does the fit of CEO-CFO high promotion focus predict new venture initial public offering fraud? *Corporate Governance-an International Review* 2023. DOI: 10.1111/corg.12536
(3) Firk, S., Detzen, N., Hennig, J., & Wolff, M. Strengthening the CEO-CFO interplay: The role of regulatory focus and similar compensation plans. *Accounting Organizations and Society* 2024, 113. DOI: 10.1016/j.aos.2024.101563

(4) Wang, S., & Luan, K. How do employees build and maintain relationships with leaders? Development and validation of the workplace upward networking scale. *Journal of Vocational Behavior* 2024, 150. DOI: 10.1016/j.jvb.2024.103985
(5) Chartrand, T., & Lakin, J. The antecedents and consequences of human behavioral mimicry. In *Annual Review of Psychology* 2013, 64, 285–308.
(6) Bowen, R., Jollineau, S., Lyon, S., Malhotra, S., & Zhu, P. CEO-CFO compatibility and audit risk. *British Journal of Management* 2024. DOI: 10.1111/1467-8551.12887
(7) Weinberg, C. At Airbnb, tensions bubble between Chesky and Tosi. https://www.theinformation.com/articles/at-airbnb-tensions-bubble-between-chesky-and-tosi: The Information, 2018.
(8) Cook, J. Former HP boss describes "poisonous" management rift over $11 billion Autonomy deal. https://www.telegraph.co.uk/technology/2019/04/02/former-hp-chief-executive-describes-poisonous-management-rift/#:~:text=Mr%20Apotheker%20said%20he%20was,days%20before%20it%20was%20announced: The Telegraph, 2019.
(9) Murphy, H., & Bradshaw, T. Snap's finance chief resigns after clashing with CEO Evan Spiegel. https://www.ft.com/content/8a1aae3e-191a-11e9-b93e-f4351a53f1c3: Financial Times, 2019.
(10) Flood, E. Disney: The "Game of Thrones" C-suite. https://www.cfodive.com/news/disney-game-thrones-c-suite/654463/: CFO Dive, 2023.
(11) Gryta, T. GE Finance Chief Jeff Bornstein to leave company in high-profile shake-up. https://www.foxbusiness.com/markets/ge-finance-chief-jeff-bornstein-to-leave-company-in-high-profile-shake-up: Fox Business, 2017.
(12) Egon_Zehnder. CFO research survey: The changing CFO role. https://www.egonzehnder.com/the-super-cfo: Egon Zehnder, 2024.
(13) Holley, C. Forging a strong relationship with the board: Charles Holley, CFO-in-residence. *The Wall Street Journal*: https://deloitte.wsj.com/cfo/forging-a-strong-relationship-with-the-board-charles-holley-cfo-in-residence-1507608131, 2017.
(14) CFO_Drive. How to build and maintain trust with the board as CFO. CFO Drive: https://cfodrive.com/qa/how-to-build-and-maintain-trust-with-the-board-as-cfo/, 2025.
(15) Remis, A. CFO lessons learned and benefits from being an outside board director. https://cfo.university/library/article/cfo-lessons-learned-and-benefits-from-being-on-an-outside-board-of-director-remis: CFO University, 2023.
(16) Bunea, E., Stolin, D., & Elias, M. Leadership in director bios: Substance or impression management? *Corporate Governance, an International Review* 2025, 1. DOI: 10.1111/corg.12659
(17) Heidrick. First-time CFO guide: Advice from U.S. CFOs. https://www.heidrick.com/en/insights/financial-officers/first-time-cfo-guide: Heidrick & Struggles, 2023.
(18) Egon_Zehnder. Time for audit committees to step up. https://www.egonzehnder.com/functions/cfo-audit-chair/insights/time-for-audit-committees-to-step-up#:~:text=That%20points%20to%20the%20need,fielding%20criticism%20from%20the%20executive: Egon Zehnder, 2017.

11

LEADING YOURSELF

In previous chapters, we saw short selections from Crossroads Life, most of them showing Clara struggling. As we enter the realm of leading oneself, let's dive deeper into where Clara's struggle comes from.

When Clara got the call up to become CFO of Europe for Crossroads, she knew she was swinging for the fences. She was suddenly the functional boss of all country CFOs in the region. It was a big leap. But the scarier part? Crossroads Europe was in the middle of rolling out "Project ACE," an Everest-sized initiative to centralize every bit of operations and IT. As many large-scale transformations, ACE was not going well. It was unclear whether the project was floundering because of the consultants driving it or because the country CEOs were quietly resisting. Likely both. In short: messy.

Technically, Clara wasn't on the hook for Project ACE's budget or performance. The project had its own finance team, and its financials were carefully quarantined from the regular reporting lines. But Clara, being the

DOI: 10.4324/9781003581734-14

newly minted regional CFO, felt responsible nonetheless. Money was being spent, after all.

And Clara wasn't one to shy away from a mess. She was a former investment banker, ex-CFO at a major health insurer, and now four years into her tenure at Crossroads. She had a reputation for turning chaos into clarity. She could untangle a gnarly cost allocation issue in the morning, then sketch out a regional strategy by lunch. She was, by all definitions, an ace.

Eighteen months later, she was on the verge of burnout.

The physics of pressure: Demands vs. resources

Psychologists have a tidy explanation for what happened to Clara. It's called the **Job Demands–Resources Model** (JD-R) (1). Think of it as the workplace equivalent of a scale: stress happens when the *demands* of your job outweigh the *resources* you have to meet them.

Seems obvious, right? And yet we rarely break it down that way. Instead, stress tends to arrive as a foggy, overwhelming "too much" sensation. We collapse into our chairs, muttering, "I have too much on my plate," and dream of magical 26-hour days.

Finance professionals, in particular, often see **time** as their only real resource. Blame our formative years. We cut our teeth solving logic puzzles under time constraints – math tests, finance cases, accounting or CFA exams. But the real world isn't a test. The problems are murkier, the logic fuzzier, and time is just one of many resources you need.

Demands: Thrill rides vs. traffic jams

Let's get specific. Demands at work come in two varieties: **challenge demands** and **hindrance demands**.

Challenge demands are the good kind of stress. For CFOs, they include things like leading M&A efforts, designing investor strategies, and rolling out change programs – essentially, all the high-impact work that you signed up for. Yes, it's demanding. But it also makes the job worthwhile.

Hindrance demands are the villains: bureaucracy, broken systems, toxic politics, outdated tech stacks, and that one team member who needs a GPS to navigate a pivot table.

Aradhana Sarin, CFO for AstraZeneca, describes her challenge and hindrance demands this way:

> Learning gives me a lot of energy. So when I'm learning new stuff, even if it's about reading 100 pages for tomorrow's meeting, but if I'm learning stuff, that gives me a lot of energy. What drains my energy: a lot of arguing about allocating things when it's really a left pocket-right pocket type of issue. You know, at some point you should be able to follow an 80–20 rule, right? Like some juice is just not worth the squeeze.[1]

But here's the twist: the same demand might be a challenge for one person and a hindrance for another. Nurses in home care, for instance, saw emotional demands as energizing (2), while for an introverted CFO, an emotionally charged conversation might be the monster under the bed. Stress isn't all in your head – but your **interpretation** of it plays a huge role.

Now, back to Clara.

Clara's DIY demands

Clara stepped into her new role not just with a packed agenda but with a self-imposed mission. She wanted to

1. Reassess independently whether Project ACE made business sense.
2. Upgrade the quality of regional quarterly reporting, turning tables and commentary into actual analysis.
3. Customize cost-cutting targets for each country, ditching the blunt "10% off everyone's Opex" formula in favor of a data-driven approach.

All noble goals. All textbook "CFO as strategic partner" material.

But – no one asked her to do any of it.

Henk, the regional CEO and Clara's boss, had long ago buried the idea of reopening the ACE business case. He believed that this would only offer the country CEOs an opportunity to kill the project. The reports? No complaints. And individualized cost-cutting targets? A surefire way to get dozens of angry emails from country CFOs defending every last euro.

Still, Clara forged ahead – without first checking whether she had the *resources* to match her ambitions.

Resources: Not just time and tools

Resources come in two buckets: **job resources** and **personal resources**.

Job resources: What the organization gives you (or doesn't)

For a CFO, job resources might include

- Clear-cut position power (see Chapter 5)
- A high-performing finance team
- Support from the CEO and board
- Collaborative relationships across departments
- Functional systems and tools

Clara, unfortunately, didn't win the jackpot here. Her role had *vague authority* – she was the functional boss of country CFOs, but not their direct line manager. The HQ finance team was underwhelming, and employment laws made *upgrading the team* nearly impossible. Her boss, Henk, wasn't exactly a "*people-first*" leader and saw her mainly as a means to a goal. As for *collaboration* with other departments, in the storm of project ACE each team closed itself within a fortress and pulled up the drawbridge. Oh, and every country had its own finance system – no centralized, transparent truth in sight.

Could she have worked on *acquiring* some more job resources? Absolutely. A seasoned, politically hardened CFO would *build alliances* with the more powerful country CEOs, establish several *trusted connections* at lower levels within the ACE project and within the countries that could provide valuable information, and form a close relationship with the CHRO to *find ways around* the draconian labor laws that prevented her from overhauling her own team (as she found out years later, there were always ways). But Clara was a political newbie. She was used to more formal power and less backroom dealing. Her values – transparency, logic, professionalism – weren't well suited for navigating palace intrigue.

Still, even leaders who are more politically endowed than Clara can get caught in a downward stress spiral that makes them not only *less able to acquire new resources* but also *more prone to destroying resources they have*. This is where a saboteur enters the scene: **self-handicapping**.

The Trap of Self-Handicapping

Self-handicapping is when we (consciously or not) undermine our own chances of success – so we have *something other than our own ability* to blame if things go south (3). It's the exec who procrastinates before a board presentation and then says, "Well, I only had a day to prepare." Or the leader who refuses to ask for help, so they can say, "I had to do it all myself."

CROSSROADS LIFE: CLARA'S SELF-HANDICAPPING

After a rather confrontational meeting where Clara presents the new cost allocation method to the country CEOs, she chooses to skip the evening's social activity with the same group. This is an example of self-handicapping or self-undermining: avoiding the opportunity to network and build trust. Part of it is because Clara feels powerless in interaction with the country CEOs. She feels like she has nothing to offer. After having seen the rich variety of "currencies" one can offer in an influence exchange (in Chapter 8), we know better.

Watch the selected scene at: https://www.ed.movie/self-handicapping or scan the QR code.

My executive development students, when I teach Clara's case, judge her quite harshly: "I would never do that!" And yet Indra Nooyi, former CEO of PepsiCo, describes an eerily similar situation in her biography (4) when, as senior vice-president for corporate strategy and planning, she chose to leave after a difficult executive meeting, forfeiting the chance to socialize with important stakeholders during the evening's program. "This was very unlike me", she comments in her book, perfectly illustrating how we can see ourselves self-handicapping after the smoke has cleared, but not in the heat of the battle.

Personal resources: your power beyond the title

A CFO's personal resources might include

- Expertise
- Leadership skills
- Political savvy
- And that precious fuel: **psychological capital**

Clara's leadership style? "Lead by example." Translation: work harder than anyone else, dazzle with intellect, and let the weak fall off the back of the sled. That approach was fraying. Like many finance leaders who climb the first rungs of the career ladder fast on the strength of their intellectual abilities only, she had reached that fated seniority level that demanded something very different: influence, social astuteness, and politics. And the worst part? *She did not realize it*. She still tried to fight this new battle with the skills and mindsets that had gotten her so far.

Unsurprisingly, her psychological capital was waning. Her usually rock-solid self-confidence and robust optimism were eroding. Her resilience? Worn thin.

Psychological capital: Your survival kit

In Chapter 2, we introduced psychological capital (PsyCap), a combination of optimism, self-confidence, resourcefulness, and resilience. PsyCap is an important part of a leader's make.

PsyCap has both **trait** (your baseline) and **state** (your fluctuating daily level) components. Even naturally upbeat leaders can find themselves in a funk. And when stress starts chewing away at your PsyCap, your coping abilities decline – triggering a vicious cycle. Once you've reached burnout, it can take a long time to rebuild your natural psychological capital levels. Trying to work with a low PsyCap feels like marathon running after you've hit the dreaded "wall": those wooly legs won't carry you for much longer.

You want to hit the running track with high PsyCap – and stay high throughout.

Strong psychological capital will support you in finding creative solutions to apparently unsolvable problems and will put you back on your feet when you take a fall. This explains, for example, why entrepreneurs report relatively low levels of stress despite facing hairy challenges: because they tend to have high PsyCap levels (5). Crucially, psychological capital fuels your transformational leadership, which in turn gives you access to more resources, creating a virtuous spiral (6).

How to refill the tank

Let's start simple: good **sleep**, proper **nutrition**, and **exercise** (7–9).

Yes, I know. When you're cranking on an M&A deal, kale smoothies and 10 p.m. yoga are not top of mind. That's why habits matter – build them *before* the chaos hits.

Next up: **active recovery**. That's right – your Netflix binge and glass of Malbec don't count. What does? Engaging activities: maybe sports that you love (so not just exercise), painting, playing guitar, building furniture (10). Even gaming, if it challenges you (sorry, Candy Crush) (11).

Connection is another fuel source. Gratitude, belonging, affection – these aren't fluffy add-ons. They trigger *powerful chemicals* in our brains that are essential for our resilience and optimism (12). And, no, your work team cannot be your only support network. *Diversify* – friends, family, your soccer fan gang to hug in tears of joy when your team scores.

Just about this point in our PsyCap-building discussion, you are probably wondering: "Yes, it makes sense; but *who has the time* for all of this?" To answer this question, allow me to first introduce a simple but profound formula that was discovered half a century ago by the visionary sociologist Stephen Marks (13):

$$T = E$$

Time equals energy. What actually limits people's investment in various life activities is not time, but energy. When you have multiple things going on, in your home and work life, but most of them are energizing, you will find you have more room on your "life plate" than you thought possible. Marks' proposition is confirmed by recent studies: when an energizing activity was introduced in subjects' lives on a recurring basis, they not only found time *for it* but also felt like they had *more time for work and family* than before (14).

Which brings us to the secret weapon: **passionate hobbies**. They are highly energizing because they hit all three psychological sweet spots (15): control (you run the show), mastery (you get increasingly better), and connection (shared passion = deeper bonds). Moreover, they have the rare power of fully detaching your mind from work.

Complete detachment is a powerful but rare source of psychological capital for the busy CFO. Most CFOs I spoke with confessed to never being able to completely leave work behind, even when they spend time with their loved ones. A passionate nonwork interest will afford complete detachment because it fully occupies your mind. Condoleezza Rice, former U.S. secretary of state and a dedicated piano player, once said:

> It's not exactly relaxing when you're struggling to play Brahms. But when you're playing there is only room for Brahms or Shostakovich. It's the time I'm most away from myself, and I treasure it (16).

Best of all, you don't need to remind yourself to engage in your hobby, for the sake of your PsyCap. It will *pull* you out of the hamster wheel by itself: time to go to that tango practice, you've got a competition coming up! In times of high stress, when you tend to throw self-care out the window, this automatic self-protection role of passionate hobbies becomes especially precious.

In my research with Fortune 500 and S&P 500 CEOs, I found that passionate hobbies made them **more energized, more creative**, and even **more present** with their families. When things went south, those hobbies brought perspective and resilience (17).

Don't have one? Get one. It takes time for such a passion to develop, so you need to start early, before you hit the high stress patch at work. Winston Churchill picked up painting at forty and developed it into a great personal passion, an invaluable fountain of detachment and joy to draw from, when work demands were overwhelming. He even wrote a book about painting as a hobby, in which he cautions:

> The cultivation of a hobby is therefore a policy of first importance to a public man. But this is not a business that can be undertaken in a day or swiftly improvised by a mere command of the will. The growth of alternative mental interests is a long process. The seeds must be carefully chosen; they must fall on good ground; they must be sedulously tended, if the vivifying fruits are to be at hand when needed (18).

The Moral of Clara's story

Clara's trials[2] end well (no spoilers), but let's be honest – although it's a true story, real life rarely ties itself up so neatly. For every Clara who makes it, there are several who burn out and are thrown off the leadership trajectory.

None of the leadership ideas in this book – none of the transformational leadership behaviors, the individual motivation magic, the political wizardry – is sustainable unless you **lead yourself first**.

And that just might start with trading burnout for Brahms.

Notes

1 Interview with the author.
2 Crossroads Life trailer: https://www.youtube.com/watch?v=xDjSeRJqZrU

References

(1) Bakker, A., Demerouti, E., Sanz-Vergel, A., & Rodriguez-Munoz, A. Job Demands-Resources theory: New developments over the last decade. *Journal of Work and Organizational Psychology* 2023, 39 (3), 157–167. DOI: 10.5093/jwop2023a17
(2) Bakker, A., & Sanz-Vergel, A. Weekly work engagement and flourishing: The role of hindrance and challenge job demands. *Journal of Vocational Behavior* 2013, 83 (3), 397–409. DOI: 10.1016/j.jvb.2013.06.008
(3) Bakker, A., & Wang, Y. Self-undermining behavior at work: Evidence of construct an predictive validity. *International Journal of Stress Management* 2020, 27 (3), 241–251. DOI: 10.1037/str0000150
(4) Nooyi, I. *My Life in Full: Work, Family, and our Future*; Penguin Random House, 2021.
(5) Baron, R. A., Franklin, R. J., & Hmieleski, K. M. Why entrepreneurs often experience low, not high, levels of stress: The joint effects of selection and psychological capital. *Journal of Management* 2016, 42 (3), 742–768. DOI: 10.1177/0149206313495411

(6) Peterson, S. J., Walumbwa, F. O., Byron, K., & Myrowitz, J. CEO positive psychological traits, transformational leadership, and firm performance in high-technology start-up and established firms. *Journal of Management* 2009, 35 (2), 348–368. DOI: 10.1177/0149206307312512

(7) Opoku, M., Kang, S., & Choi, S. The influence of sleep on job satisfaction: Examining a serial mediation model of psychological capital and burnout. *Frontiers in Public Health* 2023, 11. DOI: 10.3389/fpubh.2023.1149367

(8) Salvador-Ferrer, C., Diaz-Fúnez, P., Carrera-Ruiz, A., Monserrat-Hernández, M., Artero, E., & Mañas-Rodríguez, M. Effects of workplace supervised exercise on psychological capital: An intervention study. *Sports* 2025, 13 (1). DOI: 10.3390/sports13010002

(9) Wei, X., Lai, Z., Tan, Z., Ou, Z., Feng, X., Xu, G., & Ai, D. The effect of physical activity on depression in university students: the mediating role of self-esteem and positive psychological capital. *Frontiers in Psychology* 2024, 15. DOI: 10.3389/fpsyg.2024.1485641

(10) Sonnentag, S., Cheng, B., & Parker, S. Recovery from work: Advancing the field toward the future. *Annual Review of Organizational Psychology and Organizational Behavior* 2022, 9, 33–60. DOI: 10.1146/annurev-orgpsych-012420-091355

(11) Koçak, O., Gorgievski, M., & Bakker, A. Recovery from work by playing video games. *Applied Psychology: An International Review* 2024, 73 (3), 1331–1360. DOI: 10.1111/apps.12519

(12) Pressman, S., Jenkins, B., & Moskowitz, J. Positive affect and health: What do we know and where next should we go? *Annual Review of Psychology* 2019, 70, 627–650.

(13) Marks, S. R. Multiple roles and role strain. Some notes on human energy, time and commitment. *American Sociological Review* 1977, 42 (6), 921–936. DOI: 10.2307/2094577

(14) Clayton, R. W., Thomas, C. H., Schaffer, B. S., Stratton, M., Garrison, E., & Mathews, L. G. Exercise and work-family conflict: A field experiment. *Journal of Managerial Psychology* 2017, 32 (3), 225–238. DOI: 10.1108/jmp-08-2015-0324

(15) Deci, E., & Ryan, R. Self-determination theory: A macrotheory of human motivation, development, and health. *Canadian Psychology - Psychologie Canadienne* 2008, 49 (3), 182–185. DOI: 10.1037/a0012801

(16) Tommasini, A. Condoleezza Rice on piano. https://www.nytimes.com/2006/04/09/arts/music/condoleezza-rice-on-piano.html: The New York Times, 2006.

(17) Bunea, E. "Grace under pressure": How CEOs use serious leisure to cope with the demands of their job. *Frontiers in Psychology* 2020, 11. DOI: 10.3389/fpsyg.2020.01453

(18) Churchill, W. *Painting as a Pastime*. Odhams Press Limited: London, 1948.

TIME TO PART WAYS
Where do you go from here?

So here we are, at the end – or, perhaps more accurately, at a junction. You've journeyed through the entire LIFE model. You've peeked into the leadership toolbox, maybe tried a tool or two for size. You've wrestled with paradoxes, read through stories of failure and redemption, explored research that punctures myth, and hopefully felt a few uncomfortable truths land a bit too close to home.

I, too, faced some uncomfortable truths while writing this book. And not just when realizing I'd written an entire section that sounded like a management consultant on too much coffee (don't worry, I rewrote that one). As I worked through each chapter, I kept asking myself: *Would my past self – the CFO version of me – actually become a better leader after engaging with this?*

Time and time again, research finds that leadership development programs can make a big difference: but *only* if participants take an *active role* in them instead of being passive observers (1, 2).

Would Emilia the CFO have treated this book like she would a work on brain science or human evolution – interesting, even thought-provoking,

DOI: 10.4324/9781003581734-15

but not something that changes how you show up on Monday? Or would she have crossed the invisible line and done something with it? I hope it's the latter, but I cannot know for sure.

So as I conclude with your "next steps", I am fully aware that you might stop at just reading them. But I also believe that you are *really close* to crossing that fated line and acting on them. Maybe all that's missing is someone to hold you to it. If you feel that flicker of "maybe now", reach out.[1] Sometimes, the difference between intention and action is someone who says: *I'll hold you to it.*

Here is your "what next?" list.

Reflect and recalibrate

The first thing to do is pause and reflect. Not in the vague, "go journal about your journey" way. No – in a CFO way. Audit yourself. Run the leadership equivalent of a financial review. For example:

- Where in the LIFE model are you strongest?
- Where do you tend to over-rely on yourself and under-leverage others?
- Which relationships are overdue for recalibration?
- Where does the environment – company culture, organizational politics, outdated expectations – constrain or shape your leadership?

Rather than introspect, recalibrate. Ask: *If I were starting fresh today – in this role, in this company, with this team – what would I do differently?*

Don't fall for the "Leadership as Optics" trap

CFOs are not immune to a modern virus: performative leadership. You attend the highly branded courses, post the right articles on LinkedIn, pepper your earnings call with "people-first" language – and yet your team is disengaged, your peer relationships are brittle, and your influence has plateaued.

Leadership isn't what people hear from you. It's what they *feel* around you.

So be wary of branding over substance. Your organization can smell the difference. So can you.

Build a personal board

Every CFO needs a personal board of directors. A CEO might get this naturally, through mentors or investor interactions. You? You'll need to be more deliberate.

Who challenges your assumptions?
Who has no vested interest in flattering you?
Who will call you out when your "leadership" is just ego dressed in logic?

Surround yourself with people – from within and outside your industry – who make you think harder, not feel better. Use them. And let them use you.

Invest in development – but wisely

Should you take that leadership course? Hire a coach? Read more books?
Maybe. But be strategic.

- Choose programs that are research-backed, not jargon-laden.
- Pick coaches who don't just nod empathetically but who push you into working with yourself.
- And don't just seek knowledge – seek transformation. Find spaces where you're not the smartest person in the room. It's uncomfortable. That's the point.

Rethink "success"

CFOs are conditioned to optimize. But leadership is not an optimization problem. There is no formula. No 100% solution.

Success in leadership is ambiguous and subjective. Still, if you think of your legacy, it becomes clearer. Your legacy will probably not be that you saved 2.4% on procurement. But it may be that your controller became a COO. That a quiet analyst found her leadership path and credits you for that, years after. That your team stayed calm when the market didn't.

That is leadership. It doesn't have to show up in the P&L. But it endures.

And finally – stay uncomfortable

You may be tempted now to close this book with a satisfied sigh, tuck it into your shelf, and feel a little smug. Resist that. Leadership, especially in finance, is never "done." Stay curious. Stay unsettled. Keep working with the tension between who you are and who the moment requires you to be. Revisit this book. Disagree with parts of it. Annotate the margins with "Yes, but…" or "Not in this company." Good. That means you're leading. Remember: CFOs are not just finance people who manage others. You are force multipliers, cultural architects, strategic co-pilots.

So, where do you go from here? Wherever your courage, your curiosity, and your conviction take you.

But go as a leader.

Note

1 e.m.bunea@vu.nl or emilia@ed.movie

References

(1) Gigliotti, R., Shavelsky, M., Goldthwaite, C., Spear, S., & Waran, V. Retrospective review of leadership development programs: Alumni perceptions of value, influence, and organizational outcomes. *Journal of Leadership Studies* 2025-01-26 2025, 18(4), 18–35. DOI: 10.1002/jls.21917

(2) Lacerenza, C., Reyes, D., Marlow, S., Joseph, D., & Salas, E. Leadership training design, delivery, and implementation: A meta-analysis. *Journal of Applied Psychology* 2017-12-01 2017, 102(12), 1686–1718. DOI: 10.1037/apl0000241

APPENDIX 1

TRANSFORMATIONAL LEADERSHIP

Reconciling two schools of thought

Recent developments in leadership research have sparked significant debate around the conceptualization and measurement of **transformational leadership (TL)**. In this appendix, I briefly outline two contrasting academic perspectives on TL – the traditional view and the more recent signaling theory-based approach – and present a synthesis that integrates both perspectives for practical use in leadership development, particularly for finance leaders.

The traditional view of transformational leadership

TL has long been defined by a set of behaviors that inspire and develop followers beyond transactional exchanges. The **Multifactor Leadership Questionnaire (MLQ)** is the most widely used instrument to measure TL, capturing four dimensions:

- Idealized influence
- Inspirational motivation

- Intellectual stimulation
- Individualized consideration

However, the traditional approach has been criticized on several grounds. Scholars (1) have pointed out that some MLQ items confound **leader behaviors with their effects**. For instance, items like "makes me proud to be part of the team" blend observable behaviors with emotional responses. More generally, there are increasing concerns that TL scores may, in practice, reflect general liking for the leader rather than distinct behavioral patterns. In other words, it becomes difficult to determine whether we are measuring leadership or simply followers' sentiment, that could be dictated by a host of other factors, from last month's bonus cuts to a great personal relationship.

The signaling-based perspective

In response to such concerns, a newer school of thought – prominently featured in *The Leadership Quarterly* – has proposed a **signaling theory-based reinterpretation** of transformational and related leadership styles (1–3). This perspective narrows the focus of TL (and of charismatic and ethical leadership) to specific leader behaviors that **can be explicitly signaled**, particularly through **verbal communication**, such as speeches or presentations.

This paradigm offers several advantages:

- It enables **more rigorous causal testing** by isolating behaviors in controlled, experimental settings.
- It identifies clear **verbal cues** (e.g., expressions of confidence, moral conviction) that lead to positive follower outcomes.

However, this approach has an important limitation:

- Many **critical leadership behaviors** – especially those related to sustained interaction that wins (or loses) followers' **trust** over time – **cannot be captured** within the constraints of speech-based signaling experiments.

An integrated approach for practice

To reconcile these perspectives, I propose a **practical synthesis** that retains the conceptual richness of the traditional model while incorporating the clarity of the signaling-based view.

- I **map the four MLQ dimensions** onto the signaling theory framework:
  - Behaviors categorized as **charismatic leadership techniques** (e.g., use of moral conviction, shared identity, visionary language) roughly correspond to **idealized influence** and **inspirational motivation**.
  - Behaviors aligned with **transformational leadership** under the signaling framework (e.g., supporting individual development, encouraging new ideas) align with **individualized consideration** and **intellectual stimulation**.
- For continuity and usability in leadership development, I continue to refer to this entire behavioral set as **"transformational leadership"**, even though signaling-based literature often separates these into "charismatic" and "transformational" subsets.
- Crucially, I adopt a **broader interpretation** of signaling behaviors beyond the experimental setting. If a behavior shown in a speech (e.g., signaling moral conviction) has positive effects in controlled studies, I infer that **similar behaviors, demonstrated consistently in day-to-day leadership rather than in rhetoric only**, are likely to produce similar or stronger outcomes.

The table below presents the original list of transformational leadership behaviors, as per the Multifactor Leadership Questionnaire (4), the list of the "signaling school" (1, 5), and my synthesis, for use by practitioners.

Transformational leadership (TL) behaviors according to the MLQ	**TL behaviors according to the "signaling school"**	**Synthesis of TL behaviors for practitioner use**
Idealized influence		
Talks about their most important values and beliefs	Shows moral conviction (states personal values)	Demonstrates strong values
Considers the moral and ethical consequences of decisions	Moral conviction (assesses a situation that is value-laden)	Demonstrates strong values
Instills pride in others for being associated with them [*No specific behavior. Conflates behavior with effect of behavior*]	—	—
Acts in ways that build others' respect for them [*No specific behavior. Conflates behavior with effect of behavior*]	—	—
Displays a sense of power and confidence	*Missing, but part of the "idealized influence-attributes" scale which according to "new school"* (5) *is* "the *best-validated neo charismatic leadership instrument, and has the strongest predictive effects*" (p. 380)	Displays a sense of power and confidence
Emphasizes the importance of having a collective sense of mission	Sentiment of the collective [*partially*]	Represents the team [*reflects both "sentiment of the collective" and having a collective sense of mission*]
Specifies the importance of having a strong sense of purpose	—	—

(Continued)

Transformational leadership (TL) behaviors according to the MLQ	**TL behaviors according to the "signaling school"**	**Synthesis of TL behaviors for practitioner use**
Goes beyond self-interest for the good of the group	*Partly in "sentiment of the collective". Also part of the "idealized influence-attributes" scale which according to "new school" (5) is "the best-validated neo charismatic leadership instrument, and has the strongest predictive effects" (p. 380)*	Puts the team before self
Inspirational motivation		
Talks optimistically about the future	*Missing, but implied by "sets high goals" + "confidence that goals can be achieved"*	Shows optimism and enthusiasm about the future
Talks enthusiastically about what needs to be accomplished	*Partly reflected in non-verbal charismatic leadership techniques aiming to "demonstrate passion" (voice, body, face)*	Shows optimism and enthusiasm about the future
Articulates a compelling vision of the future	—	Articulates a compelling vision of the future
—	Sets high goals	Sets high goals
Expresses confidence that goals can be achieved	Shows confidence that goals can be achieved	Expresses confidence that goals can be achieved
—	Uses metaphors, stories, lists, rhetorical questions, body, face, and voice	— *These can enhance, but are not a condition for, TL*

(Continued)

Transformational leadership (TL) behaviors according to the MLQ	**TL behaviors according to the "signaling school"**	**Synthesis of TL behaviors for practitioner use**
Individual consideration		
Spends time teaching and coaching	Teaches life lessons	Spends time teaching and coaching
Treats me as an individual, not just as a member of the group	—	Treats me as an individual and considers my specific needs, abilities, and aspirations
—	Speaks words of affirmation	Speaks words of affirmation
Considers me as having needs, abilities, and aspirations that are different from others	*Missing, but partly addressed through developmental opportunities*	Treats me as an individual and considers my specific needs, abilities, and aspirations
Helps me to develop my strengths *[covers only part of "offers developmental opportunities"]*	Introduction to developmental opportunities	Offers me developmental opportunities
Intellectual stimulation		
Re-examines critical assumptions to question whether they are appropriate	Questions critical assumptions	Questions critical assumptions
Seeks differing perspectives when solving problems	Seeks different perspectives	Seeks differing perspectives when solving problems
Gets me to look at problems from many different angles	—	Challenges me to think creatively
Suggests new ways of looking at how to complete assignments	Provides different perspectives	Suggests new ways of looking at old problems

References

(1) Stock, G., Banks, G., Voss, E., Tonidandel, S., & Woznyj, H. Putting leader (follower) behavior back into transformational leadership: A theoretical and empirical course correction. *Leadership Quarterly* 2023, 34 (6). DOI: 10.1016/j.leaqua.2022.101632

(2) Banks, G. C., Engemann, K. N., Williams, C. E., Gooty, J., McCauley, K. D., & Medaugh, M. R. A meta-analytic review and future research agenda of charismatic leadership. *Leadership Quarterly* 2017, 28 (4), 508–529. DOI: 10.1016/j.leaqua.2016.12.003

(3) Banks, G. C., Fischer, T., Gooty, J., & Stock, G. Ethical leadership: Mapping the terrain for concept cleanup and a future research agenda star. *Leadership Quarterly* 2021, 32 (2). DOI: 10.1016/j.leaqua.2020.101471

(4) Avolio, B., Bass, B., & Jung, D. Re-examining the components of transformational and transactional leadership using the Multifactor Leadership Questionnaire. *Journal of Occupational and Organizational Psychology* 1999, 72, 441–462.

(5) Antonakis, J., Fenley, M., & Liechti, S. Can charisma be taught? Tests of two interventions. *Academy of Management Learning & Education* 2011, 10 (3), 374–396. DOI: 10.5465/amle.2010.0012

APPENDIX 2

HOW POLITICALLY SKILLED ARE YOU?

Below is the Political Skill Inventory (1). For each of the 18 statements, write how much you agree with it in the corresponding box. For example, if for statement 4: "It is easy for me to develop good rapport with most people" your answer is "slightly disagree", write the number 3 in row 4, column 3.

Calculate your Political Skill (PS) score by averaging the 18 numbers you have filled in.

How do you compare?

So, you've calculated your PS score. What does it actually mean in context? Are you in the diplomatic elite – or more of an unassuming operator? Here's how your score stacks up against managers around the world:

United States: Confident Operators

In the U.S., most managers consider themselves at least *somewhat* politically skilled. In fact, it's rare to find a manager with a PS score below 4. Studies

		1 Strongly disagree	2 Disagree	3 Slightly disagree	4 Neither agree nor disagree	5 Slightly agree	6 Agree	7 Strongly agree
1	I spend a lot of time and effort at work networking with others.							
2	I am able to make most people feel comfortable and at ease around me.							
3	I am able to communicate easily and effectively with others.							
4	It is easy for me to develop good rapport with most people.							
5	I understand people very well.							
6	I am good at building relationships with influential people at work.							
7	I am particularly good at sensing the motivations and hidden agendas of others.							

8	When communicating with others, I try to be genuine in what I say and do.							
9	I have developed a large network of colleagues and associates at work whom I can call on for support when I really need to get things done.							
10	At work, I know a lot of important people and am well connected.							
11	I spend a lot of time at work developing connections with others.							
12	I am good at getting people to like me.							
13	It is important that people believe I am sincere in what I say and do.							

(Continued)

		1 Strongly disagree	2 Disagree	3 Slightly disagree	4 Neither agree nor disagree	5 Slightly agree	6 Agree	7 Strongly agree
14	I try to show a genuine interest in other people.							
15	I am good at using my connections and network to make things happen at work.							
16	I have good intuition or savvy about how to present myself to others.							
17	I always seem to instinctively know the right things to say or do to influence others.							
18	I pay close attention to people's facial expressions.							

across industries show that scores under 4 are nearly nonexistent, while **6% to 16%** of American managers place themselves firmly in the high-skill category, with scores above 6 (2–4). In other words, most believe they know how to play the game—and some believe they play it very well.

Germany: A Wider Spectrum

German managers, while no less savvy, show a bit more range in their self-perceptions. Between **2% and 10%** report PS scores below 4, and a somewhat higher share – **15% to 19%** – see themselves as highly politically skilled, with scores above 6 (5–7). It's a more evenly distributed landscape, suggesting either greater introspection or a more nuanced cultural relationship with workplace politics.

China: Modesty or Mistrust?

Chinese managers rate themselves significantly lower on the PS scale. About **80%** score below 4, and scores above 6 are extremely rare – *virtually nonexistent* in the data (8, 9). Whether this reflects a cultural tendency toward modesty in self-assessment, or more negative perceptions of political behavior in the workplace, is a question worth exploring.

What now?

If your score is higher than most of your peers – especially in your cultural context – it may indicate strong interpersonal agility, influence, and strategic awareness. If it's lower, you may want to reflect on how you navigate complex organizational dynamics – or how comfortable you feel doing so.

Political skill, like any leadership capability, can be developed over time. The key is not to "play politics" in the negative sense but to use political acumen in service of team alignment, ethical influence, and meaningful results.

References

(1) Ferris, G., Treadway, D., Kolodinsky, R., Hochwarter, W., Kacmar, C., Douglas, C., & Frink, D. Development and validation of the political skill inventory. *Journal of Management*, (2005), 31(1), 126–152. DOI: 10.1177/0149206304271386

(2) Feitosa, J., Verhoeven, D., Shuffler, M., & Wiper, D. Political skill across health care leaders: A longitudinal analysis. *Journal of Leadership & Organizational Studies*, (2021), 28(1), 45–59. DOI: 10.1177/1548051820956651

(3) Palanovic, A., & Kovacic, M. Does political skill arise from the power motive? The role of political skill as a mediator between the power motive and leadership. *Current Psychology*, (2024), 43(8), 6923–6938. DOI: 10.1007/s12144-023-04865-x

(4) Rice, D., Taylor, R., & Forrester, J. The unwelcoming experience of abusive supervision and the impact of leader characteristics: Turning employees into poor organizational citizens and future quitters. *European Journal of Work and Organizational Psychology*, (2020), 29(4), 601–618. DOI: 10.1080/1359432X.2020.1737521

(5) Dietl, E., & Reb, J. A self-regulation model of leader authenticity based on mindful self-regulated attention and political skill. *Human Relations*, (2019). DOI: 10.1177/0018726719888260

(6) Ewen, C., Wihler, A., Blickle, G., Oerder, K., Ellen, B., Douglas, C., & Ferris, G. Further specification of the leader political skill-leadership effectiveness relationships: Transformational and transactional leader behavior as mediators. *Leadership Quarterly*, (2013), 24(4), 516–533. DOI: 10.1016/j.leaqua.2013.03.006

(7) Genau-Hagebölling, H., Meurs, J., Kückelhaus, B., & Blickle, G. Fearless dominance and leader effectiveness: A chance for excellency in leadership. *Applied Psychology-An International Review-Psychologie Appliquee-Revue Internationale*, (2024), 73(3), 1131–1157. DOI: 10.1111/apps.12504

(8) Li, F., Zhou, X., Zhang, H., & Zhang, X. A sociopolitical perspective on sensegiving and team commitment to change: The role of leader's change-supportive willingness and political skill. *Journal of Organizational Change Management*, (2025). DOI: 10.1108/JOCM-07-2024-0385

(9) Sun, L., Pan, W., & Chow, I. The role of supervisor political skill in mentoring: Dual motivational perspectives. *Journal of Organizational Behavior*, (2014), 35(2), 213–233. DOI: 10.1002/job.1865

INDEX

Pages followed by "n" refer to notes.